Beyond the Big Six Religions

First published 2019
by University of Chester Press
Parkgate Road
Chester CH1 4BJ

Printed and bound in the UK by the
LIS Print Unit
University of Chester
Cover designed by the LIS Graphics Team
University of Chester

© University of Chester, 2019

Cover image
© Clara Bonner, kommafee.de

The moral right of the author
of this work has been asserted

All Rights Reserved
No part of this publication may be reproduced, stored in a retrieval system or transmitted in any form or by any means without the prior permission of the copyright owner, other than as permitted by UK copyright legislation or under the terms and conditions of a recognised copyright licensing scheme

A catalogue record of this book is available
from the British Library

ISBN 978-1-908258-35-9

Beyond the Big Six Religions

Expanding the Boundaries in the Teaching of Religion and Worldviews

James D. Holt

University of Chester Press

*For Ruth
Eleanor, Abi, Gideon and Martha*

CONTENTS

List of figures and tables	viii
Acknowledgements	ix

Section 1: Expanding the boundaries

Chapter 1: Expanding the boundaries	1

Section 2: Extending the understanding of Christianity

Chapter 2: The boundaries of Christianity	21
Chapter 3: The Church of Jesus Christ of Latter-day Saints	30
Chapter 4: Jehovah's Witnesses	64

Section 3: Extending the understanding of Islam

Chapter 5: The boundaries of Islam	91
Chapter 6: Shi'a Islam	100
Chapter 7: Ahmadiyya Islam	140

Section 4: Beyond the Big Six

Chapter 8: Bahá'í	171
Chapter 9: Humanism	203
Chapter 10: Jainism	231
Chapter 11: Paganism	265
Chapter 12: Rastafari	297

LIST OF FIGURES AND TABLES

Figures

Figure 3.1	The plan of salvation based on an illustration by Abigail Holt, used by permission	42
Figure 5.1	Comparison of Shi'a and Sunni prayer	137
Figure 8.1	Life of Bahá'u'lláh Fortune Line	200
Figure 10.1	Jain symbol	248
Figure 10.2	Similar and different: Ahimsa	263
Figure 11.1	Similar and different: Paganism and God	295

Tables

Table 3.1	Joseph Smith and the characteristics of religious experiences	60
Table 5.1	Sunni and Shi'a groups	97
Table 5.2	Shi'a Imams in Twelver, Musta'li and Nizari expressions	105
Table 8.1	Bahá'u'lláh and the characteristics of religious experiences	199
Table 12.1	The Twelve Tribes and their associated mental practice/function, colours and body part	301

ACKNOWLEDGEMENTS

This book seems to have been a lifetime in coming to fruition. The concerns and thoughts that led to its conception began in about the year 2000. At that early stage the thoughts focussed on my own religion, and I was grateful for the encouragement of people in the wider RE world who made me feel as though the discussion had potential. Particular thanks to Geoff Teece, Jill Maybury, Lat Blaylock and Joyce Miller for this early support.

Over the years the ideas developed and I realised that the boundaries of the RE classroom should be extended to recognise that the worldviews of all pupils should be an opportunity to develop teacher expertise and pupil experience. This was enhanced by my own children's experiences in school, but also by the encouragement of others. This encouragement was positive both from people I worked with and spoke to; there were also people from whom the reaction was negative. From both of these groups I took great encouragement and reflected on the arguments that were made. On the positive side colleagues and students from Egerton Park Arts College, Parrs Wood High School and the University of Chester were particularly supportive. There are far too many to name; but for the encouragement that I had something important to say I would like to thank Lesley Wakefield, Paul Smalley and Jane Brooke. Also, thanks to Denise Cush who provided some very helpful comments and suggestions.

People from the different faith communities have been particularly helpful. Special thanks to Luke Kerr, Waqar Ahmedi, Rubina Ahmedi, Melissa Ahmedi, Mehool Sanghrajka, Stephen Vickers, Farhad Daftary and Mike Stygal for positive responses to enquiries and suggestions. Also thanks to the members of my own faith community. Special thanks to my daughter Abigail for the creation of the illustration used in chapter 3.

Thank you also to the University of Chester Press for taking a chance on this book.

The time to write this book would not have been possible without the love and support of my wife, Ruth, and our children: Eleanor, Abi, Gideon and Martha. Innumerable thank yous.

Finally, as with everything I do, the final thanks are reserved for my Heavenly Father, His Son Jesus Christ and the Holy Ghost. Thank you for forgiving my imperfections and sustaining me every step of the way.

SECTION 1

EXPANDING THE BOUNDARIES

CHAPTER 1

EXPANDING THE BOUNDARIES

Religions and non-religious worldviews involve interconnected patterns of beliefs, practices and values. They are also highly diverse and change in response to new situations and challenges. These patterns of diversity and change can be the cause of debate, tension and conflict or result in new, creative developments (Big Idea 1 in Wintersgill, 2017, p. 17).

This book works from the premise that it is important for the boundaries of the RE classroom and curriculum to be expanded to recognise the highly diverse nature of religion and worldviews. This diversity includes both minority religions, non-religious worldviews, and also minority expressions of religions. As such 'Beyond the Big Six' is both a phrase that will explore those religions and worldviews that find themselves outside the major religions of Buddhism, Christianity, Hinduism, Islam, Judaism and Sikhism, as well as exploring the boundaries of those faiths themselves. Sometimes belief systems are explored within Religious Education using neat little boxes that suggest a monolithic and potentially univocal view of religions. *Big Ideas of Religious Education* (Wintersgill, 2017), and the observation of the twenty-first century world, suggest that a static view of religion is outdated and an RE that reflects the fluidity and diversity of belief should be developed.

Firstly, in exploring religions that lie outside the big six we are led to reflect on which might be included. One example of a book that does list more than six is *God is not One* by US author Stephen Prothero (2010). In this book he selects, as the subtitle articulates, "Eight rival religions that run the world". Interestingly he omits Sikhism but adds Confucianism, Yoruba and Daoism; a brief addendum on Atheism is also inserted. It would seem that to choose his list he used worldwide numbers, as he outlines that Sikhism is not included because "I had to draw the line somewhere, however, and I drew it on this side of the world's twenty-five million or so practitioners of Sikhism" (p. 16). This seems slightly arbitrary and perhaps is viewed through the lens of history as Judaism is included with far fewer followers. Prothero's choice of those which he claims are numerically significant link with the choice of six in the UK education system which is usually justified through numbers. The UK Census of 2011 suggests that the big six are as named earlier and highlight the breakdown of religions in the UK as follows:

- Christian   33.2 million people – 59.3% of the population
- No religion   14.1 million people – 25% of the population
- Muslim   2.7 million people – 4.8% of the population
- Hindu   817,000 people – 1.5% of the population
- Sikh   423,000 people – 0.8% of the population
- Jewish   263,000 people – 0.5% of the population
- Buddhist   248,000 – 0.4% of the population
- Other religion   240,000 people – 0.4% (this included those identifying as Jain, with 20,000 people, and Pagan (as an umbrella group) with 80,414 (Source: Office for National Statistics, 2012).

Other religions such as Bahá'í and Jainism could easily find a place in the RE classroom as appropriate.[1] One of the issues surrounding the inclusion of other religions is the pressures that are already placed on curriculum time. This is why, perhaps, the religions outside of the big six have a place within the RE classroom where appropriate rather than as a systematic exploration. This argument can also be extended to the "silent majority" (Rudge, 1998, p. 155) of those who do not identify with a religious tradition outlined above, which would include those from a non-religious background as these groups continue to grow

---

1 Please note that the anglicised versions of words and phrases from Arabic, Sanskrit and other languages have been used throughout, except in relation to the Bahá'í religion where the use of accents are the norm within Bahá'í religious writings in English.

Expanding the Boundaries

in number. As such, this book will suggest an expansion to include discussion of Humanism, Bahá'í, Paganism and Jainism as the largest religious groups or non-religious worldviews outside of the big six in the UK. Rastafari are also included as an important expression that is misunderstood, but highly visible in the world, and which has important sociological implications for the study of religions.

In expanding the boundaries of the six major religions there is a question as to why those groups within a religion should receive special treatment. One of the major issues in this area is whether these groups actually belong within or outside of the parent faith. Anyone who follows RE discussions on social media will recognise that this is a very contentious issue and one that has important implications. The questions can be asked: "Who owns a religion?" and "What is meant by this?" Essentially, those who 'own' something can determine the rules and the acceptable boundaries of use. For example, in sport there are numerous national and international bodies that are recognised as **the** authority and any change to rules or procedures has to go through them. To extend the sports analogy, sometimes there are some within the sport who feel that the rules and procedures are not correct and form breakaway groups – this is seen in particular in boxing where there are rival world title belts. Sometimes these breakaway groups flourish and become the norm (such as the English Premier League, for example) and others flounder (like the United States Football League).

Having established this analogy, it should become apparent that the question with regard to RE is "Who has the right to determine the rules and boundaries within religion?" This can be seen to have a very broad or a very narrow answer. One concern is that RE teachers and exam awarding organisations are becoming the arbiters of the boundaries. Each of the arguments surrounding the religions that are included in the 'Expanding the boundaries' section of this book will be explored as a part of the wider faith tradition within the individual chapters, but at the outset it is important to note that there are probably two different answers to the question of the boundaries of a religion. The first is personal and the second is educational.

Firstly, the personal. Every individual and group has the right to hold views that define their approach to their religion. For example, the Trinity becomes normative for a large number of Christians, or Muhammad as the final prophet for Muslims, and is this the basis on which believers identify who belongs to their religion and who does not? All people have this kind of view. People may recognise that others believe differently, but individuals cannot impose their boundaries on others. The recognition of how people from different religions view each other is a central issue in inter-faith discussions. When two groups engage in dialogue, each group should consider: is it as members of the same community or as different religions? MacIntyre argues that this type of question is not just important for the validity of the dialogue undertaken, but also for the participating groups' understanding of what they are trying to achieve and where they are coming from: "Such a person is confronted by the claims of each of the traditions which we have considered as well as by those of other traditions. How is it rational to respond to them? The initial answer is: that will depend upon who you are and how you understand yourself" (MacIntyre, 1988, p. 393). In this way, how others are viewed can become an obstacle but not an insurmountable one if groups agree to disagree. Disagreeing about this need not be rude, rather it can be an exciting starting point for dialogue. It is also an honest viewpoint of an individual.

Secondly, the educational. As much as a personal view is important, RE professionals have to be aware of prejudices and how they might affect those in the classroom. I have suggested elsewhere:

> John Hull suggests that any approach to RE should be "a syllabus which can be taught by any well trained and well informed teacher, regardless of his faith, to any pupil whose interest can be caught, regardless of his faith". It is hoped that the teacher would have a positive neutrality: "It does not mean that the teacher does not care but that he cares for them all, accepting them as they are". To enable a child to be 'true' to their own religion and culture suggests that the purpose of RE is to foster

faith; and while this may be appropriate in a school with a faith basis, in a state school this is not appropriate (Holt, 2015, p. 5).

A 'neutral' curriculum in RE, whatever that might look like, is one where 'Big tent' religion is taught. Whatever the personal view about the Christianness, Muslimness or any other religion of a particular group, the self-identification of the adherents becomes important. This is because in teaching children that their faith is outside of what is considered to be a certain religion, professionals are imposing their own bias on them and questioning their sense of self and identity. This may be at odds with the teacher's own personal views, but is the only approach open to teachers of RE.

With this as a background we are able to discuss the arguments surrounding the inclusion of minority religions, or minority expressions of religions.

Currently there appears to be an uneven mention of minority religions in Agreed Syllabi and the inclusion of such expressions seems to be left to the decision of the individual teacher.

The Case For

1. *The number of adherents and community cohesion*

When examining RE throughout England and Wales there seems to be an anomaly when comparing it with the religious composition of society. Throughout the world, the six major religions in terms of membership numbers are the 'big six'. However, in the United Kingdom there are more members of some individual minority expressions than Buddhists. This would suggest that these smaller expressions may have a stronger case for inclusion within the RE classroom than some of the major world religions.

As examples of minority expressions of religions, Latter-day Saints and Jehovah's Witnesses highlight an interesting dichotomy. They want to be considered Christian, but consider themselves as a group distinct from the 'mainstream' Christian churches. How can this tension be resolved? If these groups wish to be considered part of the Christian community then special mention in text books, Agreed Syllabi and national documents cannot always be possible. With the curriculum time that is available for Christianity, including relatively new and minor groups would not be seen as viable. At the present time, while these groups don't find themselves in the mainstream of Christianity, they may need special treatment or they will find their needs (for inclusion, understanding and tolerance) not catered for by anybody. In commissioning resources for use within the RE classroom, publishers tend to respond to the curriculum that is already in place rather than pushing the boundaries. As such, minority religions and non-religious worldviews may not find themselves receiving coverage in resources. Specific resources that highlight the place of a particular worldviews in light of 'traditional' study would enable teachers to move forward with planning for their inclusion in the RE classroom.

A justification for the inclusion of those beyond the big six can be seen in recognising that a "major focus of RE is the study of the diversity of religion and belief which exists within the UK and how this diversity influences national life" (Department for Children, Schools and Families (DCSF), 2009, p. 15). It can be seen that the case for the inclusion of minority religions in the RE classroom has not been coherently articulated (either as a whole or on an individual level). Some groups, such as Humanists UK, have been very effective in having their voice heard and concerns addressed at a national level. Other religions and worldviews could follow a similar path in seeking to involve themselves in the various aspects of RE at a national and on a local level. This is not without opposition; Humanists often find difficulty at a local level, but this should not deter others from seeking representation in statutory bodies and the curriculum itself.

2. *Inclusion and listening to the child's voice*
The RE Review (2013) does provide opportunity for the use of those religions outside the big six in the RE classroom: "all types of school need to recognise the diversity of the UK and the importance of learning about its religions and worldviews, including those with a

significant local presence" (p. 15). The current experience of children from minority religions is articulated by Head (2009) when exploring the experience of Latter-day Saint (Mormon) students in English classrooms:

> Only 33% of my respondents noted that Mormonism was discussed at school and even then, it was not always done in ways that reflected the children's own religious experiences. One student responded that the church was mentioned "briefly, talking about polygamy"; another responded that "yes [the church was mentioned] once or twice because we are a bigotry [sic] religion apparently"; another said, "in history, we learnt about Mormons and they were given a negative view and some facts given which are untrue" (p. 202).

RE which takes account of the individual child's religious experience can be seen to be advantageous for both pupil and teacher. The interface between home and school life can sometimes be difficult for young people to negotiate. They deserve our best efforts as educationalists to ease their way. The presence in our schools of some individuals with clear religious views should be seen as an opportunity to share our common understanding and respect for each other on our overlapping journeys. Such contributions can enrich school life (Gillespie in Redbridge SACRE, 1997, p. 4), and help pupils feel as though their voices are important. Excluding pupils from inclusion or participation may make them feel isolated. McGarvey suggests that in such structures where people feel that their voices are not heard the desire to participate diminishes:

> Enthusiasm to take part and be active in communities quickly dissipates when people realise the local democracy isn't really designed with them in mind; that it's designed primarily so that people from outside the community can retain control of it, over the heads of those who live there (2018, pp. 48–49).

In 2001 Brunel University released a video resource called *Speaking for Ourselves*. This video "is made up of a wealth of testimony about the religious beliefs and practices of over fifty people with a variety of religious and ethnic identities ... Much of what they say concerns issues relating to personal, family and community life" (Lovelace, 2001, back cover). The video deals with the six principal religions, but also features a Humanist and a Jehovah's Witness. Including these groups could be seen to validate an individual child's religious experience. If it is not possible for each faith group to be represented, then allowing pupils an opportunity to speak for themselves and encounter the views of other classmates, gives RE the opportunity to be more inclusive. These insights into children's worldviews can also be beneficial for the teacher. Bolton has similarly explained the benefits she sees in this kind of experience:

> If there are children from Pagan homes in the classroom, it is important for teachers to acknowledge and respect that ... One of the best ways is through getting to know a little about their faith, as I did when I taught my first Mormon student. He talked about the newly built Temple he attended and I managed to visit it, while it was open to the public before it was dedicated. This was a fascinating experience (1999, pp. 8-4).

It could be seen that the RE teacher is always learning; one of the arguments against the inclusion of minority religions outlined later in the chapter highlights subject knowledge as a barrier to teaching. Using the pupils themselves as a resource, and also a teacher's engagement with that child's faith community can be seen to build the ability to teach about various groups. The use of individuals and small faith communities as a starting point for RE is building on the work that Jackson has done in developing the ethnographic approach to RE which emphasises "listening to believers, insiders or adherents" (Blaylock, 2004, p. 13). It further highlights the "dynamism of religion in the life of the individual" (Blaylock, 2004, p. 13).

Listening to and valuing every child as an individual is crucial. As such, if the RE classroom contains people from beyond the big six, it is crucial that they have a voice to explore and express their beliefs.

Examination of diversity
Within the redeveloped GCSE and A level specifications there is a

recognition of, and scope for, the inclusion of minority expressions in religions. Within the Islam specifications there are specific mentions of Shi'a and Sufi expressions alongside the majority Sunni view. There are also underpinning principles in the GCSE content which suggests that in all religions "Common and divergent views within [the chosen religion] in the way beliefs and teachings are understood and expressed should be included throughout" (Assessment and Qualifications Alliance (AQA), 2017). All GCSE specifications make reference to the inclusion of non-religious worldviews. This does raise an interesting question as to what will be accepted as 'divergent' within the various traditions. At Strictly RE, the National Association of Teachers of Religious Education NATRE conference in 2018, representatives of each exam board were asked a specific question about the inclusion of Jehovah's Witnesses as Christian. All but one said that they would be accepted; this exam board articulated the definition that a Christian Church sits on the World Council of Churches. Returning to the earlier point, this is worrying because awarding organisations are drawing boundaries that religions do not draw for themselves. This could, by extension, lead to a rejection of Ahmadiyya as Muslim, or others within different religious traditions.

3. *Inform*

Most teachers and pupils are unaware of the beliefs and teachings of those outside the big six. Miller discusses the centrality of the argument that RE is to be used to inform pupils of the beliefs and teachings of different religions:

> I'm convinced that RE has to move away from the 'safe six' and be far more adventurous in what is included in RE – and NRMs [New Religious Movements] are so much more obvious in society than some of the religions they study that we owe it to children to help them develop an informed understanding of Jehovah's Witnesses, Latter-day Saints, Hare Krishnas and all the others they encounter – literally – on the streets (2004, p. 3).

In essence, the goal of informing underpins all the other arguments for the inclusion of groups in the RE classroom elucidated in this section. The arguments centre on the incorporation of groups who are increasing in size in the UK. As such, these groups will have more and more children coming through the education system. As these children (as with all children) require an environment where they feel valued, and in which they and their culture matters, it would seem imperative that minority groups find their place in the RE classroom. While informing the general school population and enabling pupils to gain more enrichment through examination courses is laudable, the most convincing argument seems to be the inclusion of children's own views (while recognising that this means the widespread inclusion of minority expressions throughout the country could be negated by this argument). This provisional conclusion will be challenged through the arguments suggested against such inclusion.

The Case Against

In examining the arguments given by respondents against the incorporation of those beyond the big six into the RE curriculum there tended to be two families of concern. The first focuses on the problems associated with the practicalities of the subject as a whole, whilst the second focuses on the perceived dangers of such groups.

1. *The problems associated with the practicalities of the subject*

When examining the demands placed upon RE in the classroom (lack of time and specialist teachers, to mention only two) it may be argued that the requirement to balance the six major world religions (in various Agreed Syllabi the number to be taught at Key Stage 3 ranges between three and six) is in itself a major challenge. Finding time for further religions would place what could be seen as unreasonable demands on the curriculum and the teacher.

It was suggested by one respondent that funding should be made available for RE libraries, which would contain a wider range of material than the syllabus topics, so that pupils could access information about those beyond the big six. This would negate the need to place further demands on the teacher and enable pupils to become independent enquirers. However, this is an unsuccessful attempt to provide opportunities to enable students to study religions. It could be seen to be a 'hit and miss' solution which depends on a child's motivation and interest. A similar argument could be suggested in geography in a situation where, with no time to study Less Economically Developed Countries, then pupils could be directed towards the Internet and further resources.

Perhaps the solution to the concern about the practicalities of the subject is two-fold. Firstly, the Agreed Syllabus Conferences and curriculum designers could be less prescriptive in what is required in schools and give teachers an opportunity to respond to the interest of pupils, the religious make-up of the surrounding area or diversity in a religious tradition. This would localise RE to an even greater degree than Agreed Syllabuses already do and may not be a good thing. It would give teachers freedom, but there is no guarantee that this freedom would be consistently applied. As a suggestion, this would seem to be unworkable as it may actually increase the burden on the teacher through unfairly extending their responsibility to include the decisions around, and the defence for, the content of RE.

The second solution to the practicalities of the subject could be the inclusion of such worldviews in the RE classroom as a 'cherry picking' approach where aspects of the faiths are highlighted as appropriate. For example, in a discussion of war and peace the Jehovah's Witness rejection of all participation in wars could be inserted as an alternative viewpoint. In Key Stage 3 during a study of Rites of Passage, initiation ceremonies from different groups (especially those whose children are in the class/school) could be included.

2. *Confusion*

Teaching about groups beyond the big six could result in confusion. Children often mix up various aspects of the different traditions already studied, and adding more would only deepen the confusion. However, in studying any subject with varied (though similar) topics, confusion can result. As an example, one respondent compared his experience of teaching RE to his teaching of various psychological approaches at A level. Students often mix up the assumptions of the Behaviourist approach with the Biological approach. Confusion may be the natural result of studying more than one topic. Rather than seeing the study of wider worldviews as a negative imposition, it is possible to utilise the multiplicity as a positive aid to promote better learning.

3. *Subject knowledge*

A further argument against the use of such groups in the RE classroom is the lack of knowledge that a teacher may have about individual groups. Indeed, this is a valid concern based on the responses to the research project. In working with trainee teachers I have observed that it is rare to find an RE teacher who has qualified with a specialism in each of the six principal religions. However, it does not negate the need for the individual teacher to study and experience more in order to fill in the gaps of their subject knowledge. If there is a pupil of a particular religion in the school then they may well provide the teacher with opportunities to ask questions, or make links with communities to find information on which to build their study. For RE to be inclusive, it may be necessary to follow an approach to RE being more "centred on the experiences of pupils in the RE classroom" (Blaylock, 2004, p. 14) rather than the experience of the teacher. The fear that a lot of non-specialists have when they are teaching RE is that their subject knowledge will be insufficient. It is just the same for qualified RE teachers who need to be prepared to research.

Teachers also express the concern that through their lack of knowledge they could exacerbate misunderstandings, and in turn offend members of the faith communities. Copley observed that:

> Teachers were resigned to a continuing misunderstanding between themselves and Witness parents. Although they had learnt through experience the basic principles and in general expressed a respect for these, they knew how likely was the prospect of a foot-fault: either

they would put a foot wrong in ignorance or else be judged to have done so ... In the phrase of one respondent, the teaching of Witnesses is a 'minefield'. If that be so, it is at least possible to chart the most serious hazards and so to reduce the likelihood of injury. To that end, we endeavour to set out ... the principles which Witnesses observe (Copley, 1994, p. 154).

It is my experience, and that of many others in a research project in the early 2000s, that many parents were forgiving of honest mistakes, and the important aspect for parents is that teachers are willing to learn and develop their knowledge.

4. *The perceived dangers of smaller religions*

Holt (2010) has suggested that teachers may consider that minority religions should not be explored as they erroneously see them as dangerous or manipulative. Just as any good RE teaching involves shying away from a confessional approach (Grimmitt (2003) does not recognise this as a valid approach to the teaching of RE), this would be no less true for RE involving those beyond the big six. The teaching of any religion is not to promote acceptance, but rather for understanding of their truth claims and impact on the lives of believers and should incorporate all pupils. As with any religion though, it is possible that a pupil's interest could be stimulated and they are then led to seek information for themselves. This leads on to another concern which suggests that in teaching about minority expressions, stereotypes could be reinforced in the classroom or within the home. If Latter-day Saints were discussed, how many would speak of polygamy rather than helping and serving other people? This should not mean that the minority religions and worldviews are not taught, but that they need to be explored in an atmosphere where negative stereotypes could be challenged, as appropriate, and prejudice erased. This would enable faiths to be approached from an unbiased point of view: "Young people, as with all of us, recognise the difference between the authenticity of the individual voice and the rhetoric of ideological pronouncements. If we attend to the former and avoid the latter we shall gain their interest and engagement and advance their learning and development" (Erricker & Erricker, 2003, p. 204).

The problem still remains, however, of making normative expressions that may be considered to be 'fringe' or even dangerous. This can be exemplified through the inclusion and discussion of groups such as the Westboro Baptist Church. This is a group whose actions are condemned by the vast majority of Christians as antithetical to the central message of Christianity. RE professionals need to be careful about the groups that are included, and the way that they are taught. If such groups are included for 'entertainment' or as attention grabbers, the teacher and curriculum writers may want to consider the educational validity of such a choice. If they are used as a way to explore the various expressions of religion, and to develop skills of religious enquiry and literacy, then there may be an argument for their inclusion. Such groups, however, are not a focus of this book as their followings in the UK are not significant, but the discussion surrounding their inclusion may be extended to some of the groups who are.

Conclusion
It would be wrong to dismiss those beyond the big six from the teaching of RE because of parental and teacher prejudice, or arguments for the sake of striving to limit the scope of RE and the professionalism of RE teachers. The most persuasive argument against the inclusion in the RE classroom is that great pressures are already placed upon on the RE curriculum. A cohesive Phenomenological approach to individual religions may be seen to be the ideal by members of faith communities who are seeking parity with the major world religions. Indeed, most adherents to a faith community would like to see their particular group given a curriculum block, where all aspects of belief and values could be explored in depth. However, with the great stresses already placed on the time given to RE, including every single faith group or worldview is not a realistic option.

Expanding the Boundaries

The most persuasive argument for the inclusion is in those environments where they may constitute pupils' own worldviews and the good teacher should build upon the experiences of those pupils. On occasion, the bad teacher would dismiss a child's faith as not relevant or else would have an erroneous understanding of that faith which makes the child and their family upset and confused. However, on those good occasions when teachers have explored the beliefs of those they encounter, an increased understanding has come to both pupils and teachers. In my experience, engaging with pupils about their faith has made the child feel valued while enhancing the teacher's knowledge. For some teachers the child and its parents may be the first members of a particular faith community that they have met.

Expanding the boundaries of the teaching of the big six can counter the approach that provides a univocal view of religion. This can serve to reinforce stereotypes, be out of step with pupils' experiences of religion and, most crucially, may be at odds with the beliefs and practices of the pupils themselves (see Moulin, 2011). Consider the Jehovah's Witness child in the classroom who is told that a Christian is someone who believes in the Trinity; they are aware that they do not believe in the Nicene view of the Trinity yet she believes she is a Christian. Or the Muslim child who is presented with a view of Islam that presents Sunni as normative and the original form of Islam, with other forms being schismatic. Whereas a Shi'a Muslim believes that Shi'a is the original form and Sunni is schismatic. The RE teacher might have particular views about the validity of these beliefs, but these need to be secondary to the recognition that what is being taught is a particular expression of the religion rather than the normative view. If RE is to be truly inclusive and representative of religion then there should be the recognition that a "major focus of RE is the study of diversity of religion and belief" (DCSF, 2010, p. 8). This does not just mean between religions, but also within religions.

The argument of this book is that the boundaries of the RE classroom should be expanded as it prepares pupils to respect people from a myriad of faiths. This is the goal of any RE classroom, and should be extended to those whose beliefs have a significant presence in the United Kingdom. It is important to note that although this book explores the expansion of the boundaries within Islam and Christianity, the same arguments can be made for Buddhism, Hinduism, Judaism and Sikhism. Within Buddhism, the focus is often on Theravada rather than Mahayana traditions, and it is important to acknowledge the newer Buddhist movements that students will come across in the West, such as Soka Gakkai, the Triratna community, and the many different Tibetan Buddhist groups. The integration of these minority religions and worldviews should be undertaken in a robust way that is educationally and religiously valid. Oftentimes on social media I see appeals for lessons about alternative religions to fill a space in the curriculum. When pressed, requesters see their inclusion as a way to capture attention, and to engage students. On further investigation, lessons are often inappropriate as they focus on why the religion is 'controversial'; one lesson considered the question "Why do people think Mormons are not Christian?" and another considered the use of marijuana in Rastafari. The argument of this book is that the inclusion of minority religions is important, but it should be done thoughtfully and not to sensationalise the subject matter. These are lived religions that demand thoughtful consideration.

To help to overcome a perceived lack of knowledge of these groups, this book will explore how teaching about those religions beyond the big six might be practically implemented, but it will also introduce selected worldviews. Each of the chapters will provide a brief overview of the main beliefs and practices of the religious or non-religious worldview as understood from the perspective of the tradition itself (while recognising the inherent diversity within each). This will mainly utilise writings of the traditions themselves and should provide a good basis for further study (while recognising the inherent diversity within each). The focus will be on how these beliefs and practices influence the lives of individuals today. Underpinning each of these will be the importance of beliefs, together with teaching ideas for the classroom.

References

AQA (2017). *GCSE Religious Studies A 8062*. Manchester, UK: AQA Education.

Blaylock, L. (Ed.). (2004). *Representing religions. Teachers of RE from six religions explain how to represent their religions in your classroom*. Birmingham, UK: Christian Education.

Bolton, J. (1999). *An investigation into the place of paganism within RE: A teacher's guide*. Oxford, UK: Farmington.

Copley, T. (1994). *Religious education 7-11* (Appendix II Jehovah's Witnesses). London, UK: Routledge.

DCSF (2009). *Religious education in English schools: Non-statutory guidance 2009*. Nottingham, UK: DCSF Publications.

DCSF (2010). *Religious education in English schools: Non-statutory guidance 2010* Nottingham, UK: DCSF Publications.

Erricker, C., & Erricker, J. (2003). The Children and Worldviews Project: A narrative pedagogy of religious education. In M. Grimmitt (Ed.), *Pedagogies of Religious Education* (pp. 188-206). Great Wakering, UK: McCrimmons.

Grimmitt, M. (Ed.) (2003). *Pedagogies of religious education*. Great Wakering, UK: McCrimmons.

Head, Ronan (2009). The experience of Mormon children in English school-based religious education and collective worship. *International Journal of Mormon Studies, 2*, 197-205.

Holt, James (2010). Beyond the big six: Minority religions in the secondary RE classroom. In J. Schmack, M. Thompson, D. Torevell, & C. Cole (Eds.). *Engaging RE* (pp. 76-91). Newcastle upon Tyne, UK: Cambridge Scholars.

Holt, James (2015). *Religious education in the secondary school: An introduction to teaching, learning and the world religions*. London, UK: Routledge.

Lovelace, A. (2001). *Speaking for ourselves. A REnSE project video*. Norwich, UK: RMEP.

MacIntyre, A. (1988). *Whose justice? Which rationality?* London, UK: Duckworth.

McGarvey, Darren (2018). *Poverty safari: Understanding the anger of Britain's underclass*. London, UK: Picador.

Miller, J. (2004). Editorial, *Resource: The Journal of the Professional Council for Religious Education* 24(3), 3.

Moulin, D. (2011). Giving voice to 'the silent minority': The experience of religious students in secondary school religious education lessons. *British Journal of Religious Education, 33*(3), 313–26.

Office for National Statistics (2012). *Religion in England and Wales 2011*. Available at: www.ons.gov.uk/ons/dcp171776_290510.pdf (accessed 28 May 2019).

Prothero, S. (2010). *God is not one: The eight rival religions that run the world – and why their differences matter*. New York, NY: HarperOne.

Redbridge SACRE (1997). *Jehovah's Witnesses and the school*. London, UK: London Borough of Redbridge.

RE Council of England and Wales (2013). *A review of RE in England*. London, UK: RE Council.

Rudge, Linda (1998). 'I am nothing' – does it matter? A critique of current religious education policy and practice in England on behalf of the silent majority. *British Journal of Religious Education, 20*(3), 155–65.

Wintersgill, B. (Ed.). (2017). *Big ideas in religious education*. Exeter, UK: University of Exeter.

SECTION 2
EXTENDING THE UNDERSTANDING OF CHRISTIANITY

CHAPTER 2

THE BOUNDARIES OF CHRISTIANITY

Defining Christianity and its boundaries is a difficult task. In 2001 it was suggested that there are over 33,000 different Christian groups (Barrett, Kurian, and Johnson, 2001). Within this there are three main groupings of Churches: Orthodox, Catholic and Protestant. This is not the complete story and there are groups who would find themselves outside of these umbrella groups; Barrett et al. categorise them as Independents and Marginals (2001). The idea that Christianity needs defining is not new; in exploring the concept of who or what a Christian is, Justin Martyr outlined:

> Those who are found not living as he taught should know that they are not really Christians, even if his teachings are on their lips, for he said that not those who merely profess but those who also do the works will be saved (Justin Martyr in Plantinga, 1999, pp. 37-38).

His criteria seem to link with the teachings of Jesus that:

> Not everyone who says to me, 'Lord, Lord,' will enter the kingdom of heaven, but only the one who does the will of my Father who is in heaven (Matthew 7:21).

This seems to indicate that only those who live the principles that Christ taught could consider themselves to be Christian. It could be ameliorated slightly by suggesting that those who try and live as Jesus taught are Christian. This still remains problematic for two reasons; firstly, there is a myriad of interpretations as to how to put the teachings of Jesus into action; secondly, in focussing on an orthopraxy is it a slightly simplistic view of Christianity? Justin Martyr suggests that it is "not those who merely profess"; this suggests that there does have a be a level of orthodoxy, or right knowledge in determining who is a Christian.

The question then arises as to who has the authority and the right to establish orthodoxy and the boundaries of acceptability within the Christian family of Churches. For the purpose of this book there are two different answers to the question of the boundaries of a religion – the first is personal and the second is educational.

Firstly, the personal. Every individual and group has the right to hold views that define their approach to their religion. In this sense, certain Christians may make certain doctrines and practices normative to be considered as belonging. All people have this kind of view; it might be recognised that others believe differently but it is questionable as to whether these boundaries should be imposed on others. This is important for inter-faith discussions and involvement in different activities. Why is this question important for dialogue? Understanding how they view each other is important to both groups of Christians. When dialogue is engaged in between the two groups it is important for each group to consider: is it as members of the same community or as different religions? This type of question is not just important for the validity of the dialogue undertaken, but also for the participating groups' understanding of what they are trying to achieve and where they are coming from. In this way, how a Christian views others can become an obstacle but not an insurmountable one if we agree to disagree. Within Christianity it is suggested that "For most Latter-day Saints in dialogue with evangelicals, the question of their Christianity is the elephant in the room. It is … an unnecessary diversion" (Holt, 2012, p. 73). Disagreeing about this need not be rude, rather it can be an exciting starting point for dialogue. It is also an honest viewpoint of an individual.

Some examples of how the boundaries have been drawn at the personal or institutional level, include the idea that people can only be considered Christian if the Churches to which they belong:

- Are members of the World Council of Churches …
- Accept the Trinity (see Holt, 2005, p. 34).

The Boundaries of Christianity

The first one has been adopted by a major awarding organisation in England in defining the acceptability of Christian groups. It is similarly adopted in application processes of certain schools; those outside of the definition belong to the category of non-Christian groups. While this is a tenable view for individuals and Churches, it provides problems from an educational view, which is the second answer to the question as to who is a Christian. Teachers should be aware of their personal prejudices and how they might affect what is taught within the classroom. By imposing their view of what a Christian is, based on their personal beliefs, it might be antithetical to a positive neutrality that is to be expected in the teaching of religions: "It does not mean that the teacher does not care but that he cares for them all, accepting them as they are" (Hull, 1984, p. 181).

Continuing the example of the 'World Council of Churches' (WCC), the unsuitability of such a definition that seems, quite reasonably, to pass the problem of definition to an outside body, means that there may be an inadvertent exclusion of other groups that the WCC may not have needed to consider, in contrast to an RE syllabus which should be inclusive. As an ecumenical organisation, to bring together all Churches, the Roman Catholic Church did not join (but has cordial relations). Following the organisation of the WCC in 1948, Pope Pius XII addressed the lack of involvement in all ecumenical organisations in 1949:

> The Catholic Church, although she does not take part in congresses and other conventions called "ecumenical," yet has never ceased, as is clear from many Pontifical documents, nor will she in future ever cease, to follow with the most intense interest and to promote by earnest prayers to God, all efforts toward the attainment of what is so dear to the Heart of Christ Our Lord, namely, that all who believe in Him "may be made perfect in one." For she embraces with truly maternal affection all who return to her as the true Church of Christ ... (Pius XII, 1949).

This may be one of the reasons that other denominations, which may be excluded from the Christian family in some people's eyes, reject involvement in the WCC, and it may appear that there is a double standard being employed. People who use this criterion are perhaps suggesting that it is more about the acceptance of the beliefs identified by the WCC that allows a Church to be considered Christian:

> The World Council of Churches is a fellowship of churches which confess the Lord Jesus Christ as God and Saviour according to the scriptures, and therefore seek to fulfil together their common calling to the glory of the one God, Father, Son and Holy Spirit.
>
> It is a community of churches on the way to visible unity in one faith and one eucharistic fellowship, expressed in worship and in common life in Christ. It seeks to advance towards this unity, as Jesus prayed for his followers, "so that the world may believe" (John 17:21) (World Council of Churches, 2017).

With Roman Catholics rejecting the second paragraph, it would seem that the first is what is being referred to as the orthodoxy evidenced by membership of the WCC. This would link with the articulation of the Trinity as the defining characteristic of a Christian. This is highlighted using the example of Jehovah's Witnesses who would self-identify as Christian supported by a belief in Jesus and the use of the Bible, but other Christians may address their Christianity "by referring to Trinitarian doctrine: those who hold the idea of God in Trinity are Christians, but those (like the Witnesses) who do not hold this belief place themselves alongside, but separate from, the main stream of Christianity" (Holt, 2004, p. 17).

This type of definition is repeated in the Amsterdam Declaration which suggests that:

> A Christian is a believer in God who is enabled by the Holy Spirit to submit to Jesus Christ as Lord and Saviour in a personal relationship of disciple to master to live the life of God's kingdom. The word Christian should not be equated with any particular cultural, ethnic, political, or ideological tradition nor group. Those who know and love Jesus are also called Christ-followers, believers and disciples (*Christianity Today*, 2000, p. 207).

There is, however, a problem with the language used by both the WCC and the Amsterdam Declaration and the identification of the boundaries

The Boundaries of Christianity

of Christianity. The two examples of denominations used in this book to suggest an expansion of the boundaries of Christianity. The Church of Jesus Christ of Latter-day Saints and Jehovah's Witnesses, would potentially be able to subscribe to both of these statements as they are written. The problem that this highlights is that Christianity and its boundaries may be muddied by a shared language with very different understandings. Would both groups understand the statements of faith in the same way as groups from what is usually considered to be, mainstream Christianity? The language may be the same but the understanding could be either subtly or blatantly different: "terminology is deceptive. Men may speak similarly but mean and feel differently. And as you know, the theological vocabulary is notoriously vague" (Madsen, 1974, p. 74). This argument is reminiscent of Wittgenstein: "One cannot guess how a word functions. One has to look at its use and learn from that" summarised as 'don't ask for meaning ask for use' (1968, p. 109). Paulsen has recently made this very point in examining the convergence and divergence of Latter-day Saint teachings with mainstream Christianity:

> One more very important reminder: when it comes to Christian fundamentals – the divinity and lordship of Jesus Christ, his redemptive atonement, his resurrection, and our victory through him over sin and death – there is little to distinguish Joseph's understandings from those of "orthodox" Christians ... And a final important reminder: Latter-day Saint views on many points of doctrine still differ, sometimes radically, from the more traditional Christian views. This is true for even those doctrines toward which ... there has been significant Christian convergence (2006, pp. 37-38).

When a Jehovah's Witness reads the Amsterdam Declaration they do so through the lens of their own understanding. It is possible for two or more different interpretations to be taken from the same statement. Those who use the Trinity as the defining characteristic of Christianity would suggest that acceptance of the idea of God as expressed in the creeds is central to Christian identity; the Nicene Creed states:

> We believe in one God, the Father, the Almighty, maker of heaven and earth, and of all that is, seen and unseen.
>
> We believe in one Lord, Jesus Christ, the only Son of God, eternally begotten of the Father, God from God, Light from Light, true God from true God, begotten, not made, *one in Being with the Father*. Through him all things were made …
>
> We believe in the Holy Spirit, the Lord, the giver of life, who proceeds from the Father and the Son. With the Father and the Son he is worshipped and glorified (Credo n.d., emphasis added).

The italicised aspect of the creed above is the point with which most non-Trinitarian Christians disagree: the idea that the three Persons are homoousios (of one substance). God is at the same time Father, Son and Holy Spirit. This belief is seen to be a mystery beyond the capacity of humans to fully understand.

Using this definition then it is possible to suggest that many 'Marginals' are not Christian. While this is a definition that could be adopted and accepted on an institutional and personal level it is problematic as an educational boundary. The reason I suggest it is problematic is because the lived reality of many of the pupils form 'marginal' expressions of Christianity and also why I suggest the following definition may be more workable in an educational setting. A Christian is:

> … somebody who considers themselves to be a Christian. If there has to be a criterion against which they can be judged, it would be a belief that Jesus is the Christ, the Son of God (Holt, 2005, p. 34).

The belief that Jesus is the Son of God is the central feature of Christianity. While there may be other areas of diversity outside of this unifying belief, recognising the importance of Jesus in all aspects of Christianity is crucial:

> In our general introduction to the study of Christianity as a world religion the rather formidable complexity and diversity of the religion was stressed and illustrated. Without in any way underestimating the significance of this complexity, we can also recognise that the one

The Boundaries of Christianity

unifying factor among this diversity is the figure of Jesus (Read, Rudge, and Howarth, 1986, pp. 5–7).

If pupils are to understand Christian belief and why Christians behave the way they do, then an understanding of the life and person of Jesus and its importance is imperative.

The other aspect of the definition as 'somebody who considers themselves to be a Christian' may be seen to be an oversimplification of a very nuanced question about the boundaries of Christianity. In following a discussion about this topic in an RE group on Facebook, one of the commenters responded with the argument that "just because I consider myself to be Miss World doesn't make it true". Although this argument is reductive it does highlight an issue with the definition offered. It can be countered that although a person may consider themselves as such, there is little evidence that they have engaged with the process or possess any of the characteristics and activities that would indicate this. From a 'Marginals' perspective it would be argued that the believers evidence characteristics and activities that seem to indicate some level of Christianity.

Despite the possible drawbacks to such a definition, the experience of pupils in the classroom make it imperative that such a wide definition is adopted. Consider the examples of two pupils; one from a Latter-day Saint background, and one from a Jehovah's Witness background:

1. Pupil 1 received a project-based task to produce a brochure for a local Christian Church. It was to focus on the internal and external features; their uses and symbolism. The only stipulation was that it should not be an Anglican Church, as they had explored this as a class. This child was a member of The Church of Jesus Christ of Latter-day Saints and decided that it would be nice to produce a brochure for her Church. After two weeks of work and the production of an in-depth brochure which met all the criteria, she handed in the assigned task. This was returned the next lesson with a note: "You did not complete the task as set. The place of worship you have chosen is not Christian and so cannot be marked."

2. Pupil 2, a Jehovah's Witness, was in a lesson learning about the crucifixion of Jesus. As the narrative unfolded she raised her hand and shared her thoughts: "You've said that in the Bible it teaches that Jesus died on a cross. In my Church we believe that he was not crucified on a cross, but on a stake, a torture stake." The teacher responded, "That is not what the Bible says, and all Christians believe that he died on the cross."

Both are very different experiences, but the result in both instances are the same: the identity of the child is challenged and rejected. This is a problem because, while it may reflect the personal beliefs of the teacher, it is establishing a person in a position of authority and power challenging some of what may be most important to a child. Yeats wrote:

> I have spread my dreams under your feet;
> Tread softly because you tread on my dreams (Yeats, 2010, p. 26).

Teachers need to be mindful of the emotional impact they have on the individuals they teach. This kind of approach in the teaching of Christianity is, perhaps, encapsulated in a poem by Edward Markham:

> He drew a circle that shut me out –
> Heretic, rebel, a thing to flout.
>
> But Love and I had the wit to win:
> We drew a circle that took him in! (Markham, 1936, p. 67).

This will also enable teachers to play in the prevention of ostracisation or the marginalisation of people in RE. This will mainly be done in the classroom through the discussions that take place and the attitudes which are shown and are allowed to flourish. This does not mean ignoring any divergent opinions or attitudes that arise, but confronting them. In effect teachers are able to transcend the boundaries that others may see, allowing a more rigorous exploration of controversial issues and areas of debate within Christianity. In exploring the reasons behind divergence of beliefs it would provide a criticality of positions held by various denominations therein. In this context there are simple things that can be done in the teaching of Christianity to include minority expressions as appropriate.

References

Barrett, David B., Kurian, George T., & Johnson, Todd M. (2001). *World Christian encyclopedia: A comparative survey of churches and religions in the modern world* (2nd ed.). Oxford, UK: Oxford University Press.

Christianity Today, (2000, 1 August). The Amsterdam Declaration: A Charter for evangelism in the 21st century. Retrieved from https://www.christianitytoday.com/ct/2000/augustweb-only/13.0.html

Credo (n.d.). In Catechism of the Catholic Church. Retrieved from http://www.vatican.va/archive/ccc_css/archive/catechism/credo.htm

Holt, James D. (2004). Jehovah's Witnesses and the R.E. Classroom. *Resource, 26*(2), 16–19.

Holt, James D. (2005). The frontiers of Christianity. *RE Today, 22*(2), 34.

Holt, James (2012). Mormon-Evangelical dialogue: A way forward in setting ground rules. *Sacred Tribes Journal, 7*(1), 70–79.

Hull, John (1984). *Studies in religion and education.* Lewes, UK: Falmer.

Justin, Martyr (1999). The first apology. In R. Plantinga (Ed.), *Christianity and plurality. Classic and contemporary readings* (pp. 29–61). Oxford, UK: Blackwell.

MacIntyre, A. (1988). *Whose justice? Which rationality?* London, UK: Duckworth.

Madsen, T. (1974). Are Christians Mormon? *BYU Studies, 15*(1), 73–94.

Markham E. (1936). Outwitted. In Hazel Felleman, *The Best Loved Poems of the American People.* New York, NY: Doubleday.

Paulsen, D. (2006). Reassessing Joseph Smith's theology in his bicentennial. *BYU Studies, 45*(1), 35–128.

Pius XII (1949, 20 December). *On the Ecumenical Movement: An instruction of the Holy Office addressed to the ordinaries of places.*

Read, G., Rudge, J., & Howarth R. B. (1986). *The Westhill Project RE 5–16. How do I teach RE?* (2nd ed.). Cheltenham, UK: Stanley Thornes.

Wittgenstein, L. (1968). *Philosophical investigations.* (G. E. Anscombe, Trans.) New York, NY: Macmillan.

World Council of Churches (2017). *About us.* Retrieved from https://www.oikoumene.org/en/about-us

Yeats, W. B. (2010). *The wind among the reeds.* Pakenham, Canada: FQ Books.

CHAPTER 3
THE CHURCH OF JESUS CHRIST OF LATTER-DAY SAINTS

Chapter Outline
What is The Church of Jesus Christ of Latter-day Saints?
What is its place within Christianity?
Message
Nature of God
Nature of humanity
Scripture
Religious expression

What is The Church of Jesus Christ of Latter-day Saints?
The Church of Jesus Christ of Latter-day Saints was organised in New York State on 6 April 1830. In the first twenty years of its history the Church was characterised by movement within the United States, and then, following the death of Joseph Smith, the majority of the members of the Church undertook a trek across the continent and established a settlement and community in the modern-day state of Utah.

The Church today has over 16 million members worldwide and over 30,000 congregations; in the UK there are reported to be over 180,000 members of the Church.

The Church of Jesus Christ of Latter-day Saints can be described as a 'restorationist' Christian Church. One of the central teachings is that following the death of the Apostles, and over a period of time the Christian Church entered a period of apostasy where the truths were lost, and the authority of the priesthood to act in God's name was removed from this earth. This was characterised by the many denominations that arose within Christianity. Latter-day Saints believe that rather than reforming Christianity from within, it was necessary for God to restore his Church through the Prophet Joseph Smith.

The Church of Jesus Christ of Latter-day Saints

This process of restoration began with what is termed the 'First Vision'. In this Joseph Smith sought to know which Church to join. Jesus Christ told him not to join any Church, but that in time the Church would be restored through him. Between the First Vision in 1820, and the formal organisation of the Church in 1830 there were many other occurrences that laid the foundation for the organisation of the Church:

- The Restoration of the Aaronic Priesthood in May 1829. Latter-day Saints believe that Joseph Smith was given this priesthood which includes the authority to baptise by John the Baptist.
- The Restoration of the Melchizedek Priesthood in the early summer of 1829. The Melchizedek Priesthood is also known as the Higher Priesthood and enables further ordinances to be carried out, and the right of presidency within the Church. This was restored to Joseph Smith by Peter, James and John.
- The process of translation and the publication of *The Book of Mormon* in March 1830.

Although these events laid the groundwork for the organisation of the Church in 1830, the process of Restoration continued during the ministry of the Prophet Joseph Smith. Other events of note include:

- In March 1832 the First Presidency was organised. This is the highest council of the Church containing the President/Prophet of the Church and two counsellors.
- February 1835, the Quorum of the Twelve Apostles is organised. The Twelve Apostles form a council, second only in authority to the First Presidency.
- April 1836, Moses, Elias and Elijah appeared to Joseph Smith and gave him priesthood keys which included the sealing power the power to bind families together for eternity.
- March 1842, The Relief Society, or women's organisation in the Church was established.

Upon the death of Joseph Smith in 1844, Brigham Young, as President of the Quorum of the Twelve Apostles, was chosen to be the next President of the Church. This method of succession has remained in place since that time. Following the death of Joseph Smith there was controversy about who should succeed him with various people claiming that right. The Church of Jesus Christ of Latter-day Saints united under Brigham Young and while there were other groups that were formed, many did not last. One that was known as The Reorganised Church of Jesus Christ of Latter Day Saints, members of whom felt that the leadership should have passed to Smith's son, Joseph Smith III. This Church is known today as The Community of Christ and is based in Independence, Missouri.

The Church of Jesus Christ of Latter-day Saints has continued to grow into many countries during the past two hundred years. The 'succession in the presidency' is generally now considered to be fixed, in the sense that the most senior Apostle (the President of the Quorum of the Twelve Apostles) is ordained the next Prophet and President of the Church, following the death of the previous Prophet. The organisation of the Church is structured at General (world) level and at more of a local level. The organisation of the leadership of the Church includes:

- *The First Presidency* which includes the Prophet and President of the Church, along with two counsellors who are usually chosen from among the Apostles.
- *The Quorum of the Twelve Apostles* which is composed of Twelve Apostles who are viewed as witnesses of Christ who travel the world.
- *The Quorums of the Seventy* who are responsible for representing the Quorum of the Twelve Apostles and providing guidance and leadership, often in an 'Area' that is constituted of many countries.
- *General Auxiliary Presidencies* which replicate organisations on a local level such as the Relief Society, Sunday School, Primary, Young Men and Young Women. They are responsible for overseeing the work of these auxiliaries on a local level.

On a local level, the Church is organised into wards (the equivalent of parishes) and stakes (similar to dioceses). A ward is led by a Bishop, which is an unpaid office to which a person is called, usually for a period of approximately five years. He is supported by two counsellors and auxiliary presidencies. The auxiliaries and their equivalents are led by a President and two counsellors, they include the following:

- *Relief Society*: the organisation for all women aged eighteen and over. The work of the Relief Society is run by women and is for the support of everyone.
- *Elders' Quorum* is the organisation for all men aged eighteen and over. The term 'Elder' refers to the priesthood office that most worthy men over eighteen hold. Those who do not are known as 'prospective Elders'. This quorum is seen to be a brotherhood and a means of service to others.
- *Young Men* is the organisation for boys aged 12–18; in addition to Sunday lessons there are often weekly activities.
- *Young Women* is the organisation for girls aged 12–18; in addition to Sunday lessons there are often weekly activities.
- *Primary* is the organisation for boys and girls aged 18 months–11 years; in addition to Sunday lessons there are periodic activities.

The stake oversees the work of the wards and is presided over by a Stake President and two counsellors (the Stake Presidency); this role is also unpaid and is usually for approximately nine years. The ward auxiliaries (apart from the Elders' Quorum) have equivalents at a stake level that oversees their work.

What is its place within Christianity?
There are traditionally seen to be three main groupings of Churches: Orthodox, Catholic and Protestant. However, The Church of Jesus Christ of Latter-day Saints would place itself outside of this traditional typology, perhaps preferring the term 'restorationist'. Barrett et al. might categorise them as Independents and Marginals (2001). Some of its beliefs might be seen to place it outside of what is traditionally termed the mainstream. One Latter-day Saint has reflected on the positioning of the Church within Christianity:

> I once wrote an article for *RE Today* that outlined some of the arguments that I had heard and made suggestions as to why they may not be valid. These included:

- You can only be a Christian if you believe in the Trinity – I do believe in the Father, Son and Holy Spirit – just that they're not homoousios. This definition would exclude others such as Unitarians.
- A Christian Church is a member of the World Council of Churches – I suggested that as the Roman Catholic Church is not a member of such, though acts as an observer, this may not be the best definition. I have actually seen this one used recently by an awarding organisation.
- The age of the Church – thus excluding the Salvation Army and others.

I suggested that no definition was perfect and was designed to exclude rather than define. It was interesting because the next issue of *RE Today* published a rebuttal from a head teacher who suggested that I had been disingenuous in not mentioning my belief in a further book of scripture, or in a living prophet. The implication was that these were beliefs that would similarly place me outside Christianity. I wasn't being disingenuous – I just hadn't considered that these were non-Christian (Holt, 2019).

Latter-day Saints have traditionally seen the claim that they are not Christian as an "extreme" example of intolerance (England, 1999, p. 192). Some statements made by Latter-day Saints may also seem to be extreme in placing themselves apart from mainstream Christianity. Latter-day Saints sometimes place themselves as a supercessionary form of Christianity, seeing all other forms to be in error:

> … just as the early Christians believed they had found the only proper way to be Jews, so the early followers of the Mormon Prophet believed they had found the only proper way to be Christians … The Church of Jesus Christ of Latter-day Saints is best understood as a form of corporate Christianity … in much the same way that early Christianity was related to Judaism (Shipps, 1993, p. 441).

Gordon B. Hinckley, a previous President of the Church, has outlined how they differ from other forms of Christianity:

> They say we do not believe in the traditional Christ of Christianity. There is some substance to what they say. Our faith, our knowledge

is not based on ancient tradition, the creeds which came of a finite understanding and out of the almost infinite discussions of men trying to arrive at a definition of the risen Christ. Our faith, our knowledge comes of the witness of a prophet in this dispensation who saw before him the great God of the universe and His Beloved Son, the resurrected Lord Jesus Christ (2002, pp. 91–92).

Bob Millet has argued that traditional Christianity views Christ through the spectacles of the creeds, whereas Latter-day Saints view him through the spectacles of the revelations of Joseph Smith (see Millet, 2005). These are fairly large differences, and indeed, a significant belief that sets the Church of Jesus Christ of Latter-day Saints apart from the rest of Christianity.

It seems as though both 'sides' of the discussion recognise differences between themselves. Latter-day Saints self-identify as Christian, but recognise that some of their beliefs may not be orthodox. This seems to be a good starting point to work from; similar but different.

Message

The message of The Church of Jesus Christ of Latter-day Saints encompasses what is termed the Gospel, or sometimes the Restored Gospel, of Jesus Christ. For Latter-day Saints the person of Jesus Christ is at the centre of all of existence and his atonement is the pivotal event of the plan of salvation (see below: Nature of humanity).

The narrative of its message about Jesus Christ is not dissimilar to that found in mainstream Christianity. Latter-day Saints teach that at the beginning of human existence Adam and Eve were in a close relationship with God; in the Garden of Eden they lived in a paradisiacal glory, with no suffering but also no procreation. This relationship enabled them to walk and talk with God. Within the Garden of Eden they were able to use and eat freely of any of the trees which surrounded them, apart from the tree of knowledge of good and evil. Satan tempted Eve to eat of that fruit promising that if she partook "Ye shall not surely die; For God doth know that in the day ye eat thereof, then your eyes shall be opened, and ye shall be as gods, knowing good and evil" (Moses 4:10–11). In eating of the fruit, Adam and Eve transgressed the law of God and were thrust out of the Garden of Eden being separated from God.

This separation of humanity from God is the result of two things: sin and death. Both of these came into the world through Adam's transgression. Although Adam sinned, and sin entered into the world through him, there is not a concept of original sin in Latter-day Saint teaching. Adam was forgiven for his sin and the stain of that sin is not passed on to humanity: "We believe that men will be punished for their own sins, and not for Adam's transgression" (Article of Faith 2). What is passed on, however, is the capacity to sin and as such all of humanity is separated from God through sin. Also death is, for humanity by themselves, an insurmountable obstacle to an eternal relationship with God. Adam and Eve's experience is emblematic of each human's experience with God; having once been in a relationship with God (see below: Nature of humanity) they are now separated from God by sin and death, and their whole life is about striving for reconciliation with him.

The way that humanity is able to be reconciled with God is through the person and grace of Jesus Christ. For Latter-day Saints the sacrifice of Christ was an integral part of the Father's plan from the beginning. *The Pearl of Great Price*[2] records an event known as the Council in Heaven:

> And the Lord said: Whom shall I send? And one answered like unto the Son of Man: Here am I, send me. And another answered and said: Here am I, send me. And the Lord said: I will send the first (Abraham 3:27).

For Latter-day Saints, it was decreed in heaven that a Saviour, namely Jesus Christ, would be required as the world was created to "prove [humanity] herewith, to see if they will do all things whatsoever the Lord their God shall command them" (Abraham 3:25).

---

2 Latter-day Saints have different books of scripture: The Holy Bible, *The Book of Mormon*, *The Doctrine and Covenants*, and *The Pearl of Great Price*.

The Church of Jesus Christ of Latter-day Saints

The resurrection of Jesus Christ enables all people to be resurrected. Through his resurrection all are able to live again, whether that is in eternal life with God, or elsewhere. All of humanity will be brought to stand before God and be judged. This is a free gift because of the grace of Jesus Christ shown through his life, death and resurrection. This action enables all to be reconciled with God, but it may only be for the purpose of judgement. It means that the first of the obstacles produced by Adam's transgression is overcome. This act required the sacrifice of the Son of God, only he had the power to lay down his life and take it back up again.

Within Latter-day Saint theology there are the two principles of justice and mercy. *The Book of Mormon* outlines the nature of justice in terms of human sin:

> And thus we see that all mankind were fallen, and they were in the grasp of justice; yea, the justice of God, which consigned them forever to be cut off from his presence (Alma 42:14).

The eternal law of justice means that because humans sin and transgress the laws of God, they are cut off from God's presence forever. It is a 'just' judgement that separates God from his creation. However, there is a way for justice to be satisfied which is through the law of mercy. *The Book of Mormon* further explains:

> And now, the plan of mercy could not be brought about except an atonement should be made; therefore God himself atoneth for the sins of the world, to bring about the plan of mercy, to appease the demands of justice, that God might be a perfect, just God, and a merciful God also. Now, repentance could not come unto men except there were a punishment, which also was eternal as the life of the soul should be, affixed opposite to the plan of happiness, which was as eternal also as the life of the soul ... But there is a law given, and a punishment affixed, and a repentance granted; which repentance, mercy claimeth; otherwise, justice claimeth the creature and executeth the law, and the law inflicteth the punishment; if not so, the works of justice would be destroyed, and God would cease to be God. But God ceaseth not to be God, and mercy claimeth the penitent, and mercy cometh because

of the atonement; and the atonement bringeth to pass the resurrection of the dead; and the resurrection of the dead bringeth back men into the presence of God; and thus they are restored into his presence, to be judged according to their works, according to the law and justice. For behold, justice exerciseth all his demands, and also mercy claimeth all which is her own; and thus, none but the truly penitent are saved (Alma 42:15-16, 20-22).

The atonement of Jesus Christ is not a cosmic battle ransoming people from Satan's grasp, but rather from the claims of justice. Although elements of the cosmic battle remain in the sense that in being cut off from God, people are subject to the devil. The atonement of Jesus Christ enables people to be drawn back into a relationship with God and reconciled with him. While this is something that is fulfilled at judgement, it can also be developed in this life, where people live in relationship with God by abiding in his grace.

Every part of the message of the Gospel of Jesus Christ, for Latter-day Saints, means that humanity is being drawn back into this relationship with God. In Latter-day Saint belief the atonement of Christ is not just about the forgiveness of sins, but also the removal of pains and sicknesses. The whole of Jesus' life, not just the cross, becomes part of his atonement. It was necessary for Christ to experience all of the trials of humanity to be a perfect example, but also to be able to bear the burdens of humanity. By rejecting the temptations he faced, Latter-day Saints believe that, Christ was not subject to the spiritual death caused by Adam's transgression. Christ's perfection enabled the relationship with the Father to be continued even during mortality. The Father's purposeful removal (see Mark 15:34), both in Gethsemane and Calvary, was therefore a crucial part of the atonement for Christ as well as for humanity. Gethsemane was where Christ first encountered the effects of spiritual death, sin and the associated pains of mortality to the degree where he was left alone by the Father causing him to be "amazed" at the strength of sin (Mark 14:33). Especially important are Gethsemane and the cross. For Latter-day Saints, in Gethsemane, and then again on the cross, Jesus suffered for all the pains, sicknesses and afflictions of humanity; something which in Latter-day Saint theology is termed an eternal and infinite atonement.

For Latter-day Saints it is possible to encounter Jesus and utilise his atonement in every aspect of their life. This is because of the belief that Christ suffered for the pains and sickness of life, as well as for a person's sins. They should seek him and to live in his grace every day of their lives.

A further emphasis of this message of The Church of Jesus Christ of Latter-day Saints is that the Church is the Restored Church of Jesus Christ. As briefly mentioned in the introduction to this chapter, the Church has a teaching that Christianity fell into a state of apostasy and that only a Restoration could return the Church to the teachings and practices evident in the Church as established by Jesus and his Apostles. This means that while Latter-day Saints see elements of truth in other denominations of Christianity, they believe that only in the Church can the fullness of the Gospel of Jesus Christ be found.

Nature of God
The 'First Vision' establishes for Latter-day Saints an orthodoxy about the nature of God. In the spring of 1820 following a period of 'great reflection' the fourteen-year-old Joseph Smith records that he was concerned about his eternal welfare and was seeking to find the Church that Christ had established while on the earth. He describes a search for truth that incorporated attendance at different Church meetings and a study of the Bible. Following the reading of James 1:5: "If any of you lack wisdom, let him ask of God who giveth to all men liberally and upbraideth not, and it shall be given him", Smith determined to pray to God to enquire about his questions. In response to this prayer he recorded:

> I saw a pillar of light exactly over my head, above the brightness of the sun, which descended gradually until it fell upon me ... When the light rested upon me I saw two Personages, whose brightness and glory defy all description, standing above me in the air. One of them spake unto me, calling me by name and said, pointing to the other – This is My

Beloved Son. Hear Him! (Joseph Smith History 1:16–17 in *The Pearl of Great Price*).

This was recorded in 1838, and there are other narrations of this event which slightly differ; but it is seen as a foundational event through which Latter-day Saint theology and beliefs should be explored. It establishes, for Latter-day Saints, the separate nature of the members of, what they term, the Godhead.

Latter-day Saints teach that there are three members of the Godhead: the Father, Son and Holy Spirit, and that these three are separate and distinct individuals. *The Doctrine and Covenants* (see p. 49) records that in their nature, "The Father has a body of flesh and bones as tangible as man's; the Son also; but the Holy Ghost has not a body of flesh and bones, but is a personage of Spirit. Were it not so, the Holy Ghost could not dwell in us" (*Doctrine and Covenants* 130:22). The Father has a body of flesh and bone and as such is to be experienced in the form of an exalted man.

For Latter-day Saints, this does not negate a unity within the Godhead. *The Book of Mormon* teaches "The Father and I (Jesus Christ), and the Holy Ghost are one" (3 Nephi 11:36). This oneness is "a oneness of mind, of knowledge, of purpose, of will" (Roberts, 1903, p. 29). There is a unique oneness among the three members of the Godhead which, according to Jesus, in a Latter-day Saint understanding, all people must work towards:

> the mind of any one member of the [Godhead] is the mind of the others, seeing as each of them does with the eye of perfection, they see and understand alike. Under any given conditions each would act in the same way ... their unity of purpose and operation is such as to make their edicts one (Talmage, 1988 [1915], p. 41).

They are thus "one God, meaning one Godhead" (McConkie, 1979, p. 511). "This unity is so profound that there is only one power governing the universe instead of three, for what one divine person does, all do as one" (Ostler, 2001, p. 464).

The Church of Jesus Christ of Latter-day Saints

Nature of humanity

The nature of humanity within The Church of Jesus Christ of Latter-day Saints is summed up in the narrative that is termed the plan of salvation (it is also known as the plan of happiness) and is summarised in Figure 3.1 (overleaf).

Prior to life on this earth, humans were spirits who lived in the pre-mortal existence with Heavenly Parents. Humans are seen to be the spirit children of the Father. Jesus is seen to be the Firstborn of the Father in the spirit – meaning that he is a creation of the Father, but through his obedience he was designated as God the Son while in a pre-mortal existence. While in the pre-mortal existence the spirit children of God spent time learning and preparing to come to earth and receive bodies. As participants in the grand Council in Heaven, the spirit children of God were also involved in the war in heaven. In this, Satan, one of these pre-mortal spirits, rebelled against the Father's plan which enabled people to choose and required a Saviour. His alternative plan was to take away the agency (akin to free will) of humanity and force obedience meaning that all would be able to return and live with God. The Father rejected this plan along with Satan's demand for the glory associated with it. Following a war of ideologies, Satan and a third of the pre-mortal spirits were cast out of heaven never to receive bodies, or a period of probation. Thus, they were not part of the plan of the Father. This provides, for Latter-day Saints, a hopeful view of humanity. Every person who ever has, or ever will, live on the earth is a part of the two-thirds of the hosts of heaven who followed Christ in the pre mortal existence. As such, they kept what is known as their 'first estate'. This has important implications of the ultimate destiny of humanity.

The second estate occurs when the spirit children of God are born to earthly parents in mortality on this earth. Each person passes through a veil of forgetfulness, which means that they have no recollection of a pre-earth life; living in mortality by faith. With God the Father having an immortal body, in order to become like him and receive exaltation it is believed by Latter-day Saints to be necessary for humanity to live on earth to gain a body and go through a time of probation. These are the two purposes of life. People are born in a state of innocence; as such they are not required to be baptised for the forgiveness of sins until they reach the age of eight. This is seen to be the age of accountability and children are not accountable for anything they do until then. Humanity contains the spirit that is eternal and it is a central tenet of the Church that all people are sons and daughters of God. One popular hymn is "I am a child of God" which is referred to often in teaching people about their divine origin and destiny.

Referring back to the message of The Church of Jesus Christ of Latter-day Saints, throughout mortal life, Latter-day Saints should be striving to live in a relationship with God.

Death is only a step in the plan of salvation, and while people mourn for the loss of a loved one, it is believed that they have merely passed to the next stage of their existence. Upon death the spirit and the body are separated, with the body going to the grave and the spirit

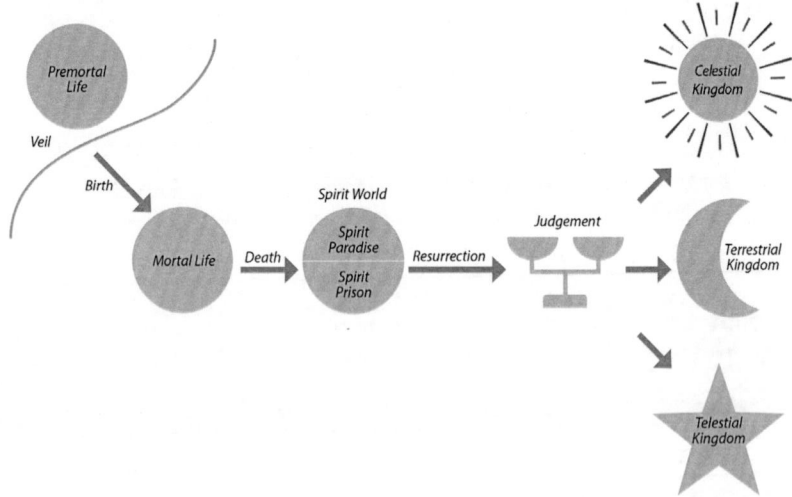

Figure 3.1 – The plan of salvation based on an illustration by Abigail Holt, used by permission.

going to the Spirit World. This Spirit World is different to the pre-mortal existence and is seen as a waiting place before the resurrection and the last judgement. The Spirit World is split into two sections, whether literally or metaphorically, Spirit Paradise and Spirit Prison. Here spirits have a temporary split in the sense that those who accepted and lived the Gospel go to Spirit Paradise, while those who are outside of that are found in Spirit Prison. When the Bible speaks of Jesus going to the spirits in prison, Latter-day Saints interpret this scripture to mean that he visited those who were in Paradise (Prison also being a term that can be used to describe the whole of the Spirit World as people are without their bodies):

> While this vast multitude waited and conversed, rejoicing in the hour of their deliverance from the chains of death, the Son of God appeared, declaring liberty to the captives who had been faithful; And there he preached to them the everlasting gospel, the doctrine of the resurrection and the redemption of mankind from the fall, and from individual sins on conditions of repentance. But unto the wicked he did not go, and among the ungodly and the unrepentant who had defiled themselves while in the flesh, his voice was not raised ... (*Doctrine and Covenants*, 138: 8–20).

Those in paradise are organised to preach the Gospel to all of those in prison. This, for Latter-day Saints, is indicative of the love of God for all of humanity; there are many people who did not have the opportunity to receive the Gospel and its attendant ordinances. As such, they receive the opportunity here. Still living by faith, with no recollection of the pre-mortal existence, people are able to accept or reject Christ. Those who reject Christ will, at some point, need to suffer for their sins:

> Therefore I command you to repent—repent, lest I smite you by the rod of my mouth, and by my wrath, and by my anger, and your sufferings be sore – how sore you know not, how exquisite you know not, yea, how hard to bear you know not. For behold, I, God, have suffered these things for all, that they might not suffer if they would repent; But if they would not repent they must suffer even as I ... (*Doctrine and Covenants*, 19:15–17)

This suffering is called eternal because God is eternal and it is his punishment, but this suffering will have an end.

At the resurrection and judgement all will be brought before God and will be judged. The resurrection will bring back the body and spirit together in a glorified immortal body like that of the Father. Latter-day Saints believe that there are three degrees of glory to which people will be assigned. Through the grace of Christ and as a result of all people choosing to follow God in the pre-mortal existence, all but a very few will be resurrected to a degree of glory – all will receive salvation. The three kingdoms or degrees of glory are the Celestial, the Terrestrial and the Telestial. *The Doctrine and Covenants* describes the qualifications for each, though it should be recognised that people are only able to receive any degree of salvation because of the atonement of Jesus Christ. The description of the Telestial kingdom links with the explanation earlier about those who will need to suffer the pains of hell in the Spirit World:

> These are they who are liars, and sorcerers, and adulterers, and whoremongers, and whosoever loves and makes a lie. These are they who suffer the wrath of God on earth. These are they who suffer the vengeance of eternal fire. These are they who are cast down to hell and suffer the wrath of Almighty God, until the fulness of times, when Christ shall have subdued all enemies under his feet, and shall have perfected his work (*Doctrine and Covenants*, 76:103–106).

In the Celestial Kingdom, where exaltation or full salvation exists, people will live together in family relationships and with the Father, Son and Holy Spirit. Only those who have been baptised and received of the gospel can be found therein. The ultimate destiny of humanity is therefore to return and live with God, and be like him.

Understanding the plan of salvation helps Latter-day Saints to understand both their divine heritage and their divine destiny. This is not, however, limited to Latter-day Saints but extends to all of humanity and as such, Latter-day Saints should strive to recognise the shared human family to which they belong, and also the divinity that is within everyone.

The Church of Jesus Christ of Latter-day Saints

Scripture
Latter-day Saints have four books of scripture. All are used in faith, study and devotion.

The Holy Bible
The Eighth Article of Faith of The Church of Jesus Christ of Latter-day Saints says: "We believe the Bible to be the word of God as far as it is translated correctly". This highlights the positive relationship that Latter-day Saints have with the Bible, but also a recognition that not everything within the Bible may have been transmitted accurately. Latter-day Saints use the King James Version of the Bible in their study and worship. This is not to indicate that this is the most correct translation, rather that it is tradition to use such, and the language of *The Book of Mormon* is similar. Members of the Church are able to use other translations to help develop their understanding.

Both the Old and New Testaments of the Bible are important; the New because the Gospels outline the life and mission of Jesus Christ, and those who established the Church of Jesus Christ in the first century CE. The Old Testament because it teaches of the Messiah who is to come and helps people understand God's dealings with the Israelites. Latter-day Saints strive to follow the example of Jesus Christ every day of their lives, and the New Testament provides the narrative of Jesus' life that enables them to know how they should act.

The Old Testament is understood Christologically. For Latter-day Saints, the Gospel of Jesus Christ is eternal and as such was known by all of the prophets of the Old Testament. These are some of the "plain and most precious" things that have been lost through the ages (1 Nephi 13:26). All things in the Old Testament, as well as a record of God's dealings with Israel, point towards the coming of the Saviour. Events such as the Exodus and the Passover are types of Jesus Christ, and should be understood as such. The Christianisation of the Old Testament is taken for granted and influences a Latter-day Saint understanding of all of the events and teachings.

Articulating a Latter-day Saint view of the inerrancy of the Bible is an interesting task. Inherent in the Eighth Article of Faith is an assumption that there is error within the Bible, and that as such not everything can be understood as literally true/accurate. In practice there is a wide range of views concerning the inspiration of the Bible. For some, it is the literal word of God, and as such events such as the creation happened exactly recorded and in the time frame listed, whereas for a large number the creation story teaches important truths, but is not a recitation of the events as they literally happened. There is room within the Church for a variety of views, though people who hold some may feel that theirs is the only correct interpretation. A further example is the story of Job which can be understood allegorically or literally. There is no official teaching on such stories, and Latter-day Saints are left to come to conclusions for themselves, as they feel they are guided by the Holy Spirit. Events as recorded that are central to the message of the Gospel of Jesus Christ would be seen to be literal – mainly those that surround the person and work of Jesus Christ.

There is an additional resource for Latter-day Saints in understanding the message of the Bible. During his lifetime Joseph Smith undertook a 'translation' of the Bible. In doing so, he did not go to manuscripts, but rather undertook an inspired reading of the Bible. Although never completed, he made some revisions to certain sections of the Bible. As a result of its incompleteness, this translation is only referred to in the footnotes of the edition of the Bible used by the Church. Examples of changes include:

> And the Lord hardened the heart of Pharaoh, and he hearkened not unto them; as the Lord had spoken unto Moses (Exodus 9:12).
>
> *And Pharaoh hardened his heart,* and he hearkened not unto them; as the Lord had spoken unto Moses (Joseph Smith Translation, Exodus 9:12, emphasis added).
>
> But I say unto you, That whosoever is angry with his brother *without a cause* shall be in danger of the judgment: and whosoever shall say to his brother, Raca, shall be in danger of the council: but whosoever shall

The Church of Jesus Christ of Latter-day Saints

say, Thou fool, shall be in danger of hell fire (Matthew 5:22 emphasis added).

But I say unto you, That whosoever is angry with his brother shall be in danger of the judgment: and whosoever shall say to his brother, Raca, shall be in danger of the council: but whosoever shall say, Thou fool, shall be in danger of hell fire (JST, Matthew 5:22).

This is used to help Latter-day Saints to understand the Bible and its message.

The Book of Mormon
In the introduction to the current edition of *The Book of Mormon*, Joseph Smith writes:

> I told the brethren that *The Book of Mormon* was the most correct of any book on earth, and the keystone of our religion, and a man would get nearer to God by abiding by its precepts, than by any other book.

This is fairly indicative of a Latter-day Saint view of *The Book of Mormon*. It is an additional book of scripture to the Bible that is seen as 'Another Testament of Jesus Christ'. For Latter-day Saints, it is an ancient book of scriptures that details God's dealings with some of the inhabitants of the Americas from approximately 600 BCE to 421 CE.[3] In line with the understanding of the eternal nature of the Gospel of Jesus Christ, all of these prophets and peoples had knowledge of the coming of Jesus Christ both prior to, and after his life in Israel. Prior to the time of Jesus' mortal life the people had prophets and were looking forward to his coming, while living the law of Moses. The first prophet recorded in *The Book of Mormon* is Lehi, who escaped from Jerusalem with his family during the reign of Zedekiah. He and his family were led to the 'Promised Land' and the rest of the book tells of his descendants. Following Jesus' resurrection, he visits the inhabitants

---

3 The dating system used throughout this book utilises CE (Common Era) instead of AD (Anno Domini), and BCE (Before Common Era) instead of BC (Before Christ). This is for uniformity throughout the book and in recognition that the majority of religions and worldviews explored are non-Christian.

of the Americas for a short period of time and establishes his Church with twelve disciples. He outlines some of the same teachings that he taught during his mortal life, and then ascends again into heaven. This is, perhaps, the crowning event of *The Book of Mormon*.

It is called *The Book of Mormon* because one of the prophets was a man called Mormon, whose responsibility it was to edit the writings that had been collected over the thousand years and collate them into one volume on golden plates.

The transmission and translation of the plates is believed, by Latter-day Saints, to be inspired. In 1823 they believe that Joseph Smith received a visitation from Mormon's son, the angel Moroni, who had buried the plates for safe keeping 1,400 years previously. He showed Joseph Smith where they were hidden and on reaching the place and finding the plates, Smith was commanded not to take them., It was not until 1827 that Latter-day Saints believe that he took possession of them. The translation of the plates was completed over the next two years; as distinct from normal translation, Latter-day Saints believe that Smith translated the plates by the gift and power of God. At the end of the translation the plates were returned to Moroni. At the beginning of *The Book of Mormon* is found the Testimony of Three Witnesses who were shown the plates by Moroni, and also the Testimony of the Eight Witnesses who were shown the plates by Smith, and were able to handle them.

Although many Latter-day Saints would recognise *The Book of Mormon* as a historical record and the events surrounding this coming forth as miraculous, there are some members of the Church who regard them as inspired, but maybe more of a reflection of ancient truths explored in the context of the nineteenth century. Whichever approach is taken, Latter-day Saints believe that the book is able to guide them and provide clarification of the teachings of the Bible. *The Book of Mormon* teaches:

> Wherefore murmur ye, because that ye shall receive more of my word? Know ye not that the testimony of two nations is a witness unto you that I am God, that I remember one nation like unto another? Wherefore, I

speak the same words unto one nation like unto another. And when the two nations shall run together the testimony of the two nations shall run together also (2 Nephi 29:8).

One of the purposes of *The Book of Mormon* is to work alongside the Bible to testify of Christ, and convince all people of the truthfulness of the Bible. The books of scripture are to work together to form a cohesive message.

Often Latter-day Saints use an analogy of two dots being joined by a line. With one dot a person is able to draw innumerable lines, or with one book innumerable interpretations, whereas with two dots there can be only one line drawn, or in terms of books, one interpretation. One such example regards the issue of baptism – the Bible records that people should be baptised (Acts 2:38), and *The Book of Mormon* outlines that the manner of baptism is by immersion (3 Nephi 11).

Latter-day Saints are encouraged to study *The Book of Mormon* each day as individuals and as families.

The Doctrine and Covenants
The full title of *The Doctrine and Covenants* includes the explanation: "Containing Revelations Given to Joseph Smith, the Prophet with Some Additions by His Successors in the Presidency of the Church". Believing in a living prophet means that Latter-day Saints have been the recipients of further revelation specifically focussed on the latter-days. The majority of these revelations recorded in *The Doctrine and Covenants* surrounded the first twenty-five years of the events of the Restoration. All but a handful were revelations to Joseph Smith. Many are in response to questions about Church government, doctrine, the will of the Lord, or events taking place in Church history. These are seen to be authoritative and help to guide Latter-day Saints in the living of their religion.

The Pearl of Great Price
The Pearl of Great Price is subtitled "A Selection from the Revelations, Translations, and Narrations of Joseph Smith First Prophet, Seer, and Revelator to The Church of Jesus Christ of Latter-day Saints".

It contains five writings that are tied together only in relation to the Gospel of Jesus Christ and their origin with Joseph Smith. These are:

- *The Book of Moses*. An excerpt from the Joseph Smith Translation of the Bible that refers to aspects of the book of Genesis.
- *The Book of Abraham*. This is a translation/midrash of the writings of Abraham inspired by some Egyptian papyri.
- *Joseph Smith – Matthew*. An excerpt from the Joseph Smith Translation (JST) of the Bible that refers to aspects of the book of Matthew.
- *Joseph Smith – History*. Excerpts from an 1838 history of Joseph Smith's life.
- *The Articles of Faith of The Church of Jesus Christ of Latter-day Saints*. An extract from a letter Smith wrote to a newspaper editor outlining thirteen beliefs of the Church.

These books are generally viewed by Latter-day Saints as inspired writings that help them understand different aspects of the Gospel of Jesus Christ.

Modern Revelation
In addition to the books of scripture outlined above, Latter-day Saints also use the writings of modern leaders of the Church. The Church has a general hierarchy that includes a Prophet/President of the Church, Quorum of the Twelve Apostles and Quorums of the Seventy. Twice a year in the General Conference of the Church they give talks/homilies that discuss issues of doctrine and practice. These can form the basis of study for the following six months, and beyond. They are seen to help people understand more about how to live their lives by following the Gospel of Jesus Christ. These are not accorded the same status as scripture, but are an important part of teachings within the Church.

On occasion the leaders of the Church publish proclamations that are of more importance than these General Conference talks. The *Encyclopedia of Mormonism* outlines that

> All such declarations have been solemn and sacred in nature and were issued with the intent to bring forth, build up, and regulate the affairs

of the Church as the kingdom of God on the earth (Matthews, 1992, p. 1151).

The most recent of these proclamations was in 1995 and was entitled: "The Family. A Proclamation to the World."

Religious expression
There are many aspects of Latter-day Saint life that could be focussed on in the remainder of this section. However, it is necessary to select only a limited number. The ones chosen are either those that seem to have most importance, such as ordinances; or those which seem to set Latter-day Saints apart in their practice, such as the Word of Wisdom. There are many other ways that Latter-day Saints express their religion, including scripture study and prayer; the omission of these is purely because of space and the reader is encouraged to explore all the different aspects of how a Latter-day Saint expresses their faith.

Ordinances
The Fourth Article of Faith says:

> We believe that the first principles and ordinances of the Gospel are: first, Faith in the Lord Jesus Christ; second, Repentance; third, Baptism by immersion for the remission of sins; fourth, Laying on of hands for the gift of the Holy Ghost.

This highlights the first two ordinances that are seen to begin a person's entrance into the faith, and the path returning to God: baptism and confirmation. Latter-day Saints believe that through participating in the ordinances of baptism and confirmation, they are able to be sanctified and cleansed from sin through the atonement of Jesus Christ. They are outward symbols of a person's belief in Jesus Christ. These ordinances are not salvific in themselves; they do "not forgive sins or save us ... for salvation is in Christ the Person. Rather, baptism and the sacrament of the Lord's Supper are channels of divine power that help to activate the power of God" (Millet, 2003, p. 76). The Holy Ghost is the active medium of the grace of Christ to make sanctification and salvation possible: "The Holy Ghost is the midwife of salvation. He is the agent of the new birth, the sacred channel and power by which men and women are changed" (Millet, 2005, pp. 146–147).

As with any action, or act of religious expression, participation in ordinances such as baptism and confirmation are an outward expression of an inner commitment to follow the Saviour, evidencing the grace that a person has received. Baptism is carried out by full immersion, and normally takes place at the age of eight, though can be performed at any age above that. The reception of the Holy Ghost by the laying on of hands takes place immediately after, or the day following, the baptism of water and is seen to be the baptism of fire spoken of in the Bible.

With each ordinance that a Latter-day Saint performs, there is an associated covenant with God. With the baptismal covenant, the promises made by the person being baptised include being willing to:

- Be called God's people.
- Bear one another's burdens.
- Mourn with those that mourn.
- Comfort those that stand in need of comfort.
- Stand as witnesses of God at all times.
- Serve God.
- Take upon them the name of Christ.
- Always remember Christ.
- Keep the commandments.

In return, Latter-day Saints believe that God promises that they will:

- Be redeemed (forgiven) by God.
- Be numbered with those of the first resurrection (receive Eternal Life).
- Have the Holy Spirit poured out upon them.
- Have their souls sanctified (purified).
- Always have the Spirit to be with them.

The effect on the daily life of a Latter-day Saint can be considerable as they strive to 'keep the covenants' they have made. These baptismal covenants are renewed each week in the sacrament. The sacrament,

The Church of Jesus Christ of Latter-day Saints

in Latter-day Saint practice, is the sharing of the bread and water in remembrance of the sacrifice of Christ, and following the example that he set at the Last Supper.

The sacrament takes place as part of the Sunday worship services. These services are two hours in length – the first hour is known as the sacrament meeting, where the sacrament is administered and talks/homilies are given by members of the congregation. The second hour is split into different classes for people of different ages, where scriptures and recent addresses from Church leaders are studied. This Church experience supplements what goes on in the home, where families and individuals are encouraged to study the scriptures together. The centre of the Latter-day Saint religious life is the home, supported by the Church.

Further ordinances take place in Temples. These buildings are different to Churches and are set apart so that only 'worthy' members of the Church, who are striving to keep the commandments can enter. The majority of the work that goes on in the Temple is for the dead; returning to the plan of salvation Latter-day Saints believe that those who accept the Gospel in the Spirit World should have the opportunity to receive the ordinances of the Gospel. In the Temple, members of the Church from the age of twelve upwards stand as proxy for their ancestors who die without baptism, and are baptised on their behalf. This, in part, explains the Latter-day Saint emphasis on family history and genealogy, as it is only for members of their family that Latter-day Saints can perform temple work.

Along with other ordinances, another ordinance that takes place in the Temple is Sealing. In this a husband and wife are sealed together for eternity, and if this is done before any children are born then all children will automatically be sealed to their parents for eternity, this is known as being born in the covenant. For converts to the Church, or for those who are not sealed prior to the birth of children, their children are sealed to them through a further ordinance in the Temple.

Ordinances are, therefore, central to the religious life and expression of Latter-day Saints. Not least because the promised blessings that they feel are associated with the covenants they make, and so cannot be fully realised unless they live up to the promises that they make.

Service
> And behold, I tell you these things that ye may learn wisdom; that ye may learn that when ye are in the service of your fellow beings ye are only in the service of your God (Mosiah 2:17).

Latter-day Saints are clear that the two Great Commandments are the centre of all their life and worship. In *The Book of Mormon* scripture above, they also recognise that living the second commandment to love thy neighbour is in reality an extension of the first commandment to love God. Latter-day Saints should seek opportunities in their individual and communal lives to serve others.

Some of these opportunities are formalised within the local Church community, known as the ward. Here, each member of the Church will usually have a 'calling' or responsibility in the running of the ward. Every calling in the ward, including that of Bishop (the leader of the ward) is a lay responsibility that people fill for a period of time, and one that they feel they are called to by God, through their leaders. Callings include teachers, youth leaders, Bishops, Relief Society President, and music leaders. One of the most important callings in the ward is that of ministering brother or sister. In this calling people are split into pairs and given responsibility for the welfare of groups of families in the community. In this way, the Church is able to ensure that all are cared for and the love of the Saviour is expressed to all.

Service, for Latter-day Saints, should extend beyond their own community and they often look for small and large ways to serve people who are not members of the Church. Organised on an institutional level there are many humanitarian projects to which the Church donates time, workers and funds. Examples include:

- Emergency Response immediately following disasters. In 2010 the Church responded to 119 disasters in 58 countries.

The Church of Jesus Christ of Latter-day Saints

- Clean Water – the Church helps to establish wells and other drinking water systems to provide access to clean water.
- Maternal and Newborn Care – the Church sends volunteer physicians and nurses to help to train birth 'attendants' in various areas of the world.
- Food Production – the Church helps to provide tools and training to improve home food production.

The Word of Wisdom

In 1833 Joseph Smith received a revelation known by Latter-day Saints as the 'Word of Wisdom' (*Doctrine and Covenants* 89). Initially revealed as a "principle with a promise" (*Doctrine and Covenants* 89:1), over the years successors to Joseph Smith, including Brigham Young, reiterated it is as a commandment for Latter-day Saints to follow. The Word of Wisdom can be seen to be a health code and is perhaps the most visible of the practices of the Latter-day Saints that is different to wider Christian practice. Although the focus tends to be on those things that are forbidden, there are positive aspects to the Word of Wisdom such as guidance/teachings on:

- Vegetables and fruits (see *Doctrine and Covenants* 89:10–11).
- Meat which is "to be used sparingly" (see *Doctrine and Covenants* 89:12–13).
- Grains (see *Doctrine and Covenants* 89:14–17).

Those things that Latter-day Saints should avoid are:

- Alcoholic drinks (see *The Doctrine and Covenants* 89:5–7).
- Tobacco (see *The Doctrine and Covenants* 89:8).
- Tea and coffee (see *The Doctrine and Covenants* 89:9). Although the revelation refers to hot drinks, latter-day prophets have taught that this means to tea and coffee.
- Harmful and illegal drugs. Although not in the revelation, later prophets have included their use as being against the Word of Wisdom.

Although at different points in time some people have tried to provide concrete explanations as to why certain things are prohibited, there has been no reason given, except only in the sense that living this law shows obedience to God. In the same revelation, Latter-day Saints believe that the Lord promised blessings to those who keep this law:

> All saints who remember to keep and do these sayings, walking in obedience to the commandments, shall receive health in their navel and marrow to their bones; And shall find wisdom and great treasures of knowledge, even hidden treasures; And shall run and not be weary, and shall walk and not faint. And I, the Lord, give unto them a promise, that the destroying angel shall pass by them, as the children of Israel, and not slay them (*Doctrine and Covenants* 89:18–21).

The Word of Wisdom is accepted to be authoritative by most Latter-day Saints, but there can be differences of interpretation in its application. One such example is the cooking of food using alcohol. Many members of the Church will avoid this as the revelations suggest that alcohol should not be drunk, while others will be happy to do so. This highlights the principle that is fundamental within the Church, that people are taught the truth and can be guided as to how to live that truth.

Tithing
Latter-day Saints recognise that God is the source of everything that they have. As such, they live in a state of thankfulness for all that he provides. In response to this belief, Latter-day Saints pay tithing, which is giving 10% of their income to the Lord through the Church. This is a principle that Latter-day Saints believe was taught in Malachi, restored to Joseph Smith and also mentioned by Jesus Christ when he visited the Americas in *The Book of Mormon*:

> Bring ye all the tithes into the storehouse, that there may be meat in my house; and prove me now herewith, saith the Lord of Hosts, if I will not open you the windows of heaven, and pour you out a blessing that there shall not be room enough to receive it (3 Nephi 24:10).

The tithes and offerings given to the Church are then used to build and maintain chapels and temples, offer aid to those in need on a local and international level, and to fund Church activities. Many Latter-day Saints will feel that it is a blessing to be able to pay tithing as a sign of their dependence on God.

Missionary Work

> Go ye therefore, and teach all nations, baptizing them in the name of the Father, and of the Son, and of the Holy Ghost: Teaching them to observe all things whatsoever I have commanded you: and, lo, I am with you always, even unto the end of the world (Matthew 28:19-20).

> Behold, I sent you out to testify and warn the people, and it becometh every man who hath been warned to warn his neighbour (*Doctrine and Covenants* 88:81).

Latter-day Saints believe that they have received the fullness of the Gospel of Jesus Christ, and that in tandem with this they are the only ones with the truth that will lead to exaltation. As such, and along with the Saviour's commission above, they feel that they have a duty to share the message of the Gospel that they have received. In so doing they are fulfilling the covenant that God made with Abraham:

> And I will make of thee a great nation, and I will bless thee above measure, and make thy name great among all nations, and thou shalt be a blessing unto thy seed after thee, that in their hands they shall bear this ministry and Priesthood unto all nations; And I will bless them through thy name; for as many as receive this Gospel shall be called after thy name, and shall be accounted thy seed, and shall rise up and bless thee, as their father (Abraham 3:9-10).

As the inheritors of the Abrahamic Covenant through membership in the Lord's Church, Latter-day Saints believe that it is their duty to teach all nations. This is done in formal and informal ways. Individual members of the Church are asked to share the truth that they receive with friends and neighbours. Formally, the Church calls young people to serve as full-time missionaries for the Church (there are retired couples who serve as well). Young men are eligible to serve missions for two years at the age of eighteen, while young women serve for eighteen months from the age of nineteen upwards. At all times it remains the choice of the individual whether to serve. They will leave their homes and serve at theirs, and their family's own expense, wherever they are called to go; after having submitted an application to serve, they receive a letter from the President of the Church assigning them to a specific place. Missions are found throughout the world and in 2019 there were over 67,000 full-time missionaries serving.

The Law of Chastity

Within the Church of Jesus Christ of Latter-day Saints one of the commandments is termed 'the law of chastity'; this is the teaching that all sexual activity should only take place between a husband and a wife. The power of procreation was given to Adam and Eve, and by extension all of humanity, in the Garden of Eden, and is to be used within the bounds the Lord has set. Sex is an important part of a married relationship, it brings a couple closer together and also enables the possibility of children to be brought into the family. Within the Church, marriage is ordained of God and it is seen to be the most desirable state within which people can live. Family relationships are eternal, and therefore should be cultivated throughout life.

All forms of sex outside of marriage are seen to be sinful; both sex before marriage and adultery. Latter-day Saints believe that Jesus Christ raised the standard for sexual behaviour when he taught in the Sermon on the Mount that:

> Ye have heard that it was said by them of old time, Thou shalt not commit adultery: But I say unto you, That whosoever looketh on a woman to lust after her hath committed adultery with her already in his heart (Matthew 5:27-28).

The law of chastity therefore extends to the films that people watch, the language people use, the material that people read, and excludes all forms of pornography. Anything that 'cheapens' or degrades the power that God has given to people should be avoided.

Latter-day Saints teach that homosexual activity is wrong and that marriage is only between a man and woman. They are clear that although this is the commandment, this does not mean that people who are homosexual should be discriminated against. All forms of homophobia are rejected based on the belief that all people are children of God, and all sin and fall short.

The eternality of family relationships does not negate the recognition that sometimes marriages and other family ties need to end. This is a major decision and should not be done without a great deal of thought and prayer, but sometimes for the physical and mental health of those involved divorce can be necessary. As such divorce is allowed, and it is at the discretion of the parties involved as to whether to end the marriage. Toxic relationships of all kinds are rejected, and if a person feels the need to remove themselves from a situation, then they will be supported in the decisions that they make.

Ideas for the RE Classroom
It is potentially unrealistic for a school to explore The Church of Jesus Christ of Latter-day Saints in a systematic way, but there are ways for elements of the Church's beliefs and practices to be used within the classroom.

- The story of Joseph Smith and the First Vision can be used at different stages throughout school. In a discussion of founders of religions, it may be a legitimate use of the story to illustrate religions that may have been founded in more recent times. For older groups the story could also be used to explore the nature of religious experiences. William James used Smith as an example in his discussion of the commonalities of religious experiences; but it could also be linked with Rudolph Otto. Table 3.1 might help pupils to categorise aspects of his experience.
- The Word of Wisdom is potentially the most identifiable feature of Latter-day Saint practice. It is the practice that is most noticeable when meeting Latter-day Saints. As such, when exploring dietary laws of religions, the Word of Wisdom can find a place. In certain ethical topics the use of legal and illegal drugs can be explored; the prohibition against the use of tobacco and alcohol should be included. Care should be taken when teaching about abstinence from tea and

Table 3.1 – Joseph Smith and the characteristics of religious experiences.

	Characteristic	Evidence
William James	**Passive** (the person having the experience does not initiate it. They feel 'done to' rather than proactive)	
	Transient (the experience is fleeting, comes and goes, cannot be retained or prolonged by their own effort)	
	Noetic (mystical experience generates knowledge, leaves people feeling sure in new ways, establishes personal certainty)	
	Inexpressible (there are no words which adequately or completely make sense of the mystical: it is beyond description)	
Rudolph Otto	**Numinous dread/awe (*Mysterium tremendum*)**	
	A feeling of **stupor**, a "blank wonder, an astonishment that strikes us dumb, amazement absolute" (1958, p. 26).	
	"The **'shudder'** reappears in a form ennobled beyond measure where the soul, held speechless, trembles inwardly to the farthest fibre of its being ... it implies that the mysterious is beginning to loom before the mind, to touch the feelings." (1958, p. 17).	
	Leading to what Otto calls "'**creature-consciousness**' or creature-feeling. It is the emotion of a creature, submerged and overwhelmed by its own nothingness in contrast to that which is supreme above all creatures" (1958, p. 10).	
	Otto develops this further to the person feeling unworthy and in a sense tainting the "holiness" by our presence. We thus need to "cover" ourselves to make ourselves able to approach the holy one (see 1958, p. 54).	

coffee; the reason that these are prohibited is unknown except that it is a commandment that was given by God. Although the fact that they contain caffeine has been suggested by some, this is not official Church teaching and, indeed, cola drinks are accepted.
- Ordinances and rites of passage are a staple of many RE classrooms; as such the opportunity to include baptism rites within the Church

The Church of Jesus Christ of Latter-day Saints

of Jesus Christ of Latter-day Saints would be a clear way that aspects of Latter-day Saints' practices can be used. They stand in distinction to both infant and adult baptism, in the sense that for most people it will take place when they are eight years of age. The covenants that a person makes are important as they underpin all aspects of living. The ordinances are also expressions of beliefs that are held by the Church of Jesus Christ of Latter-day Saints.

- GCSE courses that cover Christianity include sections on evangelism and mission. The missionary imperative of the Church for its individual members, and those members who are called to fulfil eighteen-month or two-year missions will provide a useful case study. There are usually, in the local area, members of the Church who have served missions, or even missionaries who are currently serving, who could explain their motivations for service, and their experiences in different places around the world.
- In exploring arguments about the existence of God, the religious revelation argument is sometimes used. In distinction to many forms of Christianity, Latter-day Saints believe in continuing revelation in the form of a living prophet. This may provide illustration of the role and importance of revelation in a person's life.
- The 'plan of salvation' also presents a view of life after death that is almost universalist in approach. This could provide a contrast to traditional understandings of life after death.
- An important point with regards to Latter-day Saint identity surrounds polygamy. Although practised by members of the Church until 1890, polygamy has not been allowed by the Church since that date. No member practises plural marriage and would be excommunicated if they did. There are schismatic groups who continue this practice but they are not part of the 'mainstream' Church.
- In including aspects of Latter-day Saint belief do not feel the need to include Latter-day Saint beliefs all the time in teaching; however, a use of 'some' or 'most' in a discussion of some elements of the teachings of Christianity would help in the inclusivity of the classroom. A recognition that 'most' Christians believe in the Trinity would not be untrue, but neither would it make a Latter-day Saint feel excluded.

Useful websites
ChurchofJesusChrist.org
ComeUntoChrist.org
Fairmormon.org
www.sisterholtonamission.com

References
Materials from the Church of Jesus Christ of Latter-day Saints are used by permission[4] including scriptural references from:

- *The Holy Bible*
- *The Book of Mormon*
- *The Doctrine and Covenants*
- *The Pearl of Great Price*

Barrett, David B., Kurian, George T., & Johnson, Todd M. (2001). *World Christian encyclopedia: A comparative survey of churches and religions in the modern world* (2nd ed.). Oxford, UK: Oxford University Press.

England, Eugene (1999). The Good News – and the Bad. *BYU Studies 38*(3), 191–201.

Hinckley, G. B. (2002, May). We look to Christ. *Ensign*, 90–91.

Holt, James D. (2019). Christianity. Retrieved from http://pofreonline.wpengine.com/?page_id=1150

Matthews, Robert J. (1992). Proclamations of the First Presidency and the Quorum of the Twelve Apostles. In Daniel Ludlow (Ed.), *Encyclopedia of Mormonism* (pp. 3, 1151). New York, NY: Macmillan.

McConkie, B. R. (1979). *Mormon doctrine.* Salt Lake City: Bookcraft.

Millet, R. L. (2003). *After all we can do... Grace works.* Salt Lake City, UT: Deseret Book Company.

Millet, R. L. (2005). The process of salvation. In R. Keller, & R. Millet (Eds.), *Salvation in Christ: Comparative Christian views.* (pp. 141–181). Provo, UT: Religious Studies Centre, Brigham Young University.

---

4 This chapter is neither made, provided, approved, nor endorsed by Intellectual Reserve, Inc. or The Church of Jesus Christ of Latter-day Saints. Any content or opinions expressed, implied or included in or with the material are solely those of the author and not those of Intellectual Reserve, Inc. or The Church of Jesus Christ of Latter-day Saints.

Ostler, B. (2001). *Exploring Mormon thought: The attributes of God.* Salt Lake City, UT: Kofford Books.

Otto, Rudolph (1958). *The idea of the holy.* Oxford, UK: Oxford University Press.

Roberts, B. H. (1903). *The Mormon doctrine of deity.* Salt Lake City, UT: Deseret News.

Shipps, J. (1993). Is Mormonism Christian? Reflections on a complicated question. *BYU Studies* 33(3), 438–65.

Talmage, J. (1988). [1915]. *Jesus the Christ.* Salt Lake City, UT: The Church of Jesus Christ of Latter-day Saints.

CHAPTER 4

JEHOVAH'S WITNESSES

Chapter Outline
Who are Jehovah's Witnesses?
What is their place within Christianity?
Message
Nature of God
Nature of humanity
Scripture
Religious expression

Who are Jehovah's Witnesses?
The official website of Jehovah's Witnesses indicate that in the UK there are 139,780 "ministers who teach the Bible". The exact meaning of this phrase is unclear and may refer to a total membership, or of an adult membership who are actively involved in Bible study with Jehovah's Witnesses. Worldwide there are reported to be over 8.5 million Jehovah's Witnesses.

The organisation of Jehovah's Witnesses have their roots in the life of Charles Taze Russell (1852–1916). Russell was from Pittsburgh and he is not seen to be the founder of a new religion or denomination, rather his purpose was to discover the authentic teachings of Jesus which were taught in the first century CE. To do this, in around 1870 he established a Bible reading group with his father. Through a close reading of the Bible, Russell and his associates recognised that some of the central and accepted teachings of Christian denominations were not to be found in scripture. These doctrines included the Trinity, the existence of hell, and the immortality of the soul for all people.

In 1881 Zion's Watch Tower Tract Society was founded with William Henry Conley as president and Russell as secretary-treasurer. Their purpose in organising the society was to disseminate materials including doctrinal messages and Bibles. In 1884 the Watch Tower Bible and Tract Society was incorporated with Russell as the president.

Alongside the establishment of the Tract Society, Russell continued to hold Bible studies, and his group had grown to include hundreds of members. Following Russell's death in 1916, Joseph Franklin Rutherford was elected president of the Watchtower Society. At this point, although it conducted Bible studies and published tracts, it was not regarded as a religious society. It is important to note that there were splits within the community, but those that accepted Rutherford's leadership were the precursors to the organisation that is now known as Jehovah's Witnesses.

In the late 1910s and 1920s, Rutherford embarked on establishing a structure that led to the formation of Jehovah's Witnesses. Organisation of the society and its Bible study branches became more centralised, and a director of each group was appointed who were to report the activities of the groups. In 1922 there was a new emphasis placed on door-to-door preaching. In 1931 the name of Jehovah's Witnesses was formally adopted; the name being based on a passage from Isaiah:

> "You are my witnesses," declares Jehovah, "Yes, my servant whom I have chosen, So that you may know and have faith in me And understand that I am the same One. Before me no God was formed, And after me there has been none" (*New World Translation of the Holy Scriptures*, 2013).

In 1932 Rutherford outlined a development in the understanding of biblical passages. While 144,000 people would rule with Christ in heaven, there would be a large number of people who would live on Paradise Earth. This highlights the Jehovah's Witness belief that understanding is still unfolding, and that Bible study is integral to understanding the will of Jehovah.

Following Rutherford's death in 1942, Nathan Knorr became the third president of the Watch Tower Bible and Tract Society. He expanded elements of the worldwide organisation and established a greater focus on rules surrounding the conduct of Jehovah's Witnesses.

It was during Knorr's presidency that elders and ministerial servants became a part of Witness congregations. Knorr died in 1977. The congregation of Jehovah's Witnesses has continued to grow over the years to the point where there are over eight million followers of the faith.

What is their place within Christianity?
In one sense, Jehovah's Witnesses are a part of the Christian religion. They revere Jesus, use the Bible as scripture and hold to many aspects of orthodox Christian belief, so could be seen as a denomination within Christianity. Some Witnesses use this as their own self-definition. In another sense, because of their exclusive claims, or their sociological placing on – or over – the edge of orthodox Christianity, Jehovah's Witnesses can be seen as members of a religion separate from Christianity. Homan has suggested that this is how Witnesses see themselves:

> Witnesses regard other groups claiming to be Christian as being of other faiths than their own (1988, p. 157).

Witnesses believe that the Christendom went through a period of apostasy and this only ended through the teachings and organisation of that first Bible study group and its developing society. As such Witnesses claim to be the only denomination with all truth. This 'restoration' came through the authority of the Bible and a correct understanding of it.

Copley has observed that:

> Witnesses reject as dead, or even devil inspired, mainstream Christianity, since the mainstream has not emphasized what Witnesses see as these basic biblical truths. Hence Witnesses will appear on the doorsteps of vicars and priests and try to convert them too. In that sense they are technically 'exclusivists' (= we only are right) and do not co-operate with other Churches in Christians Together and similar movements (1994, p. 89).

However, today Witnesses consider themselves to be Christians, and allow others the right to believe themselves to be Christian as well.

Jehovah's Witnesses

This may be the result of the time that has passed since Homan's work, but also may be the result of a realisation that the alternatives are not tenable.

Christian 'insiders' may tend to answer this question of identity and relationship by referring to Trinitarian doctrine: those who hold the idea of God in Trinity are Christians, but there are those (like the Witnesses) who do not place themselves alongside, but separate from the main stream of Christianity. Those, however, who use sociological categories to classify religious groups may see the Witnesses as a sect, rather than a denomination of Christianity. The exploration of the question of whether the Witnesses are Christians should include perspectives from inside the tradition. The inclusion of Jehovah's Witnesses within Christianity is an important part of their own identity.

Message

The message of Jehovah's Witnesses is of a reclamation, or restoration, of the teachings of the Bible that had been lost or corrupted over the previous centuries. This restoration has come about because of a close and inspired reading of the Bible that has revealed the truths that are found therein. The understanding of the Bible did not come all at once, but has progressed over time and so the process of reclamation of biblical truths can be seen to have been an ongoing process up until the time of Russell. This message is the only one that can bring hope to the world.

Central to the message of Jehovah's Witnesses is a belief in the different times of the earth. Working from the time of the Babylonian conquering of Israel in 607 BCE, Jehovah's Witnesses see the beginning as the dream that was given to Nebuchadnezzar which suggested that in the last days the government over the world and humanity would be under the hands of Jesus. Until that time, the world would be under the control of human governments that could be seen to have the characteristics of a 'wild beast':

> Let its heart be changed from that of a human, and let it be given the heart of a beast, and let seven times pass over it (Daniel 4:16).

These systems of government are all under the influence of Satan and seek to subdue 'Jerusalem', the kingdom of God and its peoples. The subjugation shown by these governments and systems is evident within further scripture in Daniel; where the beasts represent the systems:

> After this I kept watching, and look! another beast, like a leopard, but on its back it had four wings like those of a bird. And the beast had four heads, and it was given authority to rule. After this I kept watching in the visions of the night, and I saw a fourth beast, fearsome and terrifying and unusually strong, and it had large iron teeth. It was devouring and crushing, and what was left it trampled down with its feet. It was different from all the other beasts that were prior to it, and it had ten horns (Daniel 7:6–7).

The imagery is evocative of the corruption of the systems not ruled by God. This period of human rule would be for seven times ('seven times pass over it'). The Bible indicates that one day is equivalent to one year (see Ezekiel 4:6), and that, according to biblical time, three and a half years are 1,260 days:

> But as for the courtyard that is outside the temple sanctuary, leave it out and do not measure it, because it has been given to the nations, and they will trample the holy city underfoot for 42 months. I will cause my two witnesses to prophesy for 1,260 days dressed in sackcloth (Revelation 11:2–3).

Thus seven years would be 2,520 days, and using the biblical timing of one day to a year the ending of human rule would come 2,520 years after the Babylonian subjugation of Jerusalem in 607 BCE. By this reckoning (360 days to a year) the 2,520 years of rule by human governments came to an end in 1914. For some Jehovah's Witnesses of the time there was an expectation that all human governments would end on that day, and that Jesus would begin his rule on earth. For Jehovah's Witnesses since that time it is evident that Jesus is ruling invisibly from heaven, in preparation for his rule on Paradise Earth at the end of time.

With Jesus' enthronement in heaven as the ruler of earth, Satan was cast out:

> Be glad, you heavens and you who reside in them! Woe for the earth and for the sea, because the Devil has come down to you, having great anger, knowing he has a short period of time (Revelation 12:12).

It is for this reason that there is evil and suffering on the earth. Satan was ejected from heaven and he knows that he only has a short time to disrupt the Kingdom of God on earth. There are many indications for Jehovah's Witnesses that this time is the Last Days prophesied by the Bible:

> Nation will rise against nation and kingdom against kingdom (Matt. 24:7).
>
> There will be food shortages ... in one place after another (Matt. 24:7).
>
> There will be great earthquakes (Luke 21:11).
>
> In one place after another pestilences (Luke 21:11).
>
> Increased lawlessness accompanied by a cooling off of love on the part of the greater number (Matt. 24:11-12).
>
> Men become faint out of fear and expectation of the things coming upon the inhabited earth (Luke 21:25, 26).
>
> Christ's true followers to be objects of hatred by all nations on account of his name (Matt. 24:9).
>
> This good news of the kingdom preached in all the inhabited earth for a witness (Matt. 24:14).

Jehovah's Witnesses would see that while these signs have been in evidence throughout the history of the world, they have increased exponentially since 1914. This has now become a time to live under God's rule, to study his word and prepare for the end of times:

> Since then Christ has been supervising a work of dividing the "sheep" from the "goats" even as he foretold, a work of educating the sheeplike ones so that they can seek Jehovah, righteousness and meekness and thus be hidden in the day of his anger. This feature of Christ's presence is really a time of favour for his followers on earth and will continue until the time for his apokalypsis, or his revealing, the "revelation of

> the Lord Jesus from heaven with his powerful angels in a flaming fire, as he brings due punishment upon those who do not know God and those who do not obey the good news about our Lord Jesus." Other scriptures refer to this "revelation" as Armageddon, "the war of the great day of God the Almighty"- (2 Thessalonians. 1:7, 8; Rev. 16:14, 16) (Watchtower, 1955, pp. 103–104).

This promised safety from Armageddon, and a life on Paradise Earth is only available because of the ransom of Jesus Christ for humanity. When Adam was placed on the earth he was perfect, but through his disobedience, his sin, death came into the world and his 'perfect life' was lost. All of his descendants are under the bondage of sin and death. The Bible teaches that the penalty for the loss of life is, "Life will be for life" (Deuteronomy 19:21). Adam has lost his 'perfect life' and the only way for humanity to be removed from the consequence of this loss of life is through the ransom of another perfect life. Through the holy spirit, Jesus was born as a perfect human (see Luke 1:35) and as such was able to pay the ransom and receive the bondage under which humans found, and find, themselves.

Throughout his life Jesus acted in perfect obedience to Jehovah, until he was sacrificed as a perfect and sinless offering; his sacrifice is "once for all time" (Hebrews 10:10):

> Why was it necessary for Jesus to suffer so much? In a later chapter of this book, we will see that Satan has questioned whether Jehovah has any human servants who would remain faithful under trial. By enduring faithfully in spite of great suffering, Jesus gave the best possible answer to Satan's challenge. Jesus proved that a perfect man possessing free will could keep perfect integrity to God no matter what the Devil did (Watch Tower Bible and Tract Society of Pennsylvania, 2014, p. 53).

The ransom is paid through Jesus' death on the torture stake: Jesus dying on a torture stake (rather than a cross) is a distinctive teaching of Jehovah's Witnesses:

> Bearing the torture stake for himself, he went out to the so-called Skull Place, which is called Golgotha in Hebrew. There they nailed him to

the stake alongside two other men, one on each side, with Jesus in the middle (John 19:17-18).

People are released from the bondage of sin and death as they seek forgiveness from Jehovah.

Nature of God
Within a Jehovah's Witness worldview the name of God is Jehovah. The name Jehovah is seen to be the most common English rendering of Yahweh (the name of God in Hebrew is YHWH), but through 'superstition' the name became hidden and as such needs reclaiming in the worship of him.

Passages from the Bible help Jehovah's Witnesses to understand the nature of Jehovah:

> May people know that you, whose name is Jehovah, You alone are the Most High over all the earth (Psalm 83:18).

> Great and wonderful are your works, Jehovah God, the Almighty. Righteous and true are your ways, King of eternity (Revelation 15:3).

> Before the mountains were born Or you brought forth the earth and the productive land,
> From everlasting to everlasting, you are God (Psalm 90:2).

> You are worthy, Jehovah our God, to receive the glory and the honour and the power, because you created all things, and because of your will they came into existence and were created (Revelation 4:11).

Jehovah is Supreme (the Most High), Eternal (King of eternity, everlasting to everlasting) and the Creator. He is also a spirit person; the Watchtower rejects a misunderstanding of what it means when Jehovah is said to be omnipresent:

> God is a spirit Person, which means that he does not have a material body, but a spiritual one. A spirit has a body? Yes, for we read, "If there is a physical body, there is also a spiritual one" (1 Cor. 15:44; John 4:24). God being an individual, a Person with a spirit body, has a place where he resides, and so he could not be at any other place at the same time.

> Thus we read at 1 Kings 8:43 that the heavens are God's "established place of dwelling" (Watchtower, 1981, pp. 5–6).

His presence is felt universally through the Holy Spirit (which is his power rather than a part of a Trinity) enabling him to see, and to be felt, everywhere. A common metaphor that is used is that of a power plant. The power plant has a specific place but because of its connections to the towns and cities, its electricity can be felt, and have an influence, everywhere. Just so with Jehovah.

In explaining the power and influence of Jehovah's 'active force', Jehovah's Witnesses see its action in creation throughout history and in the world today. Genesis describes its role in Creation:

> God's active force [holy spirit] was moving to and fro over the surface of the waters (Genesis 1:2).

Then, it inspired prophets such as Moses in the works that they performed and in the scriptures that they wrote. Today Jehovah's Witnesses will strive to feel the influence of Jehovah in their lives through the holy spirit; this is attained in different ways:

> What a powerful force this spirit is! But how can Christians today avail themselves of it? First, Jesus said we should ask for it, so why not do just that? Pray to Jehovah to give you this wonderful gift not only in times of stress but on every occasion. In addition, read the Bible so that holy spirit can speak to you. (Compare Hebrews 3:7.) Meditate on what you read and apply it so that holy spirit can be an influence in your life (Psalm 1:1–3). (Watchtower, 1992, p. 13).

Although describing God as having a spirit body, this does not mean that Jehovah's Witnesses know what form that body takes. It does not necessarily mean that Jehovah is in the form of a human, but he does have characteristics and feelings.

Jehovah can be known through his 'most precious' son Jesus Christ. It is important to note that Jesus is not God, however Jehovah's characteristics can be seen most plainly in the actions and teachings of his son. He is the promised Messiah, and was pre-existing before he came to earth:

> The Bible teaches that Jesus lived in heaven before he came to earth. Micah prophesied that the Messiah would be born in Bethlehem and also said that His origin was "from ancient times." (Micah 5:2) On many occasions, Jesus himself said that he lived in heaven before being born as a human. (Read John 3:13; 6:38, 62; 17:4, 5) As a spirit creature in heaven, Jesus had a special relationship with Jehovah (Watchtower, 2014, p. 40).

Jesus Christ was God's first creation; he was involved in the creation of the world (John 1:1-3). Jehovah's Witnesses believe that he lived with God for millions of years, and as such reflects the qualities of Jehovah. The importance of Jesus as the ransom for humanity is explored in the Message section (see p. 67).

Nature of humanity

Jehovah's Witnesses teach that humanity is created in the image of God. This suggests that, rather than having a physical resemblance, humans are born with the ability to exercise the qualities that God has; including his love, justice, and mercy. Initially Adam and Eve were created in a state of perfection, but through the temptation of Satan Adam, Eve and their descendants became sinful and subject to death. Humans do not have original sin, but they inherit the sinful nature that came into the world through Adam. The sinful nature of humanity and what this leads to is described in the Bible:

> Now the works of the flesh are plainly seen, and they are sexual immorality, uncleanness, brazen conduct, idolatry, spiritism, hostility, strife, jealousy, fits of anger, dissensions, divisions, sects, envy, drunkenness, wild parties, and things like these. I am forewarning you about these things, the same way I already warned you, that those who practice such things will not inherit God's Kingdom (Galatians 5:19-21).

Despite this propensity to sin, it is possible for humans to strive to evidence the characteristics of God in their lives:

> Become imitators of God, as beloved children (Ephesians 5:1).

For Jehovah's Witnesses, despite their sinful nature this is not a hopeless exercise, rather through God's love they are able to be forgiven as they fall short:

> True, as imperfect offspring of Adam, we cannot exercise these fine qualities perfectly. Yet, remember, man was made in the image of God, and if we strive to be more and more like God, then we are in part fulfilling the reason for our existence (Ecclesiastes 12:13). If we exert ourselves to do the best we can and ask for forgiveness when we fall short, then we can hope to survive into God's righteous new world, where we may eventually attain to perfection (Watchtower, 1994, p. 28).

There are examples throughout the Bible of people who have exemplified these characteristics, showing the possibility of such for others. The greatest example is Jesus who showed the characteristics of God perfectly. In following their examples, and becoming focussed on God people are able to be transformed and "put on the new personality that was created according to God's will in true righteousness and loyalty" (Ephesians 4:24). This transformation occurs through the holy spirit which enables people to overcome their sinful nature and show the characteristics of God. This will prepare them for the time when they will be perfected and will once again truly and perfectly be in the image of God.

The traditional idea of the spirit being the 'real person' in a 'shell' of a body is rejected. Rather the spirit or life force is compared to the electric current that flows through a machine. Just as the current does not reflect or possess any of the characteristics of the machine, so the spirit remains a force reflecting of the person or animal's characteristics. When people die, the body returns to the ground:

> In the sweat of your face you will eat bread until you return to the ground, for out of it you were taken. For dust you are and to dust you will return (Genesis 3:19).

> … his spirit goes out, he goes back to his ground; in that day his thoughts do perish (Psalm 146:4).

Death is therefore a state of non-existence:

> For the living know that they will die, but the dead know nothing at all, nor do they have any more reward, because all memory of them is forgotten. Also, their love and their hate and their jealousy have already perished, and they no longer have any share in what is done under the sun … Whatever your hand finds to do, do with all your might, for there is no work nor planning nor knowledge nor wisdom in the Grave, where you are going (Ecclesiastes 3:19, 20).

Just as prior to birth, the person is not existing and is nothing; so after death the consciousness returns to this state of non-existence.

The 'spirit' does not live on, rather "the spirit itself returns to the true God who gave it" (Ecclesiastes 12:7). When a person dies, therefore, the life force does not go on existing in another realm as a spirit creature. The force returns to God, just as the force was given by God to give life to Adam, so at some future stage all those so deserving (not just Witnesses) will be recreated from the earth to inhabit the earth as themselves once more never to die. For the place on which they live will be Paradise Earth, ruled by Jesus and 144,000 chosen people from heaven. There is no hell for those who are undeserving, rather their life force will not be recreated – they remain in a state of non-existence.

Therefore, it is true that in Witness belief only 144,000 will go to heaven, but to leave the belief at that would be to give the wrong impression – for all the righteous will receive a paradisiacal glory with their loved ones.

Scripture

The whole worldview of Jehovah's Witnesses is based on one book: the Bible. The claims of Jehovah's Witnesses to truth are built upon a close reading and correct understanding of the Bible. As was outlined earlier, the religion grew from the work of Charles Russell and his study of the Bible in study groups. These study groups continue today around the world, and are the basis of Jehovah's Witness devotion and worship. The Bible is the source of all teaching, and is the guide for life.

The Jehovah's Witness view of the Bible and its use is summed up in 1 Timothy:

> All Scripture is inspired of God and beneficial for teaching, for reproving, for setting things straight, for disciplining in righteousness, so that the man of God may be fully competent, completely equipped for every good work (1 Timothy 3:16–17).

The Bible is Jehovah's word and, as such, can have an impact on the individual and the world:

> For the word of God is alive and exerts power and is sharper than any two-edged sword and pierces even to the dividing of soul and spirit, and of joints from the marrow, and is able to discern thoughts and intentions of the heart (Hebrews 4:12).

The place of Jehovah's Witnesses in the zeitgeist is possibly best represented by their witnessing from door to door. As they witness, they strive to teach people about the Bible, and as they meet with people who are interested in their message they study topics from the Bible. Although there are many ways to use the Bible within individual and communal study, the most often used will be the study of topics. A quick glance at the official website jw.org will show the various topics that are most often explored.

The version of the Bible used by Jehovah's Witnesses is *The New World Translation of the Holy Scriptures* which was first published in 1961. This is a translation of the Bible that is published by Jehovah's Witnesses and is mainly used by them. The history of this translation began in 1946, when in October Nathan H. Knorr, president of the Watch Tower Society, proposed that a new translation of the scriptures, specifically the New Testament should be undertaken. In 1947, the New World Bible Translation Committee was established. The members of this committee were not made known, but were all Jehovah's Witnesses:

> These translators were not seeking prominence; they did not desire to draw attention to themselves. In the spirit of "doing all things for God's glory," they wanted the reader to base his faith on God's Word,

Jehovah's Witnesses

not on their worldly "qualifications" (1 Cor. 10:31) (Watchtower, 1974, p. 768).

It was felt that this translation was needed for two reasons:

1. The availability of older Bible manuscripts meant that there were opportunities for a more faithful rendering in the work of translation.
2. Jehovah's Witnesses felt that the existing translation, while helpful, had been unduly influenced by prevailing beliefs of society and Christian denominations. As such the new translation would in modern language, provide a "literal translation that faithfully presented what is in the original writings and so could provide the basis for continued growth in knowledge of divine truth" (Watchtower, 1984, pp. 608–609).

In 1953 the *New World Translation of the Christian Greek Scriptures* (the New Testament) was published. Over the ensuing years the Old Testament was published as the Hebrew Scriptures in five separate volumes from 1953 to 1960. In 1961 the complete *New World Translation of the Holy Scriptures* was published for the first time. In 1984 a revised edition was published that added an appendix, 125,000 marginal references, 11,400 footnotes, and a concordance. A further revised edition was published in 2013 which changed some of the presentational structure of books. For example, the Song of Solomon was structured as a poem as it would have been read in the original. The major change, however, was the reduction of English words in the Translation by about 10%.

These changes link with what makes the *New World Translation of the Holy Scriptures* unique. Throughout the edition it is most common to see the name of God, or the Lord presented as 'Jehovah God'. In the 2013 translation this is seen 7,216 times. Jehovah's Witnesses see this as a restoration of God's true name to the scriptures, from which it had been systematically removed. There are other examples, that may be seen to remove ambiguity from certain teachings:

- When referring to Jesus' death the use of stake, or torture stake, is used to indicate the means of his death, rather than 'cross' that is found in most other translations:

Finally, after they had mocked him, they stripped him of the cloak and put his outer garments on him and led him off to be nailed to the stake (Matthew 27:31).

This had already been in place for the majority of references in the 1951 edition, but further adjustments were made in 2013.

- When translating the word Sheol or Hades, to avoid the indication that it is a separate place the words were translated as 'the grave', such as:

    Whatever your hand finds to do, do with all your might, for there is no work nor planning nor knowledge nor wisdom in the Grave, where you are going (Ecclesiastes 9:10).

- The previous use of the word 'soul' was replaced in 2013 to avoid the inference that it is the immaterial part of a human. Rather the word was translated according to its context, as to whether it referred:

    (1) to a person, (2) to the life of a person, (3) to living creatures, (4) to the desires and appetite of a person or, in some cases, (5) even to dead individuals. However, since such use of the word "soul" is not common in English, the decision was made to render these original-language words according to their intended meaning, usually with a footnote that reads "Or 'soul'" (*New World Translation of the Holy Scriptures (Study Edition),* Appendix A2).

Religious expression

The Lord's Supper/The Memorial

Once a year, at the time of Passover, Jehovah's Witnesses will attend the Lord's Evening Meal (the Lord's Supper) as a memorial of the Last Supper. The timing of the service is designed to fully replicate the time of Jesus' last meal on Passover evening nearly 2,000 years ago. Jehovah's Witnesses calculate that the meal took place after sundown on Nisan 14, 33 CE according to the lunar calendar used in biblical times. As such the meal is scheduled to occur on this date each year.

It is a meal of memorial of Jesus' death only, and is not of any sacramental value. With the ransom of Jesus being central to Jehovah's

Jehovah's Witnesses

Witness theology, this event is of the utmost importance in the worship of the community:

> Just as the Son of man came, not to be ministered to, but to minister and to give his life as a ransom in exchange for many (Matthew 20:28).

The meal itself is part of the wider service of the Lord's Supper where Jehovah's Witnesses and others will gather.

> If you are attending the Memorial with Jehovah's Witnesses for the first time, what can you expect? The gathering will likely be in an attractive, clean setting where all can comfortably enjoy the occasion. There may be some simple flower arrangements, but you will not be distracted by gaudy bunting or any party atmosphere. A qualified elder will consider in a clear and dignified manner what the Bible says about the occasion. He will help all to appreciate what Christ did for us. He died as a ransom that we may live (Watchtower, 2013, p. 25).

The meal utilises the bread and wine that was in evidence at the Last Supper:

> As they continued eating, Jesus took a loaf, and after saying a blessing, he broke it and giving it to the disciples, he said: "Take, eat. This means my body." And taking a cup, he offered thanks and gave it to them, saying: "Drink out of it, all of you, for this means my 'blood of the covenant,' which is to be poured out in behalf of many for forgiveness of sins" (Matthew 26:26-28).

The emblems of bread and water will be passed around the congregation but will only be eaten/drunk by a very small number. Those who partake will be among the 144,000 who will reign in heaven reflecting the teaching of Jesus that the rulers in heaven will sit down with him:

> However, you are the ones who have stuck with me in my trials; and I make a covenant with you, just as my Father has made a covenant with me, for a kingdom, so that you may eat and drink at my table in my Kingdom, and sit on thrones to judge the 12 tribes of Israel (Luke 22:28-30).

Those with an earthly hope (who will live on Paradise Earth) will respectfully refrain. The observation of the Meal is sufficient to show respect and their understanding of the importance of the ransom of Jesus Christ.

Those among the 144,000 will know that they are such through the spirit. It changes who they are and how they think, showing that they have been born again:

> He has enlightened the eyes of your heart, so that you may know to what hope he called you, what glorious riches he holds as an inheritance for the holy ones (Ephesians 1:18).

Most people are not called to be one of the 144,000 even among Jehovah's Witnesses.

The Lord's Meal combines different aspects of Jehovah's Witness theology. On the one hand it remembers the ransom through which all people are delivered from bondage, replicating the story of the Passover. It also reinforces the sense of community that is important and the various aspects of belief in life after death.

Ministry

Jehovah's Witnesses are literally called to be witnesses of Jehovah in the world. They have a duty to share the message of Jehovah wherever they find themselves. As mentioned earlier, one of the most recognisable features of Jehovah's Witness practice is the witnessing from door to door, or on the streets. They are following many biblical injunctions to do so:

> Let us hold firmly the public declaration of our hope without wavering, for the one who promised is faithful. And let us consider one another so as to incite to love and fine works, not forsaking our meeting together, as some have the custom, but encouraging one another, and all the more so as you see the day drawing near (Hebrews 10:23–25).

Every baptised member is seen to be a minister of Jehovah: "I solemnly charge you before God and Christ Jesus, ... preach the word, be at it urgently." (2 Tim. 4:1, 2) The message that they share is seen to be of inestimable valuable to all people. There are various levels of witnessing that take place throughout the Church:

> *Associates* are people who 'associate' with Jehovah's Witnesses by attending meetings, but do not engage in any work of witnessing.
> *Regular publishers* have no quotas for preaching activities, but should report one hour of preaching each month.
> *Auxiliary pioneers* commit to between thirty and fifty hours of preaching activities in a month.
> *Regular pioneers* commit to 840 hours per year (an average of seventy hours per month). A regular pioneer must have been a member of good standing for at least six months.
> *Special pioneers* are people who receive special assignments which may require at least 130 hours a month; these activities might include witnessing in isolated areas. Special pioneers may receive a living stipend.
> *Missionaries* perform at least 130 hours of preaching in foreign countries. They, too, receive a living stipend.

The commitment expected to live life as a witness of Jehovah is large. This commitment reflects a devotion to Jehovah and a recognition that they have received a message that is important to the world.

War and Nationalism

Jehovah's Witnesses reject all participation in war. They believe their duty is to preach against war. In their identifying features of the true religions they list the following:

> The true religion remains untainted by worldly politics and conflicts. It is neutral in time in time of war. (John 18:36; James 1:27).
>
> The true religion does not condone war or personal violence (Micah 4:2-4, Romans 12:17-21, Colossians 3:12-14) (Watchtower, n.d., p. 377).

They pray for the end to wars and earthly governments with the new reign of Jesus. A time when "the wolf will actually reside for a while with the male lamb" (Isaiah 11:6).

Jehovah's Witnesses also do not participate in elections, or the singing of national anthems. This is not to indicate an anti-government stance but a reflection that God is the true ruler.

> They never engage in anti-government activity of any kind. In fact, Witnesses believe that present human governments constitute an 'arrangement of God' that he has permitted to exist. So they consider themselves to be under divine command to pay taxes and respect such 'superior authorities' (Romans 13:1–7) (Watchtower, 1995, p. 23).

Linked in with this is the excellent resource produced by the Jehovah's Witnesses themselves called 'Stand Firm Against the Nazi Assault'. In this resource pack there are many testimonies and activities that could be used in a discussion of the Holocaust and Prejudice. This is particularly interesting as Jehovah's Witnesses were the only religious group to have their own symbol – the purple triangle (Jews were considered to be a race), and they could free themselves from the concentration camps by the signing of a repudiation document.

The Use of Blood

Probably the most controversial of doctrines from the Jehovah's Witnesses is the prohibition on blood transfusions. Although the penalties for contravening it have been relaxed (in 2000 leaders revoked the ruling that their members faced automatic excommunication if they accepted a blood transfusion), it is still a core tenet of their faith.

The doctrine, as all Witness beliefs do, comes from the Bible. In discussing Old Testament prohibitions on the eating and use of blood, Witnesses see that blood has symbolic meaning:

> The Law repeatedly stated the Creator's ban on taking in blood to sustain life. "You must not eat the blood; pour it out on the ground like water. Do not eat it, so that it may go well with you and your children after you, because you will be doing what is right." (Deuteronomy 12:23–25, New International Version; 15:23; Leviticus 7:26, 27; Ezekiel 33:25).
>
> Contrary to how some today reason, God's law on blood was not to be ignored just because an emergency arose. During a wartime crisis,

some Israelite soldiers killed animals and "fell to eating along with the blood." In view of the emergency, was it permissible for them to sustain their lives with blood? No. Their commander pointed out that their course was still a grave wrong (1 Samuel 14:31–35). Hence, precious as life is, our Life-Giver never said that his standards could be ignored in an emergency" (*The Watchtower*, 1999, p. 4).

It is probably the least understood, and empathised with, of Witness doctrines. Rather than being written off as unsympathetic in their adherence to this commandment, it could raise a discussion of whose wisdom should be followed – are people's ideas and feelings more important than a commandment of God? Where Witnesses might be applauded for not going against their faith in the face of death in Germany, they are condemned for not going against their faith in the face of death and the opinion of the world.

Celebration

One of the most identifiable practices of Jehovah's Witnesses is actually a non-practice. Jehovah's Witnesses do not celebrate Christmas. There are many reasons why Jehovah's Witnesses do not celebrate Christmas, and none of them surround the inappropriateness of the giving of gifts:

> The Bible ... speaks favourably of giving gifts or inviting family and friends for a joyful meal on other occasions. It encourages parents to train their children to be sincerely generous, instead of giving gifts when socially expected to do so (Matthew 6:2–3).

Reasons for this are fourfold:

1. Jesus asked his disciples to commemorate his sacrifice and death; at no point is there any indication that he asked people to commemorate his birth.
2. None of the first Christians celebrated Christmas or the events of his birth.
3. 25 December is highly unlikely to be the date of his birth.
4. The celebration itself is a continuation of the 'pagan' celebration of Saturnalia. Many of the customs of Christmas have also

5. been appropriated from 'pagan' source, for example, the yule log and the use of mistletoe.

Rather than being problematic for Jehovah's Witnesses, the non-celebration of Christmas is an important part of their identity. In discussing the rejection of Christmas it is important that the voices of the children themselves be heard:

> I have fun with my friends, and we surprise each other with gifts from time to time.
>
> I never feel left out because I don't celebrate Christmas or other holidays. During the holidays, when we are off from school and Dad is off from work, we play games, go to movies, watch TV. We spend a lot of time doing things together as a family (Watchtower, 1995, p. 18).

As with celebration of Christmas, pagan origins are attributed to the celebration of birthdays. Jehovah's Witnesses suggest that birthdays were not celebrated in the Early Church, and they were traditionally associated with pagan customs. The occurrence of birthdays in the Bible are of the Pharaoh in Egypt at the time of Joseph, and of Herod who beheaded John the Baptist on his birthday. The first event is linked with a 'pagan' and the second with an act of cruelty. These are both reasons that Jehovah's Witnesses would not seek to follow.

The 'celebration' of Hallowe'en is similarly rejected. The celebration of a world of spirits that, in a Jehovah's Witness view, does not exist and seeks to glamourise elements of evil should be rejected. It also is seen to directly contradict the teachings of the Bible:

> There should not be found in you anyone who makes his son or his daughter pass through the fire, anyone who employs divination, anyone practicing magic, anyone who looks for omens, a sorcerer, anyone binding others with a spell, anyone who consults a spirit medium or a fortune-teller, or anyone who inquires of the dead (Deuteronomy 18:10–11).

Most, if not all, of its celebrations are seen to be of non-Christian origin as they all try and appease or repel the evil spirits that people feel are around at Hallowe'en.

Jehovah's Witnesses

The rejection of what are perceived as non-Christian traditions places Jehovah's Witnesses in distinction to the wider world. It does, however, place them, they would see, in line with biblical teaching. This is a further example of Jehovah's Witnesses adopting practices that could be seen to be counter-cultural, but their desire is to please God rather than society.

Ideas for the RE Classroom
Much of the material above is useful for background for teachers who have children of Jehovah's Witnesses in their class/school. There are various aspects such as the fact that Jesus is believed to have been killed on a 'torture stake' that are of interest and should be borne in mind when exploring Christian beliefs within the classroom. These beliefs that differ from the 'mainstream' understandings may be prepared for by the sensitive teacher. There are aspects of Jehovah's Witness beliefs that can find expression in the classroom.

- The centrality of the Bible in establishing beliefs and practices is important for Jehovah's Witnesses. In exploring the biblical basis of various beliefs within Christianity, pupils can use reasoning to suggest conclusions that can be drawn from a close reading of the Bible.
- The idea of life after death for Jehovah's Witnesses establishes an interesting case study for the continuation of existence, and the invisible rule that they believe is in existence at the moment.
- Jehovah's Witness beliefs about war and nationalism are also worth exploring in the classroom. For Quakers, a non-fighting role in war is accepted, but Jehovah's Witnesses reject all participation. This provides an exploration of diversity within Christianity.
- The study of persecution of Jehovah's Witnesses can also add a dimension to various aspects of classroom topics. The *Stand Firm Against Nazi Assault* publication outlines the choice that they faced in the Holocaust (*The Watchtower*, 1997). They were the only religious group (Jews being a racial designation) targeted, and they could escape the punishment if they recanted their beliefs. A similar situation arose during 2009 onwards with Jehovah's Witnesses being

categorised as an extremist group in Russia. The opposition they face in living their religion is an important aspect to be explored.
- GCSE courses that cover Christianity include sections on evangelism and mission. The missionary imperative of Jehovah's Witnesses for its pioneers provides a useful case study. There will be pioneers in the local community who could explain their motivations for service.
- The use of blood products in medical professions is also an area that would engage pupils in the ramifications of religious belief. The issue was dramatised in the film *The Children Act* (Eyre, 2018). Jehovah's Witnesses outline alternatives to the use of blood products. This decision would not be an easy one, and the binary terms in which so many people think would be challenged through a sensitive exploration of the topic.
- The refusal to celebrate certain festivals and birthdays can also provide points for discussion at all ages of schooling. Children need to be able to recognise similarities and differences, as well as the motivations for certain practices. In the UK, many aspects of Jehovah's Witness practice can be seen to be counter-cultural; rather than being dismissed, this discussion should be regarded as an opportunity for engagement.

Useful websites

www.jw.org is a trove of materials for exploring the beliefs of Jehovah's Witnesses. This is an official website and all of the materials are easily searchable.

References

All Bible quotes taken from the *New World Translation of the Holy Scriptures* (2013) published by Watchtower Bible and Tract Society of Pennsylvania.

Copley, T. (1994). *Religious Education 7–11* (Appendix II, Jehovah's Witnesses). London, UK: Routledge.
Eyre, Richard (dir.) (2018). *The Children Act* (DVD) Toronto, Canada: Entertainment One.
Homan, R. (1988). Teaching the children of Jehovah's Witnesses. *The British Journal of Religious Education*, 10(3), 154–59.
Watchtower (n.d.). *Mankind's search for God*. New York, NY: Watchtower.

Jehovah's Witnesses

Watchtower (1955, 15 February). *The Watchtower announcing Jehovah's Kingdom*.
Watchtower (1974, 15 December). *The Watchtower announcing Jehovah's kingdom*.
Watchtower (1981, 15 February). *The Watchtower announcing Jehovah's kingdom*.
Watchtower (1984). *Jehovah's Witnesses – Proclaimers of God's kingdom*.
Watchtower (1986). *Jehovah's Witnesses. Unitedly doing God's will worldwide*. New York, NY: Watchtower.
Watchtower (1992, 1 February). *The Watchtower announcing Jehovah's kingdom*.
Watchtower (1994, 1 April). *The Watchtower announcing Jehovah's kingdom*.
Watchtower (1995). *Jehovah's Witnesses and education*. New York, NY: Watchtower.
Watchtower (1997). *Stand firm against Nazi assault*. Watchtower.
Watchtower (1999). *How can blood save your life?* New York, NY: Watchtower.
Watchtower (2000). *Jehovah's Witnesses. Who are they? What do they believe?* New York, NY: Watchtower.
Watchtower (2013, December). *The Watchtower announcing Jehovah's kingdom Study Edition*.
Watchtower (2014). *What does the Bible really teach?* New York, NY: Watchtower.

SECTION 3

EXTENDING THE UNDERSTANDING

OF ISLAM

CHAPTER 5

THE BOUNDARIES OF ISLAM

The reformed GCSE and A level specification highlights that there is a wider expression of Islam beyond Sunni. The majority of RE teaching teaches to the Sunni interpretation of Islam; the Six Beliefs and the Five Pillars are more closely identified with Sunni, rather than other expressions but form the majority of teaching within the classroom. Alan Brine (2015) has suggested:

> Do we need to actively question the idea that there is such a thing as 'true' or 'real' Islam? There are just lots of different Islams. Some forms are pleasing to the eye; others are distasteful but they are all just versions of Islam. Some Muslims will claim some kind of authority for their version, and that is 'interesting', but it cannot be taken as a baseline for our teaching about the religion (Brine, 2015).

In this short introduction to Islam, the establishment of boundaries of orthodoxy within Islam will be explored, and a discussion of the nature of God and the nature of humanity will be outlined. This will occur in this chapter rather than in the subsequent chapters that explore Shi'a Islam and Ahmadiyya Islam, as the teachings about Allah and humanity are essentially the same across the different expressions of Islam outlined in this book.

Islam is the world's second largest religion with over 1.8 billion followers, or approximately 24% of the world's population. In the UK Census of 2011 there were 2.7 million people, or 4.8% who self-identified as Muslim. The 'traditional' schools within Islam are seen to be Sunni and Shi'a, but within each of these schools are different traditions. The divisions within Shi'a will be explored in the next chapter, but the boundaries that identify someone as either Sunni or Shi'a within Islam need to be explored in greater detail.

The two central teachings of Islam seem to be developed in the context of Allah and the Prophet Muhammad. The Shahadah, which is accepted by most, if not all, Muslims in varying forms says:

> There is no god but Allah; Muhammad the Messenger of Allah.

These beliefs as the defining characteristics of orthodoxy within Islam seems to be supported within the Qur'an:

> You who believe, obey God [God] and the Messenger [Prophet Muhammad], and those in authority among you. If you are in dispute over any matter, refer it to God and the Messenger (Surah 4:59).

Acceptance of the unity of Allah, to whom there can be no partner ascribed, is the most important belief of Islam. This is reflected in the greatest sin within Islam – shirk – which is the sin of ascribing partners to Allah. The nature and unity of Allah underpins the message of the Qur'an and the message of Islam.

Nature of Allah

Islam is a monotheistic religion, and the belief in one Allah is central to all belief and worship. The most important concept about Allah to Muslims is Tawhid, or the unity of Allah.

> Say: He is God, the One and Only; God, the Eternal, Absolute; None is born of Him, nor is He born; And there is none like Him (Surah 112).

Allah is ultimately incomprehensible and can only begin to be understood through a reflection on his names. The Qur'an contains ninety-nine Beautiful Names of Allah; through these names Muslims hope to reflect upon the nature of Allah and their relationship to him. The first chapter of the Qur'an (Surah al-Fatihah) explores the various beliefs about Allah within Islam outlined in some of his names:

> In the name of God, Most Gracious, Most Merciful.
> Praise be to God, the Cherisher and Sustainer of the worlds;
> Most Gracious, Most Merciful;
> Master of the Day of Judgment.

The Boundaries of Islam

> Thee do we worship, and Thine aid we seek.
> Show us the straight way;
> The way of those on whom Thou hast bestowed Thy Grace, those whose (portion) is not wrath, and who go not astray.

The nature of Allah is explicitly linked with his relationship with his creation, in particular through the Prophet Muhammad and the revelation of the Qur'an. Muhammad is the most important of the messengers of Allah, and is taught to be the 'seal of the Prophets'. The Qur'an is the definitive revelation of Allah. The primacy of Muhammad and of the Qur'an can be used to draw elements of the boundaries of Islam. If we use Bahá'í as an example (see Chapter 8), they were a movement who, while having their roots in Islam, placed themselves outside of the realm of Islam because of their teaching about the person of Bahá'u'lláh and the position of Muhammad as one Manifestation of God. While teaching the Qur'an as authoritative it is not the definitive word of God and the teachings of Bahá'u'lláh are seen to take precedence. As such, both Bahá'ís and Muslims recognise that they stand outside of Islam, though the Bahá'í view is slightly more nuanced and will be discussed in Chapter 8. They provide a useful case study in that other people/books are placed before/alongside the Qur'an and the Prophet, as well as recognising themselves that they are outside of the ummah (community of Muslims).

Could this be used to draw the boundaries of Islam? A further discussion of the orthodoxy within Islam could be linked to further beliefs. A Hadith[5] reports:

> He (the inquirer) said: Inform me about Iman (faith). He (the Holy Prophet) replied: That you affirm your faith in Allah, in His angels, in His Books, in His Apostles, in the Day of Judgment, and you affirm your faith in the Divine Decree about good and evil. He (the inquirer) said: You have told the truth. He (the inquirer) again said: Inform me about al-Ihsan (performance of good deeds) (Sahih Muslim 8).

This does not create a list of things that can be believed by Muslims, rather this is the baseline. To be a Muslim, to live in submission to

---
5 Hadith are the traditions and sayings of the Prophet Muhammad.

Allah one believes in these six beliefs. It may be self-evident that this Hadith does not contain all of the nuances of these teachings and that it is possible to have divergent understandings of what is meant by each of the above. Thus, within Sunni Islam there are the Six Beliefs that relate to the beliefs outlined exactly, whereas within Shi'a, the five roots of 'Usul ad-Din could be seen to incorporate the beliefs outlined in the Hadith (see next chapter).

Nature of humanity
A further discussion of who can be considered to be a Muslim could focus on right practice, or orthopraxy. To be precise in definition, a Muslim is one who submits to the will of Allah. This submission is shown in the actions that a person performs. It is not just to be found in declarations of iman (faith) but in the living of that faith. One Hadith reports:

> The Messenger of Allah (peace be upon him) said: Al-Islam implies that you testify that there is no god but Allah and that Muhammad is the messenger of Allah, and you establish prayer, pay Zakat, observe the fast of Ramadan, and perform pilgrimage to the (House) if you are solvent enough (to bear the expense of) the journey (Sahih Muslim 8a).

This links explicitly with what Muslims believe about the nature of humanity.

Within Islam humanity is a special creation of Allah; humans were created from clay and the spirit of life was breathed into them. They are distinct from the rest of creation by virtue of their soul, their conscience, intelligence, free will and the ability to worship. These gifts make humanity superior to the rest of creation including the angels and every aspect of the natural world. The three parts of human: body, soul and intellect all combine to enable a person to worship Allah and live in submission to his will.

The initial purity of the soul is shown through the Islamic belief in reversion. All people are born in submission to Allah, it is only through life's experiences and choices that they rebel against him.

The Boundaries of Islam

Thus, when a person chooses to follow Islam they are 'reverting' to the state of submission into which they were born.

This 'battle' between living in submission to Allah and not, can be found in two elements of the human soul that have differing emphases in the various traditions of Islam, and are linked to the concept of greater jihad. The greater jihad is the struggle to live in submission to Allah, that can be seen in a discussion of 'nafs' and the 'qalb'.

For some Muslims these are what can be termed the 'downward nafs' (though some Muslims would suggest that nafs are neutral and that they are made negative or positive by human action). Geaves suggests that nafs can refer to "impurities such as anger, greed, jealousy, hatred and lust" (2007, p. 44). The purpose of life is to overcome the downward nafs, and develop those nafs that evidence a person's standing before Allah. When this mastery is attained a person is prepared for paradise.

The qalb, or heart, can be seen to be the spiritual nature of humanity which is capable of learning both good and evil. The outward actions of a person reflect the purity of a person's qalb. As a person gains wisdom and performs good deeds then the person is prepared to receive paradise. The purification of the qalb is made possible by worship of, and submission to, Allah.

Where are the boundaries of Islam?

Having established two aspects of Islam that could be seen to be normative: the nature of Allah and the nature of humanity, are we any closer to understanding how to define Islam and, more particularly, to identify who is a Muslim? A further case study, not explored in this book, is that of the Nation of Islam who are predominantly found in the USA. The Nation of Islam began with two figures: Wallace Fard and Elijah Muhammad. Fard is variously identified as the Mahdi, a prophet, and by Elijah Muhammad as God, and the source of his teachings. Elijah Muhammad himself is seen to be a prophet within the Nation of Islam. Although members of the Nation of Islam accept Muhammad and the Qur'an, and can be seen to live the Five Pillars of

Sunni Islam, most Muslims would place them outside of the ummah, though relations are ambiguous. In one sense the beliefs held by the Nation of Islam are outside of the realm of Islamic norms; their teachings about God becoming incarnate, the role of the Prophet Muhammad, and the after-life are "heterodox, or even heretical":

> But despite its vast ideological differences from the international Muslim community, the NOI has come to be seen like a partner, even an ally, by many in the Arab and Muslim worlds (Fishman & Soage, 2013, p. 59).

Fishman and Soage go on to suggest that the reasons why they are seen as an ally is political expediency and a shared political outlook. This lays open an interesting discussion: which considerations take precedence when deciding on the Islamicness of a group. Maybe because of their geographical isolation, and also because of their usefulness, the heterodoxy of the Nation of Islam can be seen to be overlooked.

In some ways the unity of Islam can be seen to be a myth; Muslims can be seen to be unified by certain teachings, but even within the same traditions there can be seen to be different expressions and emphases. Table 5.1 suggests some of the different groups that can be found within the two main traditions of Islam. Missing from this table are Sufi schools or traditions that can be found across Sunni and Shi'a expressions of Islam.

Sufism is an expression of Islam that could have been explored within this book. Within GCSE and A level specifications the distinctive teachings and practices of Sufis are featured. However, it is important to note that Sufism is not a separate school or tradition; rather it is a way of seeing and living Islam that can be found in Sunni and Shi'a expressions. Chittick has described Sufism as:

> ... the interiorisation and intensification of Islamic faith and practice (2000, p. 23).

It is possible, to the outside observer and even some Muslims, to see Islam as a very mechanistic faith. A faith where people believe and do.

The Boundaries of Islam

Table 5.1 – Sunni and Shi'a groups.

ISLAM									
Sunni				Shi'a					
Hanafi				*Ismaili*		*Jafri*			*Zaidiyyah*
Barlevi	Deoband	Hanbali	Maliki	Shafi	Sevener	Nizari	Musta'li	Twelver		Alawi	Alevi
					Qaramira		Tayyibi	Akhbari	Usull		
							Bohras	Shaykhi			

Most Muslims would reject this characterisation, but the caricature is based in two expressions of Islam: action (the body) and the tongue (the thought) and their expression in, for example, the Five Pillars. There is a third aspect to Islam, which is seen to be the heart:

> In short, the Islamic tradition recognises three basic domains of religiosity – body, tongue, and the depths of the heart. These are the domains of right doing, right thinking, and right seeing. The last is an inner awareness of the reality of things that is inseparable from our mode of being in the world (Chittick, 2000, p. 8).

The focus on Sufi teaching, belief and practice is on the heart. The awareness of the motivation of acts, and the development of a relationship with Allah, enables Sufi approaches to be "an invisible spiritual presence that animates all expressions of Islam" (Chittick, 2000, p. 11). This is a contested area though, and in the last century or so some traditions of Islam have rejected Sufi beliefs and practices. Distinctive practices include:

- The passing of knowledge/light from the teacher's (Sheikh) heart to the pupil. The teacher has an integral role within Sufism.
- Dhikr (remembrance of the name of Allah). This is a principle in all schools of Islam, and is commanded by Allah. It perhaps takes on greater emphasis within Sufism; acts of remembrance and recitation of his name include singing, dancing (the Mevlevi Order of Sufism whirl as an act of dhikr), and meditation. This enables the name of

Allah to be written upon the heart, and for the worshipper to come into a close relationship with Allah.
- Saints and pilgrimage to the place of saints of Sufism. These are people who have been "marked by divine favour ... [and] holiness" and were "loved by God and developed a close relationship of love to Him" (Radtke, 2004, p. 520). This kind of relationship sets an example to believers.

It would be useful for teachers to understand how different expressions of Sufi can be found in the different traditions of Islam.

Returning to Alan Brine's suggestion that we teach 'Islams' within the classroom, it is this that perhaps gives the teacher the ability to draw a big tent of Islam. Within the community there will always be lines that are drawn, or not drawn for one reason or another. Teachers function as "border crossers: able to listen critically to the voices of their students as well as able to critique the language in which histories of conflict was expressed" (Davies, 2008, p. 93). It would also allow for a more rigorous exploration of controversial issues and areas of debate within religions. In exploring the reasons behind divergence of beliefs it would provide a criticality of positions held by various religions and the groups therein.

Teachers, regardless of their own opinions, should be able to recognise the messiness of the boundaries of Islam, and help pupils to draw their own conclusions based on all of the evidence as to where the boundaries should be, or whether there should be boundaries at all. This is consistent with the approach adopted within Christianity, and indeed, an approach that could be applied to all religions in recognising their internal diversity.

References

All Qur'an quotes taken from the Sahih International Translation
Hadith are taken from sunnah.com

Brine, Alan (2015, 27 February). Investigating Islam: A Moroccan perspective. Retrieved from http://www.reonline.org.uk/news/alans-blog-investigating-islam-a-moroccan-perspective-alan-brine/

Chittick, William (2000). *Sufism*. London, UK: One World.
Davies, L. (2008) *Educating against extremism*. Stoke on Trent, UK: Trentham Books.
Fishman, J. E., & Soage, A. B. (2013). The nation of Islam and the Muslim world: Theologically divorced and politically united. *Religion Compass*, 7: 59–68.
Geaves, Ron (2007). 'A reality without a name': A repositioning of Sufism from the margins. *World Religions in Education. Journal of the SHAP Working Party*, XXX, 42–44.
Radtke, B. (2004). Saint. In Jane Dammen McAuliffe (Ed.), *Encyclopaedia of the Qur'ān*, (Vol. V, p. 520) Leiden, Germany: Brill.

CHAPTER 6

SHI'A ISLAM

Chapter Outline
What is Shi'a Islam?
What is its place within Islam?
Message
Nature of God
Nature of humanity
Writings
Religious expression

What is Shi'a Islam?

Shi'a is the second largest expression of Islam in the world. The word Shi'a comes from a contraction of Shī'atu 'Alī ("adherent of Ali"). This designation highlights the major difference between Shi'a Islam and other forms: a recognition of Ali as the rightful successor of Muhammad as the leader of the Muslim community. Shi'a claims surrounding the succession of Ali, rather than the Sunni Caliph Abu Bakr, hinge on the interpretation of the Hadith of Ghadir Khumm:

> "O people, God the Most Kind the Omniscient has told me that no apostle lives to more than half the age of him who had preceded him. I think I am about to be called (to die) and thus I must respond. I am responsible and you are responsible, then what do you say?" They said, "We witness that you have informed, advised and striven. May God bless you." He said, "Do you not bear witness that there is no god but God and that Muhammad is His servant and Apostle, and that His Heaven is true, His Hell is true, death is true, the Resurrection after death is true, that there is no doubt that the Day of Judgment will come, and that God will resurrect the dead from their graves?" They said, "Yes, we bear witness." He said, "O God, bear witness." Then he said, "O people, God is my Lord and I am the lord of the believers. I am worthier of believers than themselves. Of whomsoever I had been

Mawla, Ali here is to be his **Mawla**. O God, be a supporter of whoever supports him (Ali) and an enemy of whoever opposes him and divert the Truth to Ali" (emphasis added).

In this sermon, which is accepted as authentic by Sunnis and Shi'as, the interpretation hangs on the interpretation of the word 'mawla'. There seem to be over twenty different ways that the word can be used. From a Shi'a perspective, the word in this context refers to 'leader' or 'guardian', placing the leadership of the Muslim community upon Ali and the family of the Prophet. This takes on additional importance when placed alongside a verse of the Qur'an revealed as a part of this sermon by Muhammad:

> O Messenger! proclaim the (message) which hath been sent to thee from thy Lord. If thou didst not, thou wouldst not have fulfilled and proclaimed His mission. And God will defend thee from men (who mean mischief). For God guideth not those who reject Faith (Surah 5:67).

The appointment of Ali as mawla thus completes the message which Muhammad had to declare. While Sunnis accept this recitation of events, they see mawla to mean 'friend', having no connotation of leadership.

This is not the only event or saying of Muhammad that leads Shi'a Muslims to assert the claim of Ali to be the rightful leader of Islam following Muhammad's death. In the fourth year of Islam Muhammad gathered some people around him and asked:

> Who among you will support me in carrying out this momentous duty? Who will share the burden of this work with me? Who will respond to my call? Who will become my vicegerent, my deputy and my wazir? (Razwy, 2001, p. 54).

Only Ali volunteered. This event was repeated three times with only Ali volunteering each time. In response Muhammad "drew [Ali] close, pressed him to his heart, and said to the assembly: 'This is my wazir, my successor and my vicegerent. Listen to him and obey his commands'" (Razwy, 2001, pp. 54–55).

A further event used by Shi'as to suggest that Ali was wrongly prevented from assuming leadership is reflected in the Hadith of the Pen and the Paper. Both Sunnis and Shi'a accept that this event happened but have differing interpretations of what it means:

> When Allah's Messenger was on his death-bed and in the house there were some people among whom was `Umar bin Al-Khattab, the Prophet said, "Come, let me write for you a statement after which you will not go astray." `Umar said, "The Prophet is seriously ill and you have the Qur'an; so the Book of Allah is enough for us." The people present in the house differed and quarrelled. Some said "Go near so that the Prophet may write for you a statement after which you will not go astray," while the others said as `Umar said. When they caused a hue and cry before the Prophet, Allah's Messenger said, "Go away!" ... Ibn `Abbas used to say, "It was very unfortunate that Allah's Messenger was prevented from writing that statement for them because of their disagreement and noise" (Sahih al-Bukhari 5669).

Sunnis would, perhaps, accept Umar's view of the Hadith; Shi'as suggest that on this document Muhammad was to appoint Ali as his successor.

The events preceding, and following, Muhammad's death, from a Shi'a perspective, were designed to usurp the leadership of the Muslim community away from Ali. While Ali and his wife, Fatimah (the daughter of Muhammad) and other family members were preparing Muhammad's body for burial, a meeting of a small number of Muslim leaders took place at Saqifah. From a Sunni perspective this meeting was essential as the community, which was unified under the leadership of Muhammad, was in danger of fracturing. It seems as though it is portrayed as a dispute of leadership between the Ansar and Qureshi tribe. During this 'heated' meeting Abu Bakr was declared as leader of the Muslim community, and successor/Caliph to the Prophet Muhammad.

The party of Ali (Shi'at 'Ali) refused to submit to the leadership of Abu Bakr, and Ali was only coerced to do this after six months, by offering allegiance for the unity of Islam. At no point did he reject his own claim to the Imamate which, it is possible, he felt he could fulfil without fighting. At each of the next two appointments of the Caliphs it is felt by Shi'as that Ali accepted the choices made for the sake of the unity of Islam; indeed, his acceptance of the Caliphate can be seen to be taken with reluctance, again for the unity of Islam. His time as Caliph was during a time where there was great conflict about who was the rightful Caliph.

It is sometimes confusing for some observers as to why there was/is still the split between Sunni and Shi'a when Ali eventually assumed the leadership of Islam as the fourth Rightly Guided Caliph. Aside from the significant differences between the role of an Imam and a Caliph, it again, comes down to a controversy and civil war about who was the successor of Ali. His son, Hasan, succeeded him, but to avoid civil war and more bloodshed, soon abdicated the Caliphate in favour of Muawiyah I, the founder of the Umayyad Caliphate. While sharing a grandfather with Ali and Muhammad, he was an opponent of Muhammad at first, and was part of the group that chased Muhammad during the events of the hijrah. It has been suggested that his acceptance of Islam on Muhammad's return was for political, rather than religious reasons.

Although Islam and its organisation to this point had always had a political dimension, and could be seen to rely on religious and political principles; the Ummayad dynasty is a sign, for Shi'as, that the balance had tipped completely towards political leadership.

Despite retaining some hope of regaining political leadership during the lifetimes of Hasan and Husayn (his brother, and Ali's son by Muhammad's daughter, Fatimah), in some ways Shi'a Muslims recognise that these claims, while legitimate, did not come to fruition, and the Imamate as a spiritual leader is what became important. The split became irreparable through the actions of Muawiyah who appointed his son, Yazid as his successor in direct contravention of the treaty signed with Hasan when he abdicated. Understanding the precariousness of his Caliphate, Yazid demanded obeisance from

Husayn, which he refused to give as he felt that Yazid was not living according to Muslim principles and changing some aspects of the faith.

The events of the Battle of Karbala (remembered in the Shi'a festival of Ashura) is seen today as solidifying the split in the community. Although ostensibly a battle, the leader of the Kufah army, which was ostensibly part of Yazid's empire, Umar ibn Sa'ad, cut off Husayn and his family and retinue, including women and children, from water and slaughtered most of them. One survivor was Ali, the son of Husayn and the fourth Imam, who had been ill and whose life had been saved by the pleading of his aunt, Zaynab.

The exact role of an Imam in Shi'a Islam will be explored later (see Message: Imamah), but at this point it will be useful to outline the various branches (also known as traiqah/paths) of Shi'a Islam and the Imams they accept (see Table 5.2). The main branches of Shi'a are Twelver (the largest group); Nizari Isma'ili; and Musta'li Isma'ili (also known as Bohra). Sometimes the two Isma'ili groups are included in a designation of Sevener Shi'a Islam; although there was a branch of Isma'ili Islam known as Sevener which is now defunct, this is not an accurate description of the Isma'ili groups.

What is its place within Islam?
For Shi'a Muslims they are the original expression of Islam taught by the Prophet Muhammad. It is Sunni Islam that is seen to be schismatic. Sometimes within the classroom it can be seen that Sunni is taught as the normative expression of Islam, and Shi'a split from Sunni. This is perhaps an inevitable result of a large percentage of Muslims in the UK, and around the world, being Sunni (estimates range from 85–90% with the remainder generally being found within Shi'a Islam). The typical Sunni view is summarised by Cyril Glasse:

> Shi'ites are Muslims because their doctrines coincide for the most part with orthodox Islam; the Shi'ite belief in the mystic role of the Imams, while deplorable does not put them beyond the pale (2001, p. 427).

Shi'a Islam

Table 5.2 – Shi'a Imams in Twelver, Musta'li and Nizari expressions.

Twelver	Nizari Ismaili	Musta'li Ismaili
Ali	Ali	Ali is not numbered as the first Imam he is regarded wasi (successor and executor) and asas (foundation) in the sense that he embodies the principles, and is the foundation, of the Imamate. Musta'li numbering beings with Hasan.
Hasan ibn Ali	Hasan is not numbered in the listing of Nizari Imams, though he is regarded as an entrusted/trustee Imam. He was temporary Imam for a period of time but the Imamate did not pass down his line.	Hasan ibn Ali
Husayn ibn Ali	Husayn ibn Ali	Husayn ibn Ali
Ali ibn Husayn Zayn al-Abidinm	Ali ibn Husayn Zayn al-Abidinm	Ali ibn Husayn Zayn al-Abidinm
Muhammad al-Baqir	Muhammad al-Baqir	Muhammad al-Baqir
Ja'far al-Sadiq	Ja'far al-Sadiq	Ja'far al-Sadiq
Musa Al-Kadhim	Isma'il ibn Jafar	Isma'il ibn Jafar
Ali Al-Ridha	Muhammad ibn Isma'il	Muhammad ibn Isma'il
Muhammad Al-Jawad (also al-Taqi)	Ahmad al-Wafi (Abadullah)	Ahmad al-Wafi (Abadullah)
Ali Al-Hadi (also Al-Naqi)	Muhammad at-Taqi (Ahmed ibn Abadullah)	Muhammad at-Taqi (Ahmed ibn Abadullah)
Hasan Al-Askari	Radi Abdullah	Radi Abdullah
Muhammad Al-Mahdi. Imam Al-Mahdi is the living but concealed Imam	Abdullah al-Mahdi Billah	Abdullah al-Mahdi Billah
Twelvers believe that the Hidden Imam is in a period of occultation (see footnote 6 on p. 123), and will return with Isa.	Muhammad al-Qaim Bi-Amrillah	Muhammad al-Qaim Bi-Amrillah
	Ismail al-Mansur	Ismail al-Mansur
	Ma'ad al-Mu'izz li-Din Allah	Ma'ad al-Mu'izz li-Din Allah
	Abu Mansur Nizar al-Aziz Billah	Abu Mansur Nizar al-Aziz Billah
	al-Hakim bi-Amr Allah	al-Hakim bi-Amr Allah
	Ali az-Zahir	Ali az-Zahir
	Abu Tamin Ma'add al-Mustansir Billah	Abu Tamin Ma'add al-Mustansir Billah
	Nizar b. al-Mustanṣir billah, al-Mustafa li Din Allah	al-Musta'li
	'Ali Al-Hadi ibn Nizar (hidden)	al-Amir bi-Ahkami'l-Lah
	Muḥammad Al-Mutadi (hidden)	at-Tayyib Abu'l-Qasim
	Hassan I Al-Qahir (hidden) Ḥassan II 'Ala Dhikrihi-s-Salam Nur-al-Din Muḥammad II	Following the occultation of the Imam, Musta'il have a Da'i al-Mutlaq - they can be considered a viceregent who rule in at Tayyib Abu'l-Qasim's name
	Jalalu-d-Dīn Ḥassan III,	
	'Ala' ad-Din Muḥammad III,	
	Ruknu-d-Din Khurshah,	
	Shamsu-d-Din Muḥammad (hidden)	
	Qasim Shah (hidden)	
	Islam Shah (hidden)	
	This line continues until the present day with Shah Karimu-l-Ḥussayni Aga Khan IV	

For Shia's this summation would be offensive; in this understanding Sunni Islam is 'orthodox' and Shi'as beliefs are 'deplorable', also described as heterodox or heretical. Contrary to this, Shi'a Muslims would describe their version of Islam as the authentic expression, taught by the Prophet Muhammad and continued by his successors, the Imams.

This is important within the teaching of different expressions of Islam. As already noted, there is a tendency to describe Shi'as as the breakaway or schismatic sect of Islam. In teaching Shi'a self-understanding it is imperative that Shi'a claims are recognised on their own terms, and not through the lenses of Sunni history and belief. This is not to suggest that the differences cannot be examined; indeed, they provide a rich area of discussion but teachers should allow both Sunnis and Shi'as to speak for themselves.

Message

The five central beliefs of Twelver Shi'a Islam are known as the 'Usul ad-Din (roots of religion) and it is a Shi'a Muslim's responsibility to come to know, understand and experience them for themselves. While a Muslim may learn prayer through imitation of others, these beliefs are so important that an individual must search and study them. Although specifically Twelver beliefs, the roots can be seen to have resonance in other forms of Shi'a Islam. The five roots are:

- Tawhid (oneness of Allah)
- Adalat (divine justice)
- Nubuwwah (prophethood)
- Imamah (divine leadership)
- Ma'ad (life after death)

The beliefs underpin all Twelver Shi'a practice. In exploring each one, any diversity of understanding within Shi'a tradition will be noted.

Tawhid

In Chapter 5: The Boundaries of Islam, the nature of Allah was explored in detail. In addition, the Shi'a belief in Allah can be seen to emphasise this oneness. It is important to note that the idea of Allah as one is not a numerical description, as numbers can be split and divided, rather it is a sense of his uniqueness of completeness. Tawhid is perhaps best explained through its opposite – shirk – of which there are seen to be three types:

- Lordship: where a person ascribes a partner to Allah in his supremacy and might as Lord.
- Names and attributes: this is the idea that people and other created beings can be elevated to the status of Allah by being seen to independently possess his attributes. There is none other like him; people can only be said to have attributes of Allah by dependence on him.
- Worship: where other entities are worshipped besides/instead of Allah.

Adalat

This is Divine Justice, or the Justice of Allah. One of Allah's names is Al-Adl (the Just). He is the source and arbiter of justice. It is only possible to understand justice when it is in Allah's hands as he is the perfection of justice. It is against his nature to be unjust in any way. Humanity is to recognise the justice of Allah:

> Say: 'My Lord has enjoined justice' (Surah 7:29).

Allah's justice is perfect, and it is recognised that Allah is not unfair in his rewarding and punishment of humans. Good actions are rewarded and evil doings are punished justly. The judgements of Allah are based on the things that he has clearly laid out in the Qur'an to be lawful, encouraged and unlawful. Thus, his judgements are always just because they are set against his laws which have been revealed to humanity.

While humans may judge in an imperfect way, without knowing intentions or the complete facts, or out of prejudice, Allah does not act in any of these ways. He is omniscient and knows all, and therefore the judgement he gives is just and fair.

An important facet of the judgement of Allah is that he does not force humans to do anything, anything they do is subject to their free will, in which they can choose to follow his law or not. In this, and all ways, Allah's judgement is just. This last part highlights an important difference between many Shi'as and Sunnis in their interpretation of predestination. In Shi'a teaching 'hard' predestination is rejected and a more middle way between free will and predestination is adopted. There will be things that are predestined, recognising that although humans are free to act in any way, the event decreed by Allah will always be accomplished. There is diversity within Shi'ism surrounding the doctrine of predestination. The concept of bada (alteration of divine will) suggests that, while in some circumstances, it may seem to humans that Allah's will has changed, it actually only appears so; he always knew what was to happen. Examples of this include Moses and the children of Israel:

> And We appointed with Musa a time of thirty nights and completed them with ten (more), so the appointed time of his Lord was complete forty nights (Surah 7:142).

The time was changed from thirty to forty nights because of disobedience.

> And remember We appointed forty nights for Moses, and in his absence ye took the calf (for worship), and ye did grievous wrong (Surah 2:51).

Nubuwwah

Linked with the idea of justice, the idea that people will be judged justly because Allah has revealed his truth, Nubuwwah (Prophethood) reflects the belief that throughout the history of the world Allah has sent messengers to teach his truth to all people. The Qur'an teaches:

> Certainly We raised an apostle in every nation (to preach:) "Worship God, and keep away from the Rebels (false gods)" (Surah 16:36).

There are two types of prophets within Shi'a belief:

- Rasuls (messengers) who receive scripture and are law bearing.

- Nabis (prophets) who remind people of the teachings of an earlier prophet, for example Yaqub who reminded people of Ibrahim's teaching.

In Shi'a teaching these prophets, of both types, are 'immaculate', meaning that because of their spiritual state and closeness to Allah they do not commit evil acts. If they did then it would be a distraction from the immaculate message they have been sent to deliver. If there are occasions where it seems that a prophet may have committed a sin, Shi'as would say that this is not so, that people need to understand the context and complete situation to understand the sinless nature of the prophets. One example that is often used is of the prophet Musa (Moses). The Qur'an records:

> And he entered the city at a time of inattention by its people and found therein two men fighting: one from his faction and one from among his enemy. And the one from his faction called for help to him against the one from his enemy, so Moses struck him and [unintentionally] killed him. [Moses] said, "This is from the work of Satan. Indeed, he is a manifest, misleading enemy." He said, "My Lord, indeed I have wronged myself, so forgive me," and He forgave him. Indeed, He is the Forgiving, the Merciful. (Surah 28:15-16).

Shi'as would strive to find an alternative explanation that absolves the prophet of Allah, and explains that he did not sin. In trying to help an oppressed slave, Musa punched an Egyptian, who was abusing the slave, and this inadvertently killed the Egyptian. The death is accidental, and "Satan's doing" refers to the action of the Egyptian that caused Musa to act in such a way. Musa's humility in seeking forgiveness is shown, but in the Shi'a view is not necessary. This type of explanation for the apparent 'sin' or bad action of the prophet would always be sought by Shi'as. Prophets are incapable, because of their immaculate nature, of disobedience.

There are twenty-five prophets named in the Qur'an, but Shi'as would suggest that there have been 140,000 throughout history, enabling the people of the world to have received the truth against which they will receive judgement.

Muhammad stands within, but also apart, from the other prophets. He is the 'seal of the prophets', and while each prophet before him came with a message to a specific place and time, Muhammad is the prophet for "all the worlds" (Surah 21:107). His revelation of the Qur'an is the final revelation for humanity. Since the time of his life, he has also been the ultimate example of living in submission to Allah:

> In the Apostle of God there is certainly for you a good exemplar (Surah 33:21).

All of the other prophets' lives can serve as exemplars, but Muhammad is the prophet for all time and as such his Sunnah and Hadith, while not scripture, are important sources for Muslims (see below: Scripture).

Imamah

As outlined earlier (see: What is Shi'a Islam), a distinguishing/defining characteristic of Shi'a Islam is belief in the Imamate; it is, however, the distinguishing feature between the different forms of Shi'a Islam. Imams are the divinely appointed successors to Muhammad, and for all Shi'as are of his line. The divine inspiration behind the appointment of an Imam (nass) is highlighted in the Qur'an:

> Indeed I am going to set an authority on the earth (Surah 2:30).

This verse refers specifically to the appointment of Adam, but the principle of divinely appointed leaders is seen to be illustrated in this verse. The Imam, in the absence of a prophet, leads the community of Islam. In Shi'a teaching there has never been a time where there has not been an Imam on the earth, on occasion such as in the persons of Ibrahim, Nuh and Muhammad the role of prophet and Imam has been combined.

Ali is reported to have outlined the importance of Imams in the world and in the judgement of Allah:

> God is one; He was alone in His singleness and so He spoke one word and it became a light and he created from that light Muhammad and He created me and my descendants (i.e the other Imams), then He spoke

another word and it became a Spirit and He caused it to settle upon that light and He caused it to settle on our bodies. And so we are the Spirit of God and His Word ... and this was before He created the Creation (quoted in Momen, 1985, pp. 148-49).

Imams are second only to the Prophet; Imams are seen to reflect Allah's light and spirit in their lives and message. The difference between a prophet and an Imam is sometimes discussed as a prophet seeing a vision and hearing the message, whereas the Imam hears the message but does not see a vision of an angel. The Sixth Imam, Ja'far al-Sadiq, has outlined the centrality of the Imam:

> We are the ones to whom God has made obedience obligatory. The people will not prosper unless they recognise us and the people will not be excused if they are ignorant of us (quoted in Momen, 1985, p. 150).

Within Shi'a Islam the Imams are seen to be spiritual rather than temporal leaders. Sometimes these roles may be combined, but their primary role is the spiritual leadership of the community of Muslims. They are seen as spiritual leaders, exemplars and interpreters of the Qur'an among many other qualities. Although there is no outright reference to the role of Imams within the Qur'an, Shi'as recognise many verses as referring to the role and importance of the Imam. These verses indicate something of the nature of the Imams:

- The Light of Allah (see Surah 64:8).
- The Way (see Surah 25:8).
- The Possessors of Knowledge (see Surah 3:7).
- The Cord of Allah, to which people should hold fast (see Surah 3:102).
- The Straight Path (see Surah 1:6).
- The Signs of Allah (see Surah 29:49).
- The Possessors of Authority (see Surah 4:59).
- The Family of Abraham (see Surah 3:33; 19:58).
- The Truthful Ones (see Surah 9:119).
- The Servants of the All Merciful (see Surah 25:63).
- The Guides of Men (see Surah 7:181).

This list is only illustrative and there are many other passages that are interpreted to refer to the Imams. The ones chosen above illustrate the main roles that Imams are seen to perform. They are the sources of authority following the death of the Prophet, they are to interpret the meaning of the Qur'an, they are to speak authoritatively and provide guidance for Muslims. Muslims are to follow their examples, and hold fast to their authority, knowledge and teachings. Their source of authority comes from Allah, and they also receive it as members of the family of the Prophet.

The three main attributes of the Imam are:

- Nass (designated).
- Ismah (sinless/infallible).
- Afdal an-nas (the best of people).

Nass

The divinely inspired designation of the Imam (nass) is central to Shi'a belief. Allah guides the previous Imam to name his successor prior to his death. This successor can only be named by the Imam under the inspiration of Allah, because only they among all humans are immune from error. This indicates that the judgement of others, no matter how well-intentioned, is flawed and should not be used in the selection of the successor. This is in direct opposition to the way that Abu Bakr and his successors were chosen within Sunni Islam.

This does not mean that there is agreement within the Shi'a world as to the designations that take place. As can be seen from Table 5.2 on p. 105, there have been splits within Shi'a Islam which have focussed on the succession.

Isma'ili Muslims, sometimes erroneously identified as Sevener Shi'a Muslims, and Twelver Muslims split with the identity of the Seventh Imam. The Sixth Imam, Ja'far al-Sadiq, according to Shi'a sources designated his son, Isma'il as his successor. There is general agreement on this point across Shi'a schools. It was not unusual that the successor, the Silent Imam, would be designated a long time prior to the death of the Imam himself.

The death of Isma'il prior to his father meant that for Twelvers the designation was annulled and that the Imamate could be transferred to another following the death of the Sixth Imam. The Seventh Imam was Isma'il's younger brother Musa Al-Kadhim. Others felt that the designation could not be annulled, and that Isma'il had not died, but was concealed by his father for safety. Seveners, who have died out, considered that Isma'il would return one day as the Mahdi.

For Nizari and Musta'li Isma'ili Muslims the Imamate continued and passed down through the line of Isma'il, to his son Muhammad. Isma'ili Muslims identify various 'proofs' that Isma'il became Imam following his father:

> Proof #1: Imām Ja'far designated Mawlānā Ismā'īl as the next Imam by the rule of nass as per Twelver, Ismaili, Sunni and academic sources.
>
> Proof #2: The only way to deny the nass of Mawlana Isma'il is through contradictory Hadiths presented in later Twelver Hadith books.
>
> Proof #3: Isma'il's death before Imam Ja'far is not confirmed and may have been staged to protect him – as he was reportedly seen by eyewitnesses after his alleged death.
>
> Proof #4: Even if Isma'il had died before his father, the Imamat continued in Isma'il's son, Muhammad ibn Isma'il, whom Isma'il had appointed as his own successor (Ismaili Gnostic, 2014).

For Twelver Shi'a Muslims, the succession of the Imams continued until the occultation[6] of the Twelfth Imam, Muhammad Al-Mahdi. Following the death of the Eleventh Imam, Hasan Al-Askari, it was assumed by the community that the new Imam would be his brother Ja'far. As Ja'far arrived at the Imam's house to lead the funeral prayers, a young boy stepped forward and asked his uncle to stand back as it was more fitting for him to lead the prayers for his father. This is the only recorded appearance of the Twelfth Imam during his life,

---

6 Occultation of the Imam is reflective of the belief that the world is never without an Imam. This belief is evident in both Twelver and Musta'li expressions of Shi'a Islam. The implications and nuances are different in each tradition and will be explored below, but the belief that both hold is that the Imam is currently hidden from the world and continues to be a guide. He will reappear at a time decided by Allah.

and Ja'far (known as Kadhdhab or the liar in Twelver Shi'ism) denied knowledge of who this boy was. Some Muslims followed Ja'far, while others listened to Uthman ibn Sa'id al-Asadi, who had been a trusted member of the households of the previous three Imams. Uthman confirmed that Muhammad Al-Mahdi did exist, but that he had entered a period of occultation, and that he would serve as the Imam's intermediary with the world.

This occultation is possible because Twelver Shi'a Muslims believe that there are two kinds of servants: the hidden and the apparent. The world is never left without an Imam, but in this case, he is hidden. The 'Minor Occultation' where the Imam communicated to the world through his Deputies/Gates lasted from 873–941 CE, and the deputies were:

- Uthman ibn Sa'id al-Asadi (873–980 CE).
- Abu Ja'far Muhammad ibn Uthman ibn Sa'id al-Asadi (880–917 CE).
- Abul Qasim Husayn ibn Ruh al-Nawbakhti (917–938 CE).
- Abul Hasan Ali ibn Muhammad al-Samarri (938–941 CE).

For many Shi'a Muslims this devolved nature of leadership essentially carried on a system that had already been in evidence. The opposition of the powerful Abassids of the time meant that the Tenth and Eleventh Imams had essentially been in an occultation from followers, sending messages to, and receiving taxes from, them through a series of agents (Wikalah).

This lesser occultation ended and the Greater Occultation began with the death of the final deputy. The Twelfth Imam would continue to be hidden, would affect the world through his influence, until he would return again. Al-Samarri, prior to his death, delivered a message from the Imam:

> There are but six days separating you [al-Samarri] from death. So therefore arrange your affairs but do not appoint anyone to your position after you. For the second occultation has come and there will not now be a manifestation except by permission of God ... (quoted in Momen, 1985, p. 164).

The Twelfth Imam will return again as the Mahdi and defeat evil and usher in a period of peace and justice. Following his return, Jesus, the prophets and other Imams will also return.

Within the two main traditions of Isma'ili Islam (Nizari and Musta'li) the succession continued through the line of Isma'il to Abu Tamin Ma'add al-Mustansir Billah; following his death in 1094 CE there was a split on the issue of succession. Mustansir's younger son Al-Musta'li succeeded him as Caliph of the Fatimid empire, and also was seen to succeed to the Imamate. His elder brother, an-Nizar, contested this succession but was eventually defeated and executed. Following the death of Nizar, the split in the Isma'ili community was solidified. Musta'lis tended to be found in the regions of Egypt, Yemen and western India, while those following Nizar's son, Al-Hādī ibn Nizār, were in the areas of Iran and Syria.

For Nizari Isma'ilis the Imamate has passed down, and is found in the leadership of Shah Karimu-l-Hussayni Aga Khan IV today.

For Musta'li Isma'ilis the Imamate continued until the occultation of at-Tayyib Abu'l-Qasim in 1134 CE. Before he went into occultation he asked the queen, Arwa al-Sulayhi, to select a Da'i al-Mutlaq (absolute or unrestricted missionary) or vice-regent to have spiritual and social authority over the Musta'li, who would remain in communication with him. The Da'i al-Mutlaq are chosen by their predecessor through the doctrine of nass, in the same way as an Imam. The office has continued until the present day.

Ismah (sinless/infallible)

In the discussion of prophets earlier it was outlined that they are sinless and free from error. If it appears that they have done something wrong then another explanation should be found. This sinlessness extends to the Imams, and is based on the Qur'an:

> And [mention, O Muhammad], when Abraham was tried by his Lord with commands and he fulfilled them. [Allah] said, "Indeed, I will make you a leader for the people." [Abraham] said, "And of

my descendants?" [Allah] said, "My covenant does not include the wrongdoers" (Surah 2:124).

The purity of the family (household) of the Prophet, most notably the Imams, is explained in the verse of purification from the Qur'an:

> And abide in your houses and do not display yourselves as [was] the display of the former times of ignorance. And establish prayer and give zakah and obey Allah and His Messenger. Allah intends only to remove from you the impurity [of sin], O people of the [Prophet's] household, and to purify you with [extensive] purification (Surah 33:33).

This freedom of sin also extends to freedom from error. In his role as interpreter of the Qur'an, the Imam has authority that cannot be questioned. He is the recipient of Allah's truth and only he has the authority to interpret what the revelation says.

Afdal an-nas (the best of people)
As an outworking of the justice of Allah and the sinlessness of the Imam, it follows that the Imams should be the best of people. Their example and teaching provide humanity with the perfect example, so that people are left under no illusion as to what the truth is. It is therefore necessary for the Imams to be the sinless and perfect examples.

There are many other qualities and roles that Imams show in their lives, and they are seen to be examples for Shi'as to follow. Their complementary nature to the role of the prophet is shown by the concept of walayah (guardianship).

> The Imam is seen as the spiritual friend or supporter who guides and initiates mankind into the mystical or inner truth of religion. It is through him that God's grace reaches the Earth (Momen, 1985, p. 157).

Through the prophet the outward expressions of religion are revealed; the Imam is the guide of the people for the more esoteric and internal aspects of submission and devotion.

As interpreters, and reflections, of the message of Allah Imams occupy a central place in the message and practice of Shi'a Islam.

Shi'a Islam

Historical Imams are shown respect and the places of their burial can often be sites of pilgrimage. This is not to suggest a worship of the Imam, but a respect for them and ultimately devotion to Allah.

Ma'ad (Life after death)

Muslims believe that this world is temporary and the afterlife is permanent. This life is a series of tests. A Muslim believes that Allah is the giver of life and death, and He decides when someone dies. In Sura 3 of the Qur'an it says:

> No soul can die unless by the permission of Allah.

Muslims believe that they will be judged after they die by Allah and this affects the way that they live on earth. It helps them think of others and be generous while they are here. They know that Allah will hold them accountable for everything they have done.

At death Shi'a Muslims believe that the soul remains aware of its surroundings. A body should be buried, and after burial the soul will detach itself from the body and live in Barzakh which is an intermediary or waiting stage. Here, the souls will be questioned about the beliefs that they have held, and the deeds that they have performed. While in Barzakh and the grave, those who have done good deeds will have a heaven like experience, while those who have done badly will receive torment. It is only temporary, however, and they will remain here until the Day of Judgement (Yawm-al-Qiyamah).

Between Barzakh and the world is a veil, which does not allow the two realms to see each other. When life is over it is too late to do anything to alter Allah's judgement on us. Those who did not believe in Allah will beg for a second chance. They will ask if they can go back to warn those that they loved – but they will get no second chance.

On the Last Day, all graves will be opened. The dead will be brought resurrected. Two angels will question them about the lives they have led. The deeds of everyone are weighed in Allah's balance. Judgement is passed by Allah and people will receive Paradise:

> Indeed the Godwary will be amid gardens and springs. "Enter it in peace and safety!" (Surah 15:45 46).
>
> His shall be a blissful state in a lofty garden, with clusters of fruit within his reach. We shall say to him: "Eat and drink to your heart's content: your reward for what you did in days gone by" (Surah 69:19).

or Hell:

> For those who defy their Lord is the punishment of hell, and it is an evil destination (Surah 67:6).
>
> Garments of fire have been prepared for the unbelievers. Scalding water shall be poured upon their heads, melting their skins and that which is in their bellies. They shall be lashed with rods of iron (Surah 22:19).

This is inextricably linked with the concept of Adalat and the characteristic of Allah as Al-Adl (the Just); those who have asked forgiveness and tried to perform good deeds will rely on Allah's mercy to receive Paradise. Those who go against Allah's guidance will justly be separated from Allah and be in hell. Whichever judgement is made is just.

It is possible for Allah's mercy to be requested by those who are closest to him. The Qur'an says:

> Intercession will not avail that day except from him whom the All-beneficent allows and approves of his word (Surah 20:109).

In Shi'a Islam this is through the Prophet Muhammad, the Imam, and through the family of the Prophet. This is in distinction to Sunni Islam where it is felt that only Muhammad will be able to request heaven for certain people.

Writings

Within all forms of Shi'a Islam, the Qur'an is the word of Allah which was revealed to the Prophet Muhammad. It contains the law, teachings and philosophy necessary for humanity to learn the will of Allah, and live in submission to him. It is the unaltered word of Allah and will be accepted by all Shi'as. In the early history of Shi'a there was some

Shi'a Islam

debate about differences between the Qur'an compiled by Uthman, and that in Ali's possession. This was the result of mistrust between the two factions, and the suspicion that the Caliphs would edit out any aspects of the Qur'an that extolled Ali. While early Shi'as accepted that nothing had been added, there lingered the suspicion that things had been left out. Momen (1985) outlines that while "most Shi'is eventually took the view that nothing had been omitted or added to the Qur'an, traces of the earlier view are enshrined among some of the hadith" (p. 172). It would be largely untrue to say today that this dispute still exists, but some opponents of Shi'a Islam try and keep it alive.

Where Shi'as and Sunnis do disagree, however, is with regard to the authority of the Hadith. Some of the early narrators of the Sunni Hadith are seen to be closely associated with Abu Bakr and Umar; as such not all of those Hadith are to be trusted. In addition, some of the Hadith were fabricated to support one political opinion or another. Shi'as use the sayings and examples that have been passed down through the Imams, through the line of Muhammad's daughter, Fatima. The Four Books (al-Kutub al-Arba'a) regarded as canonical by Twelver Shi'as are:

- *Kitab al-Kafi* (The Sufficient in the Science of Religion) compiled by Muhammad ibn Ya'qub al-Kulayni al-Razi (died 939 CE).
- *Man la yahduruhu al-Faqih* (He who has no Jurist present) compiled by Muhammad ibn Babawayh (died 991 CE).
- *Tahdhib al-Ahkam* (The Rectification of Judgements) compiled by Shaykh Muhammad Tusi (died 1067 CE).
- *Al-Istibsar* (The Perspicacious) compiled by Shaykh Muhammad Tusi (died 1067 CE).

There are also three other books of Hadith that can be seen to be highly regarded in Twelver Shi'a Islam:

- *Al-Wafi* (The Complete) by Muhammad ibn Murtada (died 1680 CE).
- *Wasa'il ash-Shi'a* (The Means of the Shi'a) by Shaikh al-Hur al-Aamili (1692 CE).
- *Bihar al-Anwar* (Oceans of Light) by Muhammad Baqir Majlisi (died 1699 CE).

In addition to the Hadith that provide inspiration and guidance in the living of Islam, there are also a number of books attributed to certain Imams:

- *Nahj al-Balaghah* attributed to Imam Ali and collected by Al-Sharif al-Radi (died 1015 CE).
- *Al-Sahifa al-Alawiya* by Imam Ali.
- *Al-Jafr* attributed to Imam Ali.
- *Risalah al-Huquq* attributed to Imam Ali ibn Husayn Zayn al-Abidin.
- *Al-Sahifa al-Sajjadiyya* attributed to Imam Ali ibn Husayn Zayn al-Abidin.
- *Al-Risalah al-Dhahabiah* attributed to Imam Ali al-Ridha.
- *Al-Sahifat al-Ridha* attributed to Imam Ali al-Ridha.
- *Tafsir Imam Ja'far al-Sadiq* attributed to Imam Jafar al-Sadiq.

These books are useful for inspiration and guidance. Elements of Isma'ili Shi'a Islam do not generally use the same Hadith as Twelver Shi'ism. It is suggested that a compilation by al-Qadi Abu Hanifa al-Nuʿman b. Muhammad (died 974) of Hadith is authoritative:

> He codified Ismaili law by systematically collecting the firmly established hadiths transmitted from the ahl al-bayt [family of the Prophet], drawing on earlier Shiʿi as well as Sunni authorities. After producing several legal compendia, his efforts culminated in the compilation of the Daʿaʾim al-Islam (The Pillars of Islam), which served as the official legal code of the Fatimid state (Daftary, 2005, p. 219).

Religious expression

The religious expression of Twelver Shi'a Islam can be seen in the obligatory acts (Furu' ad-Din: the branches of the religion):

- Salat (prayer).
- Sawm (fasting).
- Zakat (alms giving).
- Khums (one fifth tax).
- Hajj (pilgrimage).
- Jihād (struggle).
- Amr bil Maruf (commanding what is just).

Shi'a Islam

- Nahy Anil Munkar (forbidding what is evil).
- Tawalla (loving the family of the Prophet and their followers).
- Tabarra (dissociating oneself from the enemies of the family of the Prophet).

In some enumerations there are eight with numbers seven and eight from the list being joined together, and also nine and ten being joined together. Although not one of the obligatory acts, a belief in, and recitation of, the Shahadah underpins all of the actions of a Muslim. To become a Muslim, a person must believe and repeat three times the words of the Shahadah:

> La ilaha il Allah – there is no god but Allah.
> Muhammadu Rasul Allah – Muhammad is the Messenger of Allah.

Within Shi'a Islam a third phrase is often added to show belief in Imamah:

> Aliun wali Allah – Ali is a divinely-appointed authority (sometimes translated as 'the friend of God').

This shows that all other beliefs and actions are expressions of these three beliefs: belief in Allah, his Prophet, Muhammad and the Imamate.

Salat (Prayer)

Prayer within Shi'a Islam is a way to exemplify submission to Allah. This occurs through the various positions of prayer, especially prostration, but also through the words which are recited that praise Allah and show belief in him. The first way they show submission is through their performance, as they are commanded by Allah in the Qur'an:

> ... but when ye are free from danger, set up Regular Prayers: For such Prayers are enjoined on believers at stated times (Surah 4:103).

There are five prayers that should be recited:

- Salat al-Fajr (dawn prayer), which has two cycles (rak`ah).
- Salat al-Zuhr (midday prayer) with four cycles.
- Salat al-`Asr (afternoon prayer) with four cycles.

- Salat al-Maghrib (dusk prayer) with three cycles.
- Salat al-'Isha (night prayer) with four cycles.

Within the Shi'a community it will often be seen that the prayers are offered at three times during the day. With the following prayers being combined:

- Zuhr and Asr with eight cycles.
- Maghrib and Isha with seven cycles.

The combining of these prayers is not mandatory and people are free to pray at five different times. Many Shi'a Muslims believe that Muhammad combined these prayers at times, and allowed for them to be combined for the convenience of the ummah:

> The Prophet prayed eight rak'at for the Zuhr and 'Asr, and seven for the Maghrib and 'Isha prayers in Medina (Sahih al-Bukhari 543).

It is sometimes argued that Muhammad only allowed these in exceptional circumstances, but for those Shi'a Muslims who believe that the prayers can be regularly combined, they would point to the actions and words of Muhammad. It would also be seen to be more practical within the daily life of a Muslim.

Prayer will begin with the call to prayer (adhan) being repeated in Arabic:

> Allah is most great (repeated four times).
> I testify there is no god but Allah (repeated twice).
> I testify that Muhammad is the messenger of Allah (repeated twice).
> I bear witness that Ali is a divinely appointed authority (repeated twice) – this is not part of the
> adhan but is recommended to affirm and remind of the belief.
> Hurry to prayer (repeated twice).
> Hurry to success (repeated twice).
> Hurry to the best of deeds (repeated twice).
> Allah is most great (repeated twice).
> There is no god but Allah (repeated twice).

Shi'a Islam

Wudu will then be performed to show purity before Allah in all actions:

> O you who have believed, when you rise to [perform] prayer, wash your faces and your forearms to the elbows and wipe over your heads and wash your feet to the ankles. And if you are in a state of janabah, then purify yourselves. But if you are ill or on a journey or one of you comes from the place of relieving himself or you have contacted women and do not find water, then seek clean earth and wipe over your faces and hands with it. Allah does not intend to make difficulty for you, but He intends to purify you and complete His favour upon you that you may be grateful (Surah 5:6).

The head and feet, rather than being washed, will be wiped with already wet hands. The place of prayer should also be clean.

The cycle of prayer will include various actions including:

- Raising of the hands while standing (takbirat Ihram).
- Standing with the hands by the side to follow the example of Muhammad and the Imams (qiyam).
- Bowing from the waist with the hands on the knees (ruku).
- Prostration – placing the head on the earth (sujud).

Each of these actions is symbolic, but none more so than the prostration which symbolises complete submission to Allah: "Therefore celebrate the praises of thy Lord, and be of those who prostrate themselves in adoration" (Surah 15:98). Many Shi'a Muslims will pray using a turbah (piece of clay/earth) on which they will place their forehead during prostration. They see this to follow the example of Muhammad:

> I saw Allah's Apostle prostrating in mud and water and saw the mark of mud on his forehead (Sahih al-Bukhari 836).
>
> ... the earth has been made sacred and pure and mosque for me, so whenever the time of prayer comes for any one of you he should pray whenever he is (Sahih Muslim 521a).

In other places it suggests that he prayed on earthlike materials:

> "Allah's Messenger was praying while I was in my menses, sitting beside him and sometimes his clothes would touch me during his

prostration." Maimuna added, "He prayed on a Khumra (a small mat sufficient just for the face and the hands while prostrating during prayers)" (Sahih al-Bukhari 379).

Shi'a Muslims who use a turbah would allow any piece of natural material from the earth, while most will use clay, a piece of paper, plants, or other materials from the earth are acceptable. Sometimes, they pray on earth taken from Karbala (the site of Husayn's martyrdom). Karbala is seen to be one of the most sacred sites on which to pray, and so the earthen tablets from there which are often used reflect this belief. It is not necessary, however, to use soil from Karbala as any soil will suffice.

The use of prayer mats, while functional, can be seen to be a connection to the materiality of the world that Muslims leave behind when they come to prayer. The turbah enables them to follow the example of the Prophet and remember the true purpose of prayer.

The words used will remind Muslims of the unity of Allah (tawhid) and their reliance on, and submission to, him. Words used include:

- "In the Name of All, the All-beneficent, the All-Merciful", at the beginning of each cycle.
- "All glory to my Lord, the highest."
- "I bear witness that there is no god but Allah and Muhammad is the Messenger and servant of Allah."

They will also call for blessings to be upon Muhammad and his family.

On a Friday the Zuhr prayers are replaced by Salat al Jum'a which is always performed in congregation if people are able to. The Zuhr prayer is shortened to two cycles to allow for two sermons (khutbas) to be given before prayer. There is a strength to be found by praying in congregation.

As within each action in Shi'a Islam there is the outward observance of Salat which has been explored above, there is also the walayah or internal purpose. Within Nizari Isma'ili Shi'a Islam it has been suggested that:

Shi'a Islam

> The exterior meaning of ritual prayer is the worship of God with the body by advancing towards the qiblah of bodies, which is the Ka'ba, the house of God (the exalted) in Mecca. The esoteric interpretation (ta'wīl-i bāṭin) of the ritual prayer is the worship of God with the rational soul by turning, in the quest for knowledge of the Book and the Law (sharī'at), towards the qiblah of spirits, which is God's House, which is a house in which God's knowledge resides – the Imām of Truth (Khusraw, 2012, p. 272).

Prayer involves both the body and the soul in turning to Allah both outwardly and internally.

Sawm (Fasting)

A Muslim should fast during the daylight hours of the month of Ramadan:

> O you who have faith! Prescribed for you is fasting as it was prescribed for those who were before you, so that you may be Godwary (Surah 2:183).

During the fast a Muslim will abstain from:

- Eating, drinking or the intake of any substance.
- Sexual acts.

This abstention is important as it reflects a reliance on Allah, and also the ability to become 'Godwary' (taqwa). It helps a Muslim to put the usual distractions of the day into context, and develop their understanding of Allah. It further develops their spiritual nature and helps them focus on what is most important and will be accompanied by the performance of good acts, and the avoidance of the bad. Its primary purpose for Shi'a Muslims is spiritual rather than for any physical benefits that it may bring.

Some Muslims will be exempt from the requirement to fast, as it should be seen to be a blessing rather than a burden. The Qur'an outlines this:

> The month of Ramadan is one in which the Qur'an was sent down as guidance to humankind, with manifest proofs of guidance and

the Criterion. So let those of you who witness it fast (in) it, and as for someone who is sick or on a journey, let it be a (similar) number of other days. Allah desires ease for you, and He does not desire hardship for you, and so that you may complete the number, and magnify Allah for guiding you, and that you may give thanks (Surah 2:185).

In addition to this mentioned in the Qur'anic passage above (the sick and those on a journey), also excused are the young (prior to puberty), the old, the breast-feeding, those on medication that requires a person to eat or menstruating women. For those who miss days through illness and other temporary circumstances they are required to make up the day of fasting at some other time.

An important distinction between Twelver Shi'a practice and that of Sunni Islam is the timing of the end of the fast. The Qur'an gives the guidance that a person should "complete the fast until nightfall" (Surah 2:187). Rather than ending the fast at the moment of the sunset, Shi'a Muslims end their fast when there is darkness.

During the month of Ramadan there are two commemorations for Shi'a Muslims. The first is the Night of Power (Laylat-ul-Qadr), a night to remember the recitation of the Qur'an to Prophet Muhammad by the angel Jibr'il. This night is especially important and brings blessing to those who perform good deeds:

> Indeed We sent it (the Qur'an) down on the Night of Power. What will show you what is the Night of Power? The Night of Power is better than a thousand months. In it the angels and the Spirit descend, by the leave of their Lord, with every command. It is peaceful until the rising of the dawn (Surah 97:1-5).

Shi'a Muslims do not have an exact date but suggest that it is 21st, 22nd or 23rd of Ramadan. These three nights will be spent in the worship of Allah.

The second remembrance is of the martyrdom of Ali. While at prayer on 19th Ramadan he was stabbed with a sword, dying of his injuries on 21st Ramadan.

Shi'a Islam

Zakat (Alms giving)

Those Muslims who are aware of their standing before Allah, and the necessity of living life in submission to him will give willingly of Zakat. This is an act that will purify the believer, the wealth of those who give, and also those who receive.

> Piety is not to turn your faces to the east or the west; rather, piety is (personified by) those who have faith in Allah and the Last Day, the angels, the Book, and the prophets, and who give their wealth, for the love of Him, to relatives, orphans, the needy, the traveller and the beggar, and for (the freeing of) the slaves, and maintain the prayer and give the zakat, and those who fulfil their covenants, when they pledge themselves, and those who are patient in stress and distress, and in the heat of battle. They are the ones who are true (to their covenant), and it is they who are the Godwary (Surah 2:177).

Within Shi'a Islam Zakat is paid annually on nine specific items:

- Coins: Silver and gold coins (generally 2.5%).
- Cattle: Cows, sheep, goats and camels (generally 5%).
- Crops: Wheat, barley, dates and raisins (generally 10%).

This is usually paid to the religious authorities in the area to be used according to the guidance of Allah outlined in the Qur'an:

> Alms are for the poor and the needy, and those employed to administer the (funds); for those whose hearts have been (recently) reconciled (to Truth); for those in bondage and in debt; in the cause of Allah; and for the wayfarer: (thus is it) ordained by Allah, and Allah is full of knowledge and wisdom (Surah 9:60).

This is usually broken down into the eight different categories of purpose/recipient:

- The poor.
- The needy.
- Zakat collectors.
- For the promotion of Islam and recent converts of Islam.
- To free slaves.
- To alleviate the debt of those who are in debt to meet their basic needs.

- Those fighting for Allah whether physically or ideologically.
- Stranded travellers.

Nizari Muslims generally give approximately 10% of their income each month as payment of both Zakat and Khums. This is given to the Imam to use for the purposes that Allah has outlined.

Khums (One fifth tax)
Khums is the payment annually of a one-fifth, or 20%, tax:

> And know that anything you obtain of war booty – then indeed, for Allah is one fifth of it and for the Messenger and for [his] near relatives and the orphans, the needy, and the [stranded] traveler, if you have believed in Allah and in that which We sent down to Our Servant on the day of criterion – the day when the two armies met. And Allah, over all things, is competent (Surah 8:41).

Following the payment of all living expenses, one-fifth of the excess left over, and of all gold, silver, jewellery, mined products, war booty, items taken from the sea and increase in land worth should be paid. The money that is collected should be used for the family of the Prophet, orphans, stranded travellers and the needy. There is a tradition in some forms of Shi'a Islam that half of the khums could be considered to be the Imam's share. In Twelver Islam, with the occultation, what this means differs. There are some who feel that the Imam's share can be used to support the teaching of Islam in various means and buildings.

As Allah is the source of all that a person has, it is not considered to be a burden for a Muslim to give freely of their annual increase.

Hajj (Pilgrimage)
A Muslim should complete the pilgrimage to Makkah during the month of Dhul Hijjah on specific days at least once during their lifetime if they have the health and wealth:

> And pilgrimage to the House (al-bayt) is a duty [from] God for mankind, for him who has the means to do so. As for him who disbelieveth, (let him know that) lo! Allah is Independent of (all) creatures (Surah 3:97).

The Hajj enables the Muslim to put to one side the worries of their everyday life and draw closer in submission to Allah.

Activities of the Hajj include:

- The clothing in ihram (a white robe). Women can wear ordinary clothes whatever the colour, though a lot of Muslim women would also wear white as well. This is important in reflecting the unity of the ummah.
- Pilgrims circumambulate the Ka'bah seven times praising Allah, and asking for forgiveness. In place of kissing the black stone, pilgrims will often raise their hand towards it.
- Pilgrims pray at the station of Abraham and drink some water from the Well of Zamzam.
- Pilgrims walk seven times between two hills very near to Makkah. This is symbolic of Hagar running between the two hills seven times searching for water, before Ishmael miraculously discovered the Well of Zamzam when he put the heel of one of his feet into the ground.
- Pilgrims spend the night in Mina.
- Pilgrims will pray on the plain of Arafat (20km away) and may spend the entire day there asking Allah for forgiveness. It is believed that Adam and Eve were forgiven on Arafat.
- Pilgrims say evening prayers and camp in the village of Muzdalifah.
- In Mina pilgrims throw stones at three stone pillars remembering the stones thrown by Abraham to drive the devil away.
- In Mina the festival of sacrifice (Id-ul-Adha) is celebrated. On this day animals are sacrificed, eaten and given to the poor.
- The pilgrims will remove the ihram; women have their hair cut, while men have their heads shaved; both circumambulate the Ka'bah seven more times, before repeating the run between the two hills seven times.

These events help a Muslim show submission to Allah; they also remember events associated with prophets. The Hajj is a time of renewal and reflects many aspects of a Muslim's belief.

All of the above practices are common between Shi'a and Sunni Muslims, but in addition to these Shi'a Muslims are encouraged to extend and complete their Hajj in Madinah, also visiting the tombs of Muhammad, Fatima, and the Second, Fourth, Fifth and Sixth Imams (the tombs of Fatima and the Imams can be found at al-Baqi cemetery). This is part of the wider Shi'a practice of Ziyarah (visitation). This is the recommended pilgrimage to the graves of all of the individual Imams in Twelver expressions of Shi'ism and also Karbala, the place of the martyrdom of Husayn.

Within Nizari Isma'ili Islam, there is an additional Hajj, that of Hajj-i-Batini, the Hajj to the living Imam. This builds on an understanding of the establishment of Hajj by Ibrahim in the Qur'an:

> And proclaim the ḥajj among mankind: they will come to you (yatūka) on foot and (mounted) on every kind of camel, lean on account of journeys through deep and distant mountain highways (Surah 22:27).

The emphasis in this passage is that "they will come to you", meaning to the person of Ibrahim. The Ka'bah is only a symbol for the presence of Allah reflected in the life and person of the Imam. There are blessings which are given for being in the presence, or seeking to be in the presence of the Imam:

> ... just as, by His command the Ka'bah, the House of God, is the place of reward and peace externally, so internally the Imam of the time as the House of God, the means of every kind of reward and peace. The Imam is the spiritual Qiblah, towards whom the attention of the heart is necessary in every good deed and that this is the way of attaining reward (Hunzai, 1994, p. 113).

Just as the visit to the Ka'bah draws a person close to Allah, so being in the presence of the living Imam will help a person feel close to Allah.

Jihad (Struggle)

Ayatollah Khomeini, founder of the Islamic Republic of Iran and a revered figure in elements of Shi'a Islam, wrote a book that encapsulates the Shi'a view of Jihad. It was titled: *The Greatest Jihad: Combat with the Self* (2012). This recognises the importance placed upon the development of the self in submission to Allah, rather than self-aggrandisement or placing things as more important than Allah in life. This Jihad is also developed into a struggle against injustice and poverty that is found in the world. Mahmoud Ayoub has suggested:

> Whether through weeping, the composition and recitation of poetry, showing compassion and doing good to the poor or carrying arms, the Shi'i Muslim saw himself helping the Imam in his struggle against the wrong (zulm) and gaining for himself the same merit (thawab) of those who actually fought and died for him. The ta'ziyah, in its broader sense the sharing of the entire life of the suffering family of Muhammad, has become for the Shi'i community the true meaning of compassion (1978, p. 148).

From the words of Ayoub it is evident that the cultivation of the positive is helping the Imam in the struggle against wrong that can be found in the world. Jihad is expressed through compassion.

The meaning of Jihad as an armed struggle is also an element of Shi'a Islam. It is obligatory for all male Muslims who are able. In the Twelver expression of Shi'a Islam, the declaration of an offensive Jihad is limited to the authority of the Imam. Since the occultation, most Shi'a Muslims would suggest that the possibility of this type of conflict to be impossible, though the obligation to fight a defensive Jihad still exists.

Within Nizari Isma'ili adherents are generally pacifist and suggest that opponents to faith are the vices that people struggle with in their own lives. Physical force would only be used in defence as a last resort.

Amr bil Maruf (Commanding what is just) and Nahy Anil Munkar (Forbidding what is evil)

> There has to be a nation among you summoning to the good, bidding what is right, and forbidding what is wrong. It is they who are the felicitous (Surah 3:104).

This is very much linked with jihad and the requirement to live a virtuous life in submission to Allah. This would require a Muslim to follow Shari'ah law and eschew anything that could be considered to be evil, or draw a person away from acts that reflect this submission. It is also required that a Muslim should stand up for that which is right, enjoin other Muslims to live a submissive life and speak out to prevent evil being committed. In some ways, these aspects of the obligatory acts are two sides of the same coin. A Muslim will always strive for that which is right and avoid that which is evil.

The justice of Allah (adl) should be sought in all actions and Muslims should stand up for it. Imam Husayn is an example of this behaviour. Before his martyrdom at Karbala, and the slaughter of most of his family, he is reported to have said in a Hadith:

> I never revolted in vain, as a rebel or as a tyrant, but I rose seeking reformation for the nation of my grandfather Muhammad. I intend to enjoin good and forbid evil, to act according to the traditions of my grandfather, and my father 'Alī ibn Abī Tālib (Majlisi, Bihārul Anwār Hadith, vol. 44, p. 329).

Imam Husayn saw corruption, and because of the enjoinder to do good and forbid evil he was compelled to act without fear for himself. This follows a Hadith of the prophet Muhammad where both action and words are seen to be examples of these commands:

> Whosoever of you sees an evil, let him change it with his hand; and if he is not able to do so, then [let him change it] with his tongue; and if he is not able to do so, then with his heart – and that is the weakest of faith (40 Hadith Nawawi 34).

Even the 'weakest' of Muslims can fulfil this command. A Muslim has a responsibility to oppose evil in their heart, in their speech and in their actions. Similarly, they should do the same in doing what is good/just. One Muslim has explained how they put this into practice in their lives:

> This shows that if I cannot say or do something, then at least I can approve or disapprove of it in my heart. It can sometimes be difficult to say something when everyone around me is doing something that Islam does not agree with. For example, the people around me may drink alcohol and I have to make it clear that this is something I do not

agree with and not take part in without offending them. However, there are times where I have to speak out and make it clear that I disapprove of something. On the other hand, if I am about to do a good action, I try to encourage my friends to also join me (Bdaiwi and Hussain, 2017, p. 53).

Tawalla (Loving the family of the Prophet and their followers) and Tabarra (Dissociating oneself from the enemies of the family of the Prophet)

These two obligatory acts surround the Prophet Muhammad and his family (Ahl-ul-Bayt) which include the Imams. It builds on a command of the Qur'an:

> Say, "I do not ask you any reward for it except love of (my) relatives" (Surah 42:23).

Each of the members of the family of the Prophet are seen to be role models of how to live a life in submission to Allah. This has especial meaning when linked with the Hadith of the cloak where Muhammad takes Fatima, Ali, Hasan and Husayn under his cloak and declares them as pure. Fatima has a special place within Shi'a Islam and is particularly remembered. Her tomb will be visited, and she too is seen to be sinless and an example to the believers.

This Hadith is used to support the Imamah within Shi'a Islam, as it is the Prophet's household that is purified. Tawalla is used to help a Muslim live their life in submission, but by extension strengthens and reflects the belief in the importance of the Imam.

In contrast Tabarra means that a Muslim should not seek the guidance or teaching of someone who stands in opposition to the Prophet and his family. This might be someone today or someone who has lived and taught in the past. This could be seen to extend to those who stand in opposition to the family, which may include the Caliphs apart from Ali. The fifth Imam, Muhammad al-Baqir, is reported to have responded to a question about Abu Bakr and Umar:

> What are you asking me about them? Whoever among us (Ahl al-Bayt) or the progeny of Muhammad departed from this world, departed in a state of extreme displeasure with them. The elders among us admonished the younger ones to perpetuate it (extreme displeasure with them), Verily, the two of them have unjustly usurped our right. By Allah! These two were the first to settle on our (Ahl al-Bayt) necks.
>
> Therefore, may the la'nat (curse) of Allah, the Malaikah (angels) and of mankind be on the two of them (*Kitabur Raudhah*, p. 115 quoted in Qadri, 2013, p. 23).

It seems impossible for Shi'a Muslims to stand with both Abu Bakr and the Imams. This does not necessarily mean that Shi'a Muslims do not associate with Sunni Muslims, but means that the teachers who claim authority through the Caliphate should not be followed. This would also be extended to corrupt individuals whose teachings stand in contrast to the teachings and actions of the Prophet and his family.

Each of the obligatory acts reflects important beliefs in Shi'a Islam. The practices reinforce the central aspects of Shi'a teaching.

The Seven Pillars of Nizari Shi'a Islam

Within Nizari Isma'ili Shi'a Islam there are seen to be seven pillars, Imam Muhammad al-Baqir has said:

> Islam is based upon seven pillars: walayah – and this is the most excellent; through it and through the walī (the Imām), the true knowledge of the pillars can be obtained: ṭaharah (purification), ṣalah (prayer), zakah (purifying alms), ṣawm (fasting), hajj (pilgrimage), and jihād (striving) (Qādi al-Nu'man, Da'ā'im al-Islām, Prologue, 2 quoted in Ismaili Gnostic, 2012).

These seven are often described as a tree, the trunk is seen as walayah out of which the other six grow, and the trunk is underpinned by the five roots. As can be seen five of the seven pillars are similar/the same as some of the Twelver acts. Tabarah (purification) and the trunk of walayah are the two distinctive features.

Walayah (closeness, sanctity, friendship, love, authority, governance and saintship) refers to the closeness of the Imams and

Prophets to Allah. In turn, it refers to the closeness and love which the believer should have for the Imams. All of the other pillars and practices of Shi'a Islam grow out of this concept. The recognition of the status of the Imam, and the desire to be close to them enables a Muslim to live all aspects of their religion in a way that shows complete submission to Allah. Walayah involves the complete devotion of the believer to Allah through the Prophets and Imam; it includes their actions, their heart and their soul.

Tahara (purification) is the state of ritual purity within which a Shi'a Muslim should live. The Qur'an teaches of the importance of purity:

> A mosque founded on righteousness from the first day is more worthy for you to stand in. Within it are men who love to purify themselves; and Allah loves those who purify themselves (Surah 9:28).

Although immediately applicable to the practice of wudu within a mosque, this purity is extended to the different aspects of a person's life. The mind, the soul and actions should all be pure. A person's soul can become contaminated through various situations called Hadath which cause interaction/contact with impurities (Najis). There are two types of Hadath: major (Akbar) and minor which require two different cleansings: ghusl and wudu, both of which take place before a prayer is performed or a mosque is entered. This type of cleansing is mentioned in the Qur'an:

> O you who have believed, do not approach prayer while you are intoxicated until you know what you are saying or in a state of janabah, except those passing through [a place of prayer], until you have washed [your whole body]. And if you are ill or on a journey or one of you comes from the place of relieving himself or you have contacted women and find no water, then seek clean earth and wipe over your faces and your hands [with it]. Indeed, Allah is ever Pardoning and Forgiving (Surah 4:43).

The cleansing is physical, but is also symbolic of the cleansing of the soul. There are six circumstances that makes ghusl mandatory:

1. Janabah (sexual intercourse or the release of seminal fluid).
2. Haydh (menstruation).
3. Nifas (bleeding that occurs after childbirth).
4. Istihadha (irregular bleeding for a woman).
5. Ghusl Al-Mayyit (the washing of a dead body).
6. Ghusl Mas Al-Mayyit (touching the dead).

Within Shi'a Islam there are two types of ghusl that can be performed: ghusl tartibi and ghusl irtimasi. In ghusl tartibi the impurity is washed away, then there is a three-stage washing of the body:

- From the head down to the neck.
- Going down the right side of the body from the shoulder to the foot.
- Going down the left side of the body from the shoulder to the foot.

During ghusl irtimasi the body is completely submerged ensuring all areas of the body are cleansed.

Ideas for the RE Classroom

Whereas in the past the required study of Islam was reserved for A level, in the 2016 reformed GCSE specification study of the beliefs and practices of Shi'a Islam is now required, though a glance at the material used suggests that it is mainly, if not exclusively, focussed on the Twelver expression. This should not suggest that Shi'a should only be included at fourteen and above; children of Shi'a families are of all ages, and the inclusion of diversity within Islam is important from an early age. This may necessitate a changing in certain vocabularies that are used; 'many', 'most' and 'some' become crucial in certain aspects. One example could be the assertion that all Muslims pray five times a day. It is correct to say that Shi'as offer five prayers a day, but to an observer (from within or without Shi'a) it may appear that they pray three times a day. It is a nuance of language, but it indicates the need to be precise to be inclusive in all of our discussions of Islam. Specific areas that may have applicability within the classroom include:

Shi'a Islam

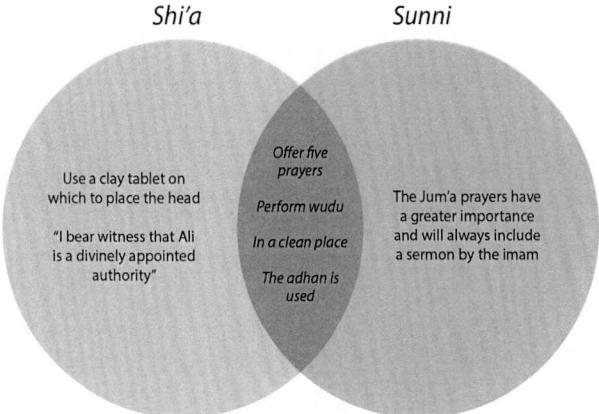

Figure 5.1 – Comparison of Shi'a and Sunni prayer.

- Although it is important for Shi'a beliefs to be explored as beliefs in their own right and not in contrast to those found in Sunni, it is possible to make no judgements about which are authentic but also to compare practices. There are many different topics and practices that can be explored in this way. For example, a simple sorting activity can construct a Venn diagram to show the similarities and differences between Shi'a and Sunni prayers.
- The concept of the Imam and Imamah in Shi'a Islam is very distinctive, and is perhaps the point which is the greatest separator from other forms of Islam. An exploration of the lives of the Imams as inspirational figures for Shi'a Muslims would not be inappropriate at different ages. There are stories that are told about each one. Some of the concepts within certain expressions of Shi'a, such as the occultation of the Imam are perhaps harder concepts that could be explored in later years. Their status within Shi'a should be reflected in aspects of classroom teaching. The story of the martyrdom is particularly important for Shi'a identity and is remembered at Ashura each year. The links between these events and the commemoration of them today form an important part of study.

- The idea found in the Nizari expression of Shi'a Islam of the tree, with its beliefs being the roots and the practices the branches, is very helpful. This will help pupils recognise the interaction between beliefs and practices. In the teaching of Islam teachers often focus on the observable, e.g. the Five Pillars and ignore the underlying beliefs. This Nizari illustration will help teachers and pupils to recognise that practices are important as expressions of more deeply held beliefs. This extends into the exoteric (outward) and esoteric (internal) expressions that each of these practices should have.

Useful websites
www.al-islam.org
www.iis.ac.uk/about-us/ismaili-community
https://the.ismaili/

References
All Qur'an quotes taken from the Sahih International Translation
Hadith are taken from sunnah.com with the exception of those noted.

Ayoub, Mahmoud M. (1978). *Redemptive suffering in Islam: A study of the devotional aspects of Ashura in Twelver Shi'ism*. The Hague, ND: Mounton.

Bdaiwi, Ahab, & Hussain, Zameer (2017). *GCSE Religious Studies Shi'a Islam teacher's edition*. London, UK: The Centre for Shi'a Studies.

Daftary, Farhad (2005). *Ismailis in medieval Muslim societies*. London, UK: I. B. Tauris Publishers/The Institute of Ismaili Studies.

Glasse, Cyril (2001). *The concise encyclopedia of Islam* (Rev. ed.). London, UK: Stacey International.

Hunzai, Allamah Nasir al-Din Nasir (1994). *Fruit of paradise* (Faquir Muhammad Hunzai, & Rashida Noormohamed-Hunzai, Trans.). Karachi, Pakistan: Khanah-i Hikmat/Idarah-i Arif.

Ismaili Gnostic (2012). The Seven Pillars of Islam: The esoterics of Walayah:. Retrieved from: https://ismailignosis.com/2012/09/30/the-seven-pillars-of-islam-the-esoterics-of-walayah/

Ismaili Gnostic (2014). Who succeeded Imam Jafar al-Sadiq? Seven proofs for the Imamat of Imam Ismail ibn Jafar. Retrieved from https://ismailignosis.com/2014/10/02/who-succeeded-imam-jafar-al-sadiq-seven-proofs-for-the-imamat-of-imam-ismail-ibn-jafar/

Shi'a Islam

Khomeini, Ayatullah Sayyid Ruhallah Musawi (2012). *Jihad al-Akbar, The Greatest Jihad: Combat with the self* (Muhammad Legenhausen Azim Sarvdalir, Trans.). Tehran, Iran: The Institute for the Compilation and Publication of the Works of Imam Khomeini.

Khusraw, Nasir-i (2012). *Between reason and revelation: Twin wisdoms reconciled* (Eric Ormsby, Trans.). I. B. Tauris Publishers/The Institute of Ismaili Studies.

Momen, Moojan (1985). *An introduction to Shi'i Islam*. New Haven, CT: Yale University Press.

Qadri, Maulana Muhammad Afroz (2013). *The reality of Shi'a*. Cape Town, South Africa: Sunni Youth Society.

Razwy, Sayed Ali Asgher (2001). *A restatement of the history of Islam and Muslims CE 570 to 661*. World Federation of KSI Muslim Communities United Kingdom. Retrieved from https://www.al-islam.org/printpdf/book/export/html/27929

CHAPTER 7

AHMADIYYA ISLAM

Chapter Outline
What is Ahmadiyya Islam?
What is its place within Islam?
Message
Scripture
Religious expression

What is Ahmadiyya Islam?
Ahmadiyya Islam takes its name from an alternative name for the Prophet Muhammad, Ahmad (see Murtaza Khan, 1945), which is also mentioned in the Qur'an as a prophecy of Isa about the Prophet:

> And [mention] when Jesus, the son of Mary, said, "O children of Israel, indeed I am the messenger of God to you confirming what came before me of the Torah and bringing good tidings of a messenger to come after me, whose name is Ahmad." But when he came to them with clear evidences, they said, "This is obvious magic." (Surah 61:6).[7]

For Ahmadi Muslims this places their faith within the sphere of the religion taught by the Prophet Muhammad himself. This is an important tenet of Ahmadiyya. It is not a new revelation, rather they are inheritors of the religion taught in its purity by Muhammad and his successors. There are approximately 20 million Ahmadis worldwide.

Its history begins in the person of Hazrat Mirza Ghulam Ahmad (1835–1908) who is seen to be the promised Messiah prophesied in the Qur'an and the Hadith. He summarised his role in his own words:

---

[7] Ahmadiyya referencing always includes 'In the name of Allah, Most Gracious, Ever Merciful' as the first verse in all but one Surahs, unlike the referencing of other Muslims. In many Surahs this will mean that there is a difference of one in the referencing of verses. This chapter uses Ahmadiyya reference numbers.

Ahmadiyya Islam

> With God-given strength and with the power of His hand, I am here to set the world back on the path of reformation, righteousness and piety, and to remove their errors in faith and in action (*Tadhkiratush Shahadatain*).

Ahmadis make an important distinction between Islam and Muslims. When discussing Islam and the message of the Qur'an and the Prophet Muhammad, these are seen to be perfect and the revelation of Allah. However, the actions of Muslims themselves meant that someone needed to reawaken them to a sense of their duty to Allah and the way to live in submission to him. In outlining this view, Hadith of the Prophet Muhammad are used:

> There will come a time upon the people when nothing will remain of Islam except its name and nothing will remain of the Qur'an except its words. Their mosques (masaajiduhum) will be splendidly furnished but destitute of guidance. Their scholars (ulemaa-uhum) will be the worst people under the heaven; evil plots will originate from them and return to them (*Mishkat al-Masabih* 1/91 Hadith 276).

The authenticity of this Hadith is disputed by some Muslims, but it provides a basis for understanding the view of Islam and Muslims held by Ahmadis. The solution to this malaise within Islam is the coming of the Messiah:

> Surely Jesus, son of Mary, will soon descend among you and he will judge mankind justly (as a Just Ruler) (*Sahih al-Bukhari* 3448).

Ahmadiyya Muslims believe that Isa/Jesus was crucified, but that he survived his time on the cross, being revived in the tomb. Isa then lived until he was about 120 when he died and was buried in Kashmir. His return, for Ahmadis, is not in the same literal form or as the same person, but as a person with a similar message and characteristics. This person is Hazrat Mirza Ghulam Ahmad. Ahmad does not just fulfil the prophesied role of the return of Jesus, he is also the promised coming of the Hidden Imam/Mahdi that is particularly important within Shi'a Islam. Whereas a large number of Shi'a Muslims believe that the Mahdi will accompany Jesus, for Ahmadiyya Muslims they are one and the same person. The Hadith talking about the return of Jesus are interpreted to mean that the set of circumstances and outcomes with the second coming would be very similar to the first. Jesus came as the Messiah for the Jews, as per the Old Testament prophecies, to restore humanity's relationship with Allah; yet he was rejected by the very people to whom he was sent, declared a heretic and persecuted along with his followers. Yet despite this they were highly successful. In the same way, Muslims were expecting a Messiah of their own but many rejected Mirza Ghulam Ahmad's claims, seeing him as an imposter. and starting a campaign of persecution against him and his followers, which continues to this day. Ahmadis believe that the second coming of any Messenger is a metaphor for the appearance of a Prophet with similar qualities as the first – in the same way that Jesus himself may have pointed to John the Baptist as the second coming of Elijah.

Ahmadis believe that the Messiah/Mahdi came not just for Muslims but to usher in an age of peace for all of humanity. Ahmad outlined his message:

> The purpose for which God has appointed me is that I should remove the malaise that afflicts the relationship between God and His creatures, and should restore the relationship of love and sincerity between them. Through the proclamation of truth I should bring about peace by putting an end to religious wars and should manifest the verities which have become hidden from the eyes of the world. I am called upon to demonstrate that spirituality, which has been overlaid by selfish darkness. It is for me to demonstrate in practice and not only in words, the Divine attributes which penetrate into the hearts of people and are manifested through prayer and concentration. Most of all it is my purpose to plant once more in the hearts of people the pure and shining unity of God which is free from every suspicion of paganism and which has completely disappeared. All this will be accomplished not through my power, but through the Power of Him Who is the God of Heaven and earth (*The Essence of Islam*, Volume IV, p. 111).

The establishment of the new community of Muslims (they would not be known as Ahmadiyya for a further ten years) took place on 23 March

Ahmadiyya Islam

1889. On this date, Ahmad took the oath of allegiance (bay'ah) as a leader of community. This was a practice that was undertaken by the Prophet Muhammad. Following the death of the Mahdi/Messiah in 1908 a Caliphate was established. For Ahmadis, a Caliph is a successor to a prophet rather than 'just' a title given to, or appropriated by, a leader. The Qur'an outlines the role of a Caliph:

> Allah had promised to those among you who believe and do good works that He will surely make them Successors in the earth, as He made Successors from among those who were before them; and that He will surely establish for them their religion which He has chosen for them; and that He will surely give them in exchange security and peace after their fear: They will worship Me, and they will not associate anything with Me. Then who so is ungrateful after that, they will be the rebellious (Surah 24:56).

The Caliphs are the spiritual successors to the prophets and have spiritual leadership. The Caliphs since Ghulam Ahmad have been:

- Hakeem Noor-ud-Din (1908–1914) – elected as Caliph the day after the death of the Messiah Noor-ud-Din, oversaw an English translation of the Qur'an, established the first Ahmadiyya Muslim mission in England and introduced various newspapers and magazines.
- Mirza Basheer-ud-Din Mahmood Ahmad (1914–1965) – elected the day after the death of the previous Caliph. He was the son of Hazrat Mirza Ghulam Ahmad by his second wife, and was elected at the age of twenty-five. Following his election, a group of Ahmadi Muslims split in disagreement over certain doctrinal tenets and became the Lahore Ahmadiyya Muslim community. As Caliph for over fifty years he established many of the structures in the community including the Majlis-ash-Shura or the Consultative Council. He also wrote a ten volume commentary on the Qur'an: Tafseer-e-Kabeer.
- Mirza Nasir Ahmad (1965–1982) – again, elected the day after the death of his father, the previous Caliph. He continued the development of missionary work around the world, and compiled the writings of Ghulam Ahmad into twenty-three volumes known as Ruhani Khaza'in (*Hidden Treasures*).

- Mirza Tahir Ahmad (1982–2003) elected the day after the death of the previous Caliph. Mirza Tahir Ahmad was also the son of the second Caliph. Following the introduction of Ordinance XX to the Pakistan Constitution (see below) he moved the headquarters of the organisation to London. During his Caliphate the translation of the Qur'an into different languages was accelerated. He also initiated developments in the global communication capabilities of the Ahmadis, notably establishing the first Muslim satellite television network, Muslim Television Ahmadiyya in 1994. This network enabled him to broadcast messages to the Ahmadiyya Community around the world. In the same year he oversaw the setting up of the charity, Humanity First.
- Mirza Masroor Ahmad (2003–) was elected in London a few days after the death of the previous Caliph. He travels the world and meets with Ahmadiyya communities as well as meeting with global leaders to pursue the path of peace. He leads Friday prayers and preaches to the worldwide community from Baitul Futuh Mosque in Morden, London.

Each of these Caliphs is to continue the work begun by Ghulam Ahmad, and prepare the world for an age of peace. This can only be done through a living of the principles of Islam (see below: Message).

What is its place within Islam?

Ahmadiyya Islam occupies a controversial place within wider Islam. If one were to attend prayers in an Ahmadiyya mosque, or converse about the central tenets of Islam a person would struggle to observe a noticeable difference between Sunni and Ahmadiyya practice and teachings. At an 'institutional' level Ahmadiyya Muslims seem to be rejected as Muslim. One example of this is in the state of Pakistan. There are elements of the Pakistani constitution that outlines their placement outside of Islam. Firstly, in 1974 the Second Amendment to the Constitution of Pakistan declared members of the Ahmadiyya Muslim Community to be non-Muslims. In 1984 Ordinance XX was added to the constitution which effectively restricted the self-identification and religious practice of Ahmadiyya Muslims. Ordinance XX outlines specific prohibitions against the Ahmadiyya community. Section 1 of this ordinance is specifically focussed on those beliefs of the Ahmadiyya that separate them from the remainder of Islam. These generally focus on the place of the Mahdi and his successors in the Ahmadiyya community, and the use of honorifics that some assume are reserved for the Prophet, his companions and family. Section 2 prohibits Ahmadiyya Muslims from praying. Section 3 suggests that Ahmadis are not Muslim, in the sense that this outlines that the government of Pakistan feel that Ahmadis 'pose' as Muslims, and are not so. Each of these 'offences' are punishable by three years imprisonment and a fine.

There are numerous other examples of anti-Ahmadiyya sentiment and action. Although most prevalent in majority Muslim countries, such as Saudi Arabia and Bangladesh, there are examples in the UK. In March 2016 Ahmadi newsagent, Asad Shah, forty, was killed by a Sunni Muslim in what police termed an act of "religious prejudice". In the same year leaflets calling for death to Ahmadis were found in mosques – the mosques themselves asserted that they were unaware of the leaflets and had not placed them there, they remain evidence of anti-Ahmadiyya feeling within aspects of Islam.

There is space for disagreement within Islam as is shown in Sunni–Shi'a relationships. What is it, therefore, that Ahmadis believe and teach that seems to create such animosity? The major point of dissension surrounds the person and role of Hazrat Mirza Ghulam Ahmad. In the introduction of Ahmadiyya Islam above it was outlined that he was the promised Messiah/Mahdi foretold in the Qur'an and by the Prophet. This is rejected by other Muslims, this also in concert with the Ahmadi belief that Ghulam Ahmad was sent to rejuvenate Muslims from their malaise. In some ways it could be argued that Ghulam Ahmad's claims are a rejection of Islamic tenets as understood by Muslims worldwide. This could lead to feelings of animosity.

The area of most contention seems to surround an understanding of Muhammad as 'seal of the prophets'. For Sunni and Shi'a Muslims this tends to indicate that Muhammad is the final prophet, and that after him there will be no further prophets. A Hadith of the Prophet is used to suggest the completeness of the message that he delivered:

> My similitude in comparison with the other prophets before me, is that of a man who has built a house nicely and beautifully, except for a place of one brick in a corner. The people go about it and wonder at its beauty, but say: "Would that this brick be put in its place!" So I am that brick, and I am the last of the Prophets (*Sahih al-Bukhari* 3535).

Further,

> The Hour shall not be established until tribes of my Ummah unite with the idolaters, and until they worship idols. And indeed there shall be thirty imposters in my Ummah, each of them claiming that he is a Prophet. And I am the last of the Prophets, there is no Prophet after me (*Jami' at-Tirmidhi* 2219).

Ahmadis would not disagree with either of these Hadith, but their interpretation of what is meant by no prophet after Muhammad differs from that held by Sunni and Shi'a Muslims. There is no disagreement about Muhammad's position as the greatest of the prophets but, in distinction to Sunni and Shi'a Muslims, Ahmadis say that there are two types of prophets: law bearing and non-law bearing. Ahmad Chaudhry suggests:

> His [Muhammad's] title being "Khataman Nabiyyeen", meaning "Father of the Prophets", gives us the logical conclusion that there can be and will be such spiritual sons who will be prophets bearing the seal of his allegiance and obedience. Such a prophet can bring no new law and will bear the seal of his law (Chaudhry, 1996, p. 39).

Ghulam Ahmad is a follower of the Prophet Muhammad, indeed, is a reflection of all of the prophets and their messages. He does not seek to add to the message of Muhammad, rather he reminds Muslims of the teachings of Muhammad and glorifies his name. In this way he is not coming as a law bearing prophet but as a prophet chosen by Allah to restore the message of Islam in the lives of Muslims:

Ahmadiyya Islam

> But I am a Messenger and a Prophet without a new law in the sense that God reveals to me that which is hidden, and because of the inner grace that has been bestowed upon me on account of my obedience to the
>
> Holy Prophet, and because of having received his name (Hazrat Mirza Ghulam Ahmad, *Spiritual Treasures of Islam*, 302).

Section 2 of Ordinance XX to the Pakistan Constitution makes it clear that this is the major issue which wider Islam has with the Ahmadiyya community. It is my belief that as teachers we are not to draw lines of demarcation within religions and that the self-identification of adherents should be respected. As will be seen, in most other aspects of Islamic belief and practice there is little, if any, difference between the Ahmadiyya ideal and those found within the wider Islamic world, even though the religiosity and observance may be different.

Message

In common with Sunni Islam, Ahmadiyya Muslims recognise the foundational basis of the Six Beliefs of Islam:

1. Tawhid (Unity of Allah).
2. Malaikah (Angels).
3. Kutub (Holy books).
4. Rossoll (Prophets).
5. Yaumul Akhir (The Day of Judgement).
6. Al Qadr khayrihi washarr (Divine Decree about good and evil).

Tawhid

The unity of Allah and submission to his will is the fundamental message and principle of Islam (see Chapter 5: Nature of Allah, p. 92). This unity of Allah is summarised in the Shahadah:

> There is no God but Allah, Muhammad is the Messenger of Allah.

Allah's uniqueness is summarised within the Qur'an:

> Say, He is Allah, the One; Allah, the Independent and Besought of all. He begets not, nor is He begotten. And there is none like unto Him (Surah 112:2–5).

This belief lies at the heart of every practice of Ahmadiyya Islam.

Malaikah

Angels are an important aspect of Ahamadiyya Islam, and indeed of wider Islam as a whole. Within Ahmadiyya beliefs there are a multitude of angels who are messengers and/or agents of Allah. They each have a role given by Allah, some will deliver messages to humanity, others are responsible for the operation of natural forces. Each angel, while they may be referred to by an individual name, such as Jibril, Mikail, and Izrail, does not work alone. Within each role/function of the angels there is a supreme angel who oversees all of that role, but there is a multitude of angels who work under that angel (this host is referred to as the Junood of the Lord). Angels are created of light, but are completely subject to the will of Allah; they do not deviate from their role and task.

One example of the work of angels is the assignation of two angels to each human. They are appointed to record the good and bad deeds that the human performs. This is not seen to be two angels with books, rather they are observing the effect that a person's deeds have on their soul and personality. These angels do not deviate from this work.

Angels are created beings and have appeared in the forms of humans when appearing to people. By nature, angels are not human but can be made to appear in human form, if Allah wills. One of the most famous examples of this is in the Hadith when Jibril came to see the Prophet Muhammad and asked the questions about what Islam, iman and ihsan are (Sahih Muslim 8). Indeed, when the Qur'an talks of angels having wings:

> All praise belongs to Allah the Originator of the heavens and the earth, Who employs the angels as Messengers, having wings, two, three and four (Surah 35:2).

This language of the Qur'an is symbolic in the sense that wings are indicative of the power of the angels. Angels have an important role in the life of Ahmadis as they are the agents by which Allah shows his power, and sustains the universe.

Kutub

The Qur'an is the authoritative source of all Muslim teachings and is seen to be 'perfection', with not one word altered since the recitation to the Prophet Muhammad. There are other holy books that should be used with discretion. This is summarised in the Six Beliefs as kutub and reflects belief in all the revelations of Allah to his prophets as they were originally given. These primarily refer to:

- The Tawrat/Torah as originally revealed to Moses.
- The Psalms/Zabur as originally given to David.
- The message given to Jesus found in the Gospels/Injil.
- The Scrolls/Sahifah of Abraham.

For Muslims these scriptures do not exist in their original form today. While the "people of the book" are respected it is important to note that their books (the Bible and TeNaKh) are not the original revelation and have changed the original message. The Scrolls of Abraham, in distinction to the other three, are unknown in today's world. Further exploration of the importance of the Qur'an is found below (Scripture on p. 155).

Rossoll (Prophets)

Elements of the Ahmadiyya understanding of prophets are outlined above in discussing the distinctiveness of the Ahmadi message within Islam. Their discussion of law bearing and non-law bearing prophets is not unique, however, the role of Ghulam Ahmad as a prophet/Mahdi in the latter days is a distinguishing feature from other Muslim traditions. The Qur'an mentions by name twenty-eight prophets including: Adam, Elisha, Job, David, Ezekiel, Hud, Abraham, Elijah, Jesus, Isaac, Ishmael, Luqman, Noah, Salih, Solomon, Jonah, John the Baptist, Jacob, Joseph and Muhammad. These, however, are just a drop in the ocean. There is a reported saying of the Prophet Muhammad that there have been over 124,000 prophets, indicative of the teachings of the Qur'an that:

> ... there is no people to whom a Warner has not been sent (Surah 35:25).
>
> And We, indeed, sent Messengers before thee; of them are some whom We have mentioned to thee, and of them there are some whom We have not mentioned to thee; ... (Surah 40:79).

This leads to the possibility that various of the founders and leaders of the world's religions prior to the coming of Muhammad were messengers sent with a purity and degree of truth, which has been lost.

> One of the principles which forms the basis of my belief refers to the established religions of the world. These religions have met with wide acceptance in various regions of the earth. They have acquired a measure of age, and have reached a stage of maturity. God has informed me that none of these religions were false at their source and none of the prophets imposters (Hazrat Mirza Ghulam Ahmad, *Hidden Treasures*, p. 256).
>
> This is a beautiful principle, which promotes peace and harmony, and which lays the foundation for reconciliation, and which helps the moral condition of man. All prophets that have appeared in the world, regardless of whether they dwelt in India or Persia or China, or in some other country, we believe in the truth of them, one and all (Hazrat Mirza Ghulam Ahmad, *Hidden Treasures*, p. 259).

Whomever the prophets may have been, they all laid the basis and looked forward to the time when the law would be sent in its completeness and purity, with a message for the entirety of humanity for all time. This message was delivered through the Prophet Muhammad in his role as 'seal of the prophets'. As mentioned before, Ghulam Ahmad has been sent to remind people of the message that Muhammad preached.

Yaumul Akhir (The Day of Judgement)

For Ahmadiyya Muslims a body should be buried at death, and after burial the soul will detach itself from the body and live in Barzakh, which is an intermediary or waiting stage. Here, the soul will remain until the Day of Judgement. At the Day of Judgement, Allah will judge humanity and assign them to Paradise or Hell. Ghulam Ahmad has explained the afterlife thus:

> The Holy Qur'an has repeatedly affirmed that the life after death is not a new phenomenon and all its manifestations are reflections of this life. It has also stated that in the Hereafter all the spiritual conditions of this world will be manifested physically, both in the intermediate state and in the resurrection. Further it has emphasized that there will be unlimited progress in the hereafter. In short, according to the Holy Qur'an, hell and heaven are both reflections of a man's life, and are not something new that comes from outside ... and will be but reflections of the spiritual conditions of man in this life (*The Philosophy of the Teachings of Islam*).

The descriptions of the afterlife found in the Qur'an are seen by Ahmadis to be a description of a state that is indescribable to the human mind. The focus of the descriptions is concrete and carnal, whereas Ahmadiyya Muslims would suggest that the rewards and punishments are much more about closeness to Allah. Allah has used things that humans like to enjoy to describe Paradise (for example, milk) and things that they fear as a description of Hell (for example, fire). This analogical description of the afterlife is alluded to in the Qur'an:

> We will raise you into a form of which you have not the slightest knowledge (Surah 56:62).

These descriptions are imperfect but reflect the state of the soul which has been influenced throughout life by actions and thoughts. The life hereafter will be reliant on spiritual rather than carnal pleasures.

In the resurrection, Ahmadiyya Muslims believe that there is one existence but in different dimensions. The state of the soul will make it a heaven or a hell. There are many descriptions of what this may be similar to, whether it is someone who is only used to the dark being blinded and hurt by the light. Ghulam Ahmad used such examples to highlight that it is the state of the soul that leads to heaven or hell:

> If a man is thirsty and hungry as well, and he needs an immediate source of energy, a chilled bunch of grapes can provide him with such deep satisfaction as is not experienced by the same in ordinary circumstances. But the pre-requisite for these pleasures is good health. Now visualise a very sick man, who is nauseating and trying to vomit whatever liquid is left in him and is on the verge of death through dehydration. Offer him a glass of cool water, or a chilled bunch of grapes, then not to mention his accepting them, a mere glance of them would create a state of revulsion and absolute abhorrence in him (Mirza Tahir Ahmad, 2010, pp. 51–52).

This view of the state of the soul is developed further in Ahmadiyya Islam where the pains and suffering of hell are seen to be temporary, and to be consistent with the belief that Allah is All-Merciful. The afterlife is a state of progress nearer towards Allah for people who are in heaven or hell. Those in hell will realise their wrongdoings and seek Allah's forgiveness, and this progression for those souls will come to such a point when they leave the state known as hell. Ahmadis feel this is supported by the Qur'an and by Hadith, as well as the writings of the Mahdi and the Caliphs:

> Abiding therein so long as the heavens and the earth endure, excepting what thy Lord may will. Surely, thy Lord does bring about what He pleases. But as for those who will prove fortunate, they shall be in Heaven; abiding therein so long as the heavens and the earth endure, excepting what thy Lord may will – a gift that shall not be cut off (Surah 11:108–109).
>
> My mercy encompasses all things (Surah 7:157).

This view of life after death stands in distinction to the version found in Sunni and Shi'a Islam. For Ahmadis this highlights the compassion and mercy of Allah. It provides a hopeful view of judgement for all people.

Al Qadr khayrihi washarr (Divine Decree about good and evil)
In discussing the Divine Decree, Ahmadiyya Muslims teach that humans are free; their actions and choices are not predetermined. This

reflects the belief that Allah does not compel anyone to believe or to act. There are things within existence that are predetermined and it is important for Ahmadis to recognise these.

The first is that Allah and his servants will always emerge victorious. This could be seen to be an eternal law in the sense that all actions in the universe will eventually work to the victory of Allah. While the parameters and destiny of the universe are set, humanity enjoys free will within those boundaries.

The second is with regard to the social, economic and other influences that are found within the lives of individuals. It is possible to suggest that these are things over which the individual has no control. They cannot influence where they are born, the socio-economic circumstances in which they grow up and much more. To some extent, some of their actions can be seen to be determined by circumstance – this does not mean, however, that humans are absolved of all responsibility and can rise above those circumstances. Ahmadis recognise the mercy and compassion of Allah and suggest that his judgement will take all of these circumstances into account.

Love For All Hatred For None

In discussing the unity of the Ahmadiyya message Ghulam Ahmad said:

> There are only two complete parts of faith. One is to love God and the other is to love mankind to such a degree that you consider the suffering and the trials and tribulations of others as your own and that you pray for them (quoted by Hazra Mirza Masroor in Ahmad, 2014, p. 69).

The first purpose of life for all of humanity is to worship Allah, to live in submission to his will:

> O ye men, worship your Lord Who created you and those who were before you, that you may become righteous; Who made the earth a bed for you, and the heaven a roof, and caused water to come down from the clouds and therewith brought forth fruits for your sustenance. Set not up, therefore, equals to God, while you know (Surah 2:22-23).

This message is for all of humanity, and as many religions point towards a messiah-like figure, Ahmadiyya Muslims would say that all of their expectations are fulfilled in the person of the Mahdi/Messiah Ghulam Ahmad. This promised figure, and his successors would establish the message of Islam again and would bring all religions under the auspices of Islam. This would usher in an age of peace.

On visiting an Ahmadiyya mosque, or one of its websites, a person cannot help but notice the phrase:

> Love For All Hatred For None

This was first coined by Hazrat Mirza Nasir Ahmad when he laid the foundation stone for the first mosque in Spain in the last 700 years on 9 October 1980. This was in the midst of the beginning of some of the laws being passed in Pakistan with regard to the Ahmadiyya community, and perhaps can be seen to have more resonance as a result. This was extended further in 2010 when there was worldwide news coverage about the possible burning of the Qur'an in Florida:

> The world needs peace, love and brotherhood. The world needs an end to wars. Instead of walls of hatred being erected we need peace to prevail and for this to occur people of all faiths must join together. There is nothing wrong with debates but they should take place in a peaceful and respectful environment (Hazrat Mirza Masroor Ahmad, 2010).

Underpinning this message of love are the qualities of loyalty, freedom, equality, respect and peace. This will be explored in greater detail in the Religious expression section of this chapter, but this belief leads Ahmadiyya Muslims to integrate into society with love for all, and love for Allah. Mirza Masroor Ahmad (2014) has outlined that:

> True Islam teaches Muslims to stop evil and cruelty wherever it exists. Thus, rather than any question of it failing to integrate, true Islam naturally pulls society towards it like a magnet (p. 126).

The message of Islam is meant to permeate all societies, and is the solution for all the ills that face the world. This gives Ahmadis the impetus to share this love to all without restriction.

Ahmadiyya Islam

Scripture

In concert with other expressions of Islam, the Qur'an is the central scripture of Ahmadiyya Islam. Ghulam Ahmad wrote about the Qur'an:

> The title Khatam al-Nabiyyin used for the Holy Prophet (on whom be peace and blessings of God) requires – the term in its own right requires – that the Book revealed to the Holy Prophet (on whom be peace and blessings) should be Khatam al-Kutub, it should be a book perfect in all dimensions. The Quran is full of such perfection (Malfoozat vol. 3, p. 36).

Alongside the above, it is an Ahmadiyya belief that Allah has sent messengers among all nations, and that the religions of the world may be seen to be imperfect revelations given to people at a certain time and in a certain place. They performed a function for a period of time, but over time some of the truths were diluted by human involvement. Some of these individuals who were recipients of divine revelation were Zoroaster, Jesus, the Buddha and Krishna. As such, the books associated with them can be seen to contain kernels of revelation and may be of use to study by Ahmadis; however, care should be taken and the truths they contain are only recognised when they are in agreement with the Qur'an.

As outlined earlier, the role of the Mahdi/Messiah was to revitalise Islam and to reclaim it from its malaise. The writings of Ghulam Ahmad are seen to be reflective of this role, and that by reading them, and listening to the teachings of his successors, the caliphs, a Muslim is able to understand the truths that are taught in the Holy Qur'an. He is not adding scripture or new messages to the Qur'an, rather he is helping people to understand it. In this manner his writings are seen to be important to Ahmadis. There are volumes of books that he wrote, as well as articles and papers. These include:

- *Barahin-e-Ahmadiyya. Arguments in Support of the Holy Quran & the Prophethood of the Holy Prophet Muhammad* (five volumes). Ghulam Ahmad outlined the purpose for the writing of these volumes:

> [The reason it] has been compiled is that the proofs of the truth of Islam and the proofs of the excellence of the Holy Qur'an and the proofs of the truth of the prophethood of the Holy Prophet (sa[8]), the Khatamun-Nabiyyeen, may God's choicest blessings be upon him, are made known to the people with the greatest clarity.

- *The Essence of Islam* (5 volumes).
- *The Philosophy of the Teachings of Islam.*
- *Tadhkirah: The Dreams, Visions and Verbal Revelations vouchsafed to Hazrat Mirza Ghulam Ahmad, The Promised Messiah and Mahdi (on whom be peace).*

Religious expression

In common with Sunni Islam, Ahmadiyya Muslims adopt the practices associated with the Five Pillars of Islam. In terms of theology (apart from the coming of the Mahdi/Messiah), practising Ahmadiyyas are closer to Sunni in their expression. The Five Pillars are:

1. Shahadah.
2. Salat.
3. Zakat.
4. Sawm.
5. Hajj.

Concepts such as Jihad, Halal/Haram and rules of modesty would also find expression within Ahmadiyya Islam.

Shahadah

The underlying principles of Islam are expressed in the Shahadah: "There is no God but Allah; Muhammad is the Messenger of Allah". The importance of the recitation of the Shahadah is shown throughout Ahmadiyya practice.

---

[8] 'sa' is a shortening of an Arabic phrase *'alayhi s-salām'*, meaning 'peace be upon him' and is added when speaking of a prophet, especially in the case of Prophet Muhammad. 'pbuh' (peace be upon him) is also a common shortening and epithet in English publications.

Ahmadiyya Islam

To become a Muslim, a person must believe and recite the Shahadah; when a child is born the first words whispered into their ears is the adhan (call to prayer) which includes the Shahadah. It is, similarly, encouraged to be the last words that a Muslim says before death. In many ways, the Shahadah can be seen to be the most important of the Pillars of Islam as it underpins every other pillar. The belief in Allah is the motivation behind all acts, and finds expression in the various different rituals associated with the other pillars.

Salat

An Ahmadiyya Muslim will pray five times a day as commanded by the Prophet Muhammad. During the cycle of prayer submission to, and praise of, Allah are evident in the words and actions associated with prayer.

Prayers begin with the adhan being called in Arabic by the muezzin; the words translated in English are:

> Allah is most great (repeated four times).
> I testify there is no god but Allah (repeated twice).
> I testify that Muhammad is the messenger of Allah (repeated twice).
> Come to prayer (repeated twice).
> Come to success (repeated twice). In the call to morning prayer the statement, "Prayer is better than sleep" is inserted after the fifth statement.
> Allah is most great (repeated twice).
> There is no god but Allah.

Wudu or ablutions are then performed in preparation for prayer. The procedure followed is:

- Wash the hands three times with water.
- Rinse the mouth three times with water.
- The nose should be cleaned inside three times.
- The face is washed three times.
- The forearms up to the elbow are washed three times (right arm first).

- Wet hands, with palms down and thumbs extended, should be passed over the head three times, ensuring the ears are cleaned at the end of each passing. And then clean one's mouth by rinsing with water three times.
- A pass is made with the back of the hands from the nape of the neck to the front of the neck.
- Feet, up to the ankles, are washed three times. If socks are placed on immediately after the ablution it is not essential to wash the feet again for 24 hours. A pass can be made over socks with wetted hands.

This washing is symbolic of getting ready to commune with Allah. The spiritual cleanliness is most important which is indicated by the accompanying recitation of:

> O Allah make me of those who seek forgiveness and make me of those who are pure and cleansed.

This process should be performed immediately before prayer as it is essential to pray while the ablution has not been broken. It is possible, if the ablution has not been broken since the last prayer, to not need to perform wudu again before the next prayer, though this is unlikely, as the ways that the ablution can be broken include: passing wind; urination; defaecation; sleeping; menstruation; ejaculation; vomiting; and bleeding.

Praying in a community brings strength and as such, when possible, men are asked to pray in mosques. Women can also pray in mosques but it is not compulsory. For prayer outside of the mosque a Muslim may pray anywhere that is clean (musulla); hence the use of a prayer mat. A prayer is always towards the Ka'bah in Makkah.

Prayers:

- Are usually read in Arabic, though it is possible to pray in the vernacular in the prostration position.
- Are offered at dawn, soon after midday, mid-afternoon, just after sunset and at night.
- Are made up, if missed through unavoidable circumstances.
- In the mosque are led by the imam.

Ahmadiyya Islam

As outlined earlier each stage of the prayer shows glorification of, and submission to, Allah. Examples include the beginning of the prayer where, in the standing position with hands by the side of the head (takbeer), a Muslim will say that Allah is most great. The most symbolic act of prayer is when saying Allah is most great three times, the worshipper will go into bowing position with hands on knees and back parallel to the floor (Rukoo).

Once a week there is a special Friday afternoon prayer (al Jumu'ah) that all men should attend, it being a requirement of faith to attend the congregational prayers. Women may also attend; this prayer is normally performed in a mosque. This prayer also involves a sermon (which is usually given by the Caliph and broadcast live on the community's satellite channel Muslim Television Ahmadiyya (MTA) International (Sky 708) as well as online (mta.tv), and watched by Ahmadis all around the world).

While anyone is welcome to recite prayers in an Ahmadiyya mosque, Ahmadis are encouraged to pray only in Ahmadiyya mosques and have been since the time of Ghulam Ahmad. The reason behind this is an issue of safety. The way that Ahmadis are viewed by other Muslims makes it a sensible precaution to pray in a place where safety is assured.

Zakat

With Islam the obligatory act of charity is Zakat, which is based on a person's wealth. In giving Zakat, the rate can differ, according to the type of wealth held, but is usually accepted by Ahmadis to be 2.5% of a person's wealth that should be donated each year. This act of charity reminds a person that they are dependent upon Allah for everything, and it also sanctifies the giver and the remainder of their wealth. The act of devotion shows submission to Allah and recognises humanity's complete reliance upon him.

Within Sunni Islam, the funds can then only be used to support Muslims in certain circumstances. Although Ahmadis stipulate the uses for which it can be utilised, non-Muslims can also be eligible.

Zakat funds can be used for the following:

- Those in poverty and distress.
- Those in debt.
- Travellers in need.
- Those in need of scholarships.
- Ransom for prisoners of war.
- Promotion of Islam.
- Zakat collection expenses.
- Other activities to benefit society.

Sadaqah is voluntary giving and is additional to Zakat, at the discretion of the individual Muslim. In addition to Sadaqah, there are numerous other voluntary schemes introduced by various caliphs to further more specific establishments and funds. Notably, there is the scheme of Wassiyat established by Ghulam Ahmad (the Messiah and reformer of the age for Ahmadi Muslims) whereby in his book 'Al-Wassiyat' he encourages members of the community to donate between one-tenth and one-third of one's income for propagate the message of Islam. This is seen as a way to purify one's wealth and earnings in addition to paying the Zakat on one's savings.

Sawm

In a similar way to Zakat, Sawm is an expression of a Muslim's belief in Allah as the source of everything in life and he has provided for the world he has created. The month of Ramadan is set aside for fasting where Ahmadis, in common with other Muslims, do not eat or drink anything during daylight hours. This has been a practice since the time of Muhammad and is required by the Qur'an (See Surah 2: 183–87). Ahmadis begin the fast an hour before sunrise.

Ahmadiyya Muslims will declare their intention to fast with the words: "I hereby express my intention to keep the fast of tomorrow during the month of Ramadan". If a Muslim inadvertently eats or drinks, when they remember the fast they should stop and continue the fast. However, if they realise and then continue to eat, the fast is broken and needs to be made up on another day.

Ahmadiyya Islam

Ahmadiyya Muslims fast during Ramadan in submission to the will of Allah. The only people who are excused are:

- The old.
- The young.
- The ill.
- Those who are expecting a baby or breast-feeding one.
- Those who are travelling.

Apart from old and the young, the others are expected to make up the fast. The time of the fast is a time of opportunity for spiritual devotion, not only through the fast but also in the reading of the Qur'an during the month. The recitation of the first revelations from Allah through Jibril came during the last ten days of Ramadan. The exact night is known as the Night of Power. This is a special night when Muslims are encouraged to perform extra worship to receive greater forgiveness of sins.

Hajj

A Muslim should complete the pilgrimage to Makkah during the month of Dhul Hijjah on specific days at least once during their lifetime if they have the health and wealth. The Hajj enables the Muslim to put to one side the worries of their everyday life and draw closer in submission to Allah.

Activities of the Hajj include:
- The clothing in ihram (a white robe). Women can wear ordinary clothes whatever the colour, though a lot of Muslim women would also wear white as well. This is important in reflecting the unity of the ummah, as well as serving as a reminder of worshippers to try to attain an almost death-like state (as Muslims are wrapped in white cloth after death before burial). This death-like state is to encourage worshippers to turn their full attention towards Allah and to remove themselves of their desires and ties to this world whilst performing the pilgrimage.
- Pilgrims circumambulate the Ka'bah seven times praising Allah, and asking for forgiveness. In place of kissing the black stone, pilgrims will often raise their hand towards it.

- Pilgrims pray at the station of Abraham and drink some water from the Well of Zamzam.
- Pilgrims walk seven times between two hills very near to Makkah. This is symbolic of Hagar running between the two hills seven times searching for water, before Ishmael miraculously discovered the Well of Zamzam when he put the heel of one of his feet into the ground.
- Pilgrims spend the night in Mina.
- Pilgrims will pray on the plain of Arafat (20km away) and may spend the entire day there asking Allah for forgiveness. It is believed that Adam and Eve were forgiven on Arafat.
- Pilgrims say evening prayers and camp in the village of Muzdalifah.
- In Mina pilgrims throw stones at three stone pillars remembering the stones thrown by Abraham to drive the devil away.
- In Mina the festival of sacrifice (Id-ul-adha) is celebrated. On this day animals are sacrificed, eaten and given to the poor.
- The pilgrims will remove the ihram; have their hair cut (for women) or shaved (for men) and circumambulate the Ka'bah seven more times, before repeating the run between the two hills seven times.

These events help a Muslim show submission to Allah; they also remember events associated with prophets. The Hajj is a time of renewal and reflects many aspects of a Muslim's belief. Sometimes Ahmadiyya Muslims can be prevented from completing Hajj as authorities in Makkah and its environs may adopt the views evidenced in the Pakistan constitution in placing Ahmadis outside of Islam. For this reason, while not hiding their faith as Ahmadiyya Muslims, individual Ahmadis will not draw attention to their identity as Ahmadiyya while entering and completing the Hajj.

Jihad
Jihad in Ahmadiyya Islam primarily refers to the 'greater' Jihad; the struggle within oneself for submission to Allah, purification and self-mastery. Each day of a Muslim's life they are striving to live their lives in submission to Allah through mastery of themselves and love for all. Essentially, for Ahmadis, based on the writings of their founder

Ahmadiyya Islam

Mirza Ghulam Ahmad, there is no need for a physical Jihad in this age, unless particular conditions apply, when only the leader of the community can give authorisation for it. To support the supremacy of the internal Jihad of love and submission, Ahmadis use a Hadith of the Prophet Muhammad:

> [Jihad] must be fought by means of the Quran and the Quranic message alone. Again, to tame one's rebellious nature into complete submission to God is another form of Jihad which is in fact the greater Jihad, according to the Holy Prophet of Islam. On returning from a battle, he is reported to have said: "We are returning from the lesser Jihad to the greater Jihad" (Mirza Tahir Ahmad, 2010, p. 47).

Hazrat Mirza Masroor Ahmad has outlined the nature of Jihad for Ahmadis that fits with their message of 'Love for all, hatred for none':

> ... our Jihad is not a Jihad of swords, guns or bombs. Our Jihad is not a Jihad of cruelty, brutality and injustice. Rather, our Jihad is of love, mercy and compassion. Our Jihad is of tolerance, justice and human sympathy. Our Jihad is to fulfil the rights of God Almighty and of His Creation (2017, p. 21).

The use of force is rejected except in the defence of the weak and practice of religion. In today's society where people are generally free to worship as they choose, there should be no need for the use of a Jihad of violence. Rather Ahmadi Muslims will combat intolerance with compassion and love. Hazrat Mirza Masroor Ahmad has engaged with the concept of Jihad through the 'Jihad of the Pen' or of the message of Islam. He has written to world leaders and travelled the globe to share the message of love and peace. He inaugurated a Peace Conference in 2004 aimed at bringing harmony between peoples; all of this is based on the message of the Qur'an.

Community Action
The phrase "Love For All Hatred For None" finds expression in a large amount of Ahmadi involvement in the local, national and international communities. There are global initiatives such as the Peace Symposium,

or the letters which Mirza Masroor Ahmad wrote to the world's leaders outlining the critical need for peace.

There is also an international charity called Humanity First, founded in 1994 and its stated aim is:

> Drawing strength from our global resources, we aim to relieve suffering caused by natural disaster and human conflict, promote peace and understanding and strengthen people's capacity to help themselves.

To complete this work the charity relies on donations and volunteers, the bulk of which will come from Ahmadiyya communities around the world. Some of their initiatives include:

> Disaster relief.
> Community care for the most vulnerable in society.
> Orphan care.
> Food banks.
> Building and running schools.
> Local access to improved water for drinking and sanitation.
> Global health.
> 'Gift of Sight'.

The most common expression of the belief of love for all can be found in local communities around the world. A quick glance at Ahmadiyya country websites (such as http://www.loveforallhatredfornone.org/press/) highlights the multiplicity of initiatives in which Ahmadis have become involved. Headlines from various press outlets include:

> Spreading the peaceful message – love for all.
> Muslim youth support the Woodland Trust.
> Muslim youth group spends New Year's Day cleaning Bradford.
> Crawley homeless helped with food served by young helpers.
> Interfaith conference to show unity.

In Manchester, for example, Ahmadiyya Muslims are at the forefront of 'Let's End Hate Crime' projects. This reflects the ideal that as Muslims integrate into society their responsibility is to spread goodness and love. Through these types of activities people are drawn together and the pathway to peace is embarked upon.

Ahmadiyya Islam

The activities are focussed on people of all faiths and none. Other examples include the serving of Christmas meals to those who are on their own. This reflects the teachings of Ahmadiyya Islam and exemplifies the responsibility they feel to enhance the world in which they find themselves.

Role of Women

Often at the forefront of the efforts within society are the women's organisations of the local Ahmadi community. These groups are known collectively as the Ahmadiyya Muslim Women's Association, or local groups have the term Lajna attached to the area they serve. Formed in 1922 Lajna has the stated purpose of:

> Provid[ing] women a structure to train, develop, and enhance their religious and academic knowledge, acquire health and fitness skills, manage trade and industry affairs and develop their financial abilities. The aim of Lajna Ima'illah (literally translated as maids of Allah) is to raise awareness amongst women of their important status and their great responsibilities in the religious organisation (Lajna Ima'illah UK, 2013).

Women enhance the community through their employment as an integral part of their daily lives, but they also organise activities to strengthen the community as well as their individual faith. A large number of the community activities are organised by the women of the Ahmadiyya faith.

Their proactive role within society can often surprise those who are familiar with stereotypes of Muslim women that have been perpetuated in society. In Ahmadiyya Islam women stand alongside men in the expression of faith in the community. This does not mean that there is no difference; men and women pray separately and there are different responsibilities within the family. They are not, however, silent participants in the expression of Islam.

In addition to the work of the Lajna there are also many other aspects of the Ahmadiyya Muslim Community which assist the individual. There are the Ansar 'the helpers of Allah' for the men above the age of forty. The companions of the Prophet Muhammad were referred to as the Ansar, hence the borrowed name. There are the Khuddam, for the men aged fifteen to forty. There is the Atfal reserved for seven- to fourteen-year-old boys. There is also the Nasirat for seven- to fourteen-year-old girls. Lajna is the title assigned for all women aged fifteen and over.

Ideas for the RE Classroom
Ahmadiyya Muslims are an interesting case study for use in the RE classroom. In most, if not all, of their practices they live Islam in the same way as that which is taught in Sunni Islam. Recognition of diversity within Islam when the beliefs and practices are almost identical is an interesting task. Perhaps the most important thing that a teacher can do is to have knowledge about Ahmadiyya Islam and be prepared for questions and comments that arise. There are, however, places that could be looked into further if a teacher wanted to explore the distinctive teachings of Ahmadiyya Islam.

- The understanding of Muhammad's role of the 'seal of the prophets' is seen by some Muslims to be different to what is seen as the traditional understanding. An exploration of law bearing and non law-bearing prophets expands the view of Islam, and what it might mean in the lives of Muslims today. The role of the Mahdi/Messiah is a part of the different expressions of Islam, and how Ghulam Ahmad has been received enables a fruitful discussion about where the boundaries of Islam lie.
- The role and work of Ahmadiyyas throughout the world and in the communities evidenced by Love for all, Hatred for None' is an important aspect of Ahmadi practice that can show how Islam finds expression in the lives of believers. The organisation of the community into the various groups, each of which have a work to do is also an important distinction from wider Islam.
- Although all of Islam can be seen to teach that women are different but equal, in Ahmadi communities this finds expression in the work of the Lajna. They provide an example of Muslim women who express their belief in all that they do. There are Ahmadiyya women

- around the country who would be more than willing to come into schools to talk about the emancipatory message that Islam has for women.
- The Ahmadi understanding of Jihad as being something that has been developed in light of the Jihad of the Pen, is also an interesting counterbalance to the narrative that might be found in aspects of the media.
- The study of persecution of Ahmadiyya Muslims can also add a dimension to various aspects of classroom topics. The laws in Pakistan, the problems they face in completing the Hajj, and persecution in communities around the world are important aspects of Ahmadis trying to find their place in the world. The opposition they face in living their religion should be explored.

Useful websites
www.alislam.org

Reference list
All Hadith taken from sunnah.com except for *Mishkat al-Masabih* 1/91 Hadith 276 which is quoted from www.alislam.org/library/books/Conditions-of-Baiat-Responsibilities-of-Ahmadi.pdf

All Qur'anic quotes are taken from Malik Ghulam Farid (Ed.) (2016). *The Holy Qur'an. Arabic text with English translation and short commentary*. London, UK: Islam International Publications Ltd.

Ahmad, Mirza Tahir (2010 [1985]). *An Elementary study of Islam*. Tilford, UK: Islam International Publications Ltd.

Ahmad, Hazrat Mirza Masroor (2010, 22 August). Press release: Ahmadiyya Muslim Jama'at condemns plans to burn Holy Qur'an in United States. Retrieved from https://www.alislam.org/library/press-release/ahmadiyya-muslim-jamaat-condemns-plans-to-burn-holy-quran/

Ahmad, Hazrat Mirza Masroor (2014). Islam – a threat or a source of peace. *Review of Religions*, 109(7), 62–71.

Ahmad, Hazrat Mirza Masroor (2015). *World crisis and the pathway to peace*. Tilford, UK: Islam International Publications Ltd.

Ahmad, Hazrat Mirza Masroor (2017). Mosques – building blocks for Peace. *Review of Religions*, January, 12–24.

Chaudhry, Aziz Ahmad (1996). *The question of finality of prophethood, the promised messiah and mahdi*. London, UK: Islam International Publications Limited.

Lajna Ima'illah UK (2013). *Lajna Ima'illah UK: A short introduction to an auxiliary organisation of the Ahmadiyya Muslim Community UK*. London, UK: Lajna Ima'illah UK. Retrieved from http://www.lajna.org.uk/images/frontpage_images/lajna%20leaflet.pdf

Murtza Khan, Maulana (1945). *The name Ahmadiyya and its necessity*. Lahore, Pakistan: Ahmadiyya Anjuman Ish'at-i-Islam.

Works by Hazrat Mirza Ghulam Ahmad used within this chapter:
Tadhkiratush Shahadatain
Hidden Treasures of Islam
The Philosophy of the Teachings of Islam
The Essence of Islam
Malfoozat

Are all available at https://www.alislam.org/library/ and are used here by permission.

SECTION 4

BEYOND THE BIG SIX

CHAPTER 8

BAHÁ'Í

Chapter Outline
What is Bahá'í?
Message
Nature of God
Nature of humanity
Scripture
Religious expression

What is Bahá'í?
Bahá'í often describe their faith as the newest 'world' religion in the sense that it developed in the nineteenth century CE. It was founded by Bahá'u'lláh (born Mírzá Husayn-Alí Nurí in 1817) but its origins are slightly more complicated than this. His message and work can be seen to have its origins in aspects of Shi'a Islam and, in particular, the teachings of the Báb (Siyyid `Alí Muhammad Shírází, 1819–1850), a descendant of Muhammad.

The Báb (the Gate) took the title as a sign that he was the long awaited 'gate'. Initially being part of Shi'a Islam, the name of the 'gate' would have particular meaning as the Hidden Imam of Twelver Shi'ism. The initial teaching was that throughout history there have been people who have served as emissaries or means of communication with the Hidden Imam who resides in a spiritual realm. At the first declaration he was largely ignored, but over the years Shi'a Muslims actively opposed him, particularly those who held authority who saw his claim as challenging the foundation of their power and leadership of the peoples of Shi'a Islam. The understanding of the Báb as the gate took on a different meaning, and it could be suggested that he was the promised Imam; he came not to reform but to initiate a new religious dispensation. During the time of the Báb, many of his followers tended to remain within Islam, though they faced increased persecution for many reasons, including the addition of the Báb to the call to prayer, as the gate. His role was articulated by Hatcher and Martin (1998):

> Thus he was a messenger of God, the founder of a new and independent religious dispensation. Just as early Christians had to free themselves from the laws and ordinances of the Torah, so were the Bábís called upon to free themselves from the requirements of the Islamic Shari'ah (p. 15).

One of his followers, Tahirih, exemplified this as she appeared at a conference of Bábís without the veil; the Bábí also rejected all types of violence and jihad except that which was fought in self-defence. For Bahá'ís the Bábí described his work as preparing the way for "Him Who God Will Make Manifest". All that he taught in his life and was written down in his most important work, the Bayán, would be confirmed or ended by this promised being. The Báb was thus the gate to the knowledge of "Him Who God Will Make Manifest". Bahá'ís regard him as a Manifestation of God, as the promised forerunner to Bahá'u'lláh and, as the closest of the manifestations of God to the time of Bahá'u'lláh, he is followed and his words are studied. The period of the Bábí dispensation is important to Bahá'ís as he laid the foundation of, and bore witness to, the Manifestation of God that was to come.

Bahá'ís describe Bahá'u'lláh's childhood and youth as one of great devotion and mystical experiences. In 1844 Bahá'u'lláh became a follower of the Báb, and quickly became one of principal figures in Bábísm. Following the execution of the Báb in 1850 he was seen as the driving force behind the remainder of the Báb's followers, though there was some argument about leadership of the Báb community. One faction of the Bábí led by a man called Azim, attempted to assassinate the Shah of Iran. In retaliation for this the leaders of the Bábí were imprisoned. This included Bahá'u'lláh who had not been involved in any militant plots. Bahá'u'lláh was imprisoned in the Siyah-Chal dungeon in the August of 1852, the same month as the assassination

Bahá'í

attempt. By negotiation, he was spared life imprisonment but instead was banished from Iran on 12 January 1853.

During his imprisonment at Siyah-Chal Bahá'u'lláh received a number of mystical experiences where he was identified as the promised fulfilment of the Báb's message: "Him Who God Will Make Manifest". Shoghí Effendí describes the events surrounding one of the visions where Bahá'u'lláh received God's revelation known as the 'Maid of Heaven':

> Wrapped in its stygian gloom, breathing its fetid air, numbed by its humid and icy atmosphere, His feet in stocks, His neck weighed down by a mighty chain, surrounded by criminals and miscreants of the worst order, oppressed by the consciousness of the terrible blot that had stained the fair name of His beloved Faith, painfully aware of the dire distress that had overtaken its champions, and of the grave dangers that faced the remnant of its followers—at so critical an hour and under such appalling circumstances the "Most Great Spirit," as designated by Himself, and symbolized in the Zoroastrian, the Mosaic, the Christian, and Muhammadan Dispensations by the Sacred Fire, the Burning Bush, the Dove and the Angel Gabriel respectively, descended upon, and revealed itself, personated by a "Maiden," to the agonized soul of Bahá'u'lláh.
>
> "One night in a dream," He Himself, calling to mind, in the evening of His life, the first stirrings of God's Revelation within His soul, has written, "these exalted words were heard on every side: 'Verily, We shall render Thee victorious by Thyself and by Thy pen. Grieve Thou not for that which hath befallen Thee, neither be Thou afraid, for Thou art in safety. Ere long will God raise up the treasures of the earth—men who will aid Thee through Thyself and through Thy Name, wherewith God hath revived the hearts of such as have recognized Him.'" In another passage He describes, briefly and graphically, the impact of the onrushing force of the Divine Summons upon His entire being—an experience vividly recalling the vision of God that caused Moses to fall in a swoon, and the voice of Gabriel which plunged Muhammad into such consternation that, hurrying to the shelter of His home, He bade His wife, Khadíjih, envelop Him in His mantle. "During the days I lay in the prison of Tihrán," are His own memorable words, "though

the galling weight of the chains and the stench-filled air allowed Me but little sleep, still in those infrequent moments of slumber I felt as if something flowed from the crown of My head over My breast, even as a mighty torrent that precipitateth itself upon the earth from the summit of a lofty mountain. Every limb of My body would, as a result, be set afire. At such moments My tongue recited what no man could bear to hear" (*God Passes By*, p. 101).

The Maiden is an important figure in the visions and revelations of Bahá'u'lláh as Shoghí Effendí identifies her with the Holy Spirit, "the Most Great Spirit" who was the same who came to Jesus, Moses and Muhammad.

Bahá'u'lláh did not declare his visions, or his identity, immediately and he was exiled to Baghdad where over the following years a group of Babí followers gathered around him. One of these followers was his younger brother, Mírzá Yahyá, who had been nominated by the Báb as the 'titular' head of the Bábí community should the Báb die. Bahá'ís suggest that this happened, with Bahá'u'lláh's support and encouragement with the aim of creating "a channel through which Bahá'u'lláh could continue to guide the affairs of the new faith, while avoiding the risk of adding a formal designation to the personal prominence he had gained" (Hatcher and Martin, 1998, p. 35). Contrary to the wishes of the Báb before he died, Yahyá tried to establish himself as the authority of the Bábí community in Baghdad. To avoid any conflict Bahá'u'lláh removed himself to the nearby mountains for months of meditations.

During this time of separation, it is said that Yahyá proved himself ineffective as a leader of a community and of a religion. The Bábís, including Yahyá, petitioned Bahá'u'lláh to return to lead the community, which he did on 19 March 1856.

Under the leadership of Bahá'u'lláh the community thrived and he wrote the *Kitáb-i-Iqan* (the Book of Certitude) which explained God's plan for humanity, the importance of the Manifestations of God and how humans could develop spiritually. In April 1863 Bahá'u'lláh was told by the Ottoman authorities that he would have to move to

Constantinople at the insistence of the Persian Shah. While preparing to leave he lived on an island on the River Tigris in a garden called by Bahá'ís, the Garden of Ridván (Paradise). In the Garden of Ridván Bahá'u'lláh revealed to his followers that he was "He Whom God Will Make Manifest".

Having spent a few months in Constantinople, he was again exiled to Adrianople. It was here in 1868 that Bahá'u'lláh announced himself to the community as "He Who God Will Make Manifest" in a statement known as Súriy-i-Amr. Following this announcement Yahyá responded by announcing himself as the promised manifestation. Shoghí Effendí has described this event as "one of the darkest dates in Bahá'í history and was the signal for the open and final rupture between Bahá'u'lláh and Mírzá Yahyá" (God Passes By, p. 167). Most Bábís rejected Yahya's claims, and it is from this point that the Bábí community began to identify themselves as Bahá'ís.

He then moved in 1877 from Acre to a nearby estate, Mazra'ih, and then to a final residence known as Bahjí (Joy). While there Bahá'u'lláh designated the place that the Báb would be interred, which has since become the international headquarters of the Bahá'í faith. During his final years he passed much of the administration for the community to his son, Abbas, who became known as 'Abdu'l-Bahá (Servant of Bahá). Bahá'u'lláh passed away on 29 May 1892.

Following his death, 'Abdu'l-Bahá was named Ghusn-i-A'zam (the Most Mighty Branch) and the successor to Bahá'u'lláh as the perfect example of his teachings, and not as a Manifestation of God. Bahá'u'lláh had so named him in a 'Covenant' with the community before he died. Under 'Abdu'l-Bahá the faith spread into Europe and North America. Newly converted Bahá'ís would visit with 'Abdu'l-Bahá and return invigorated with their faith and desire to live the principles of the religion. In 1912 he undertook a tour of forty cities in the USA.

In 1908 'Abdu'l-Bahá wrote a will in which he named two institutions that would conduct the affairs of the Bahá'í faith. He named Shoghí Effendí (Bahá'u'lláh's eldest grandson) as 'Guardian' and the authority on the interpretation of teachings. He also names the 'Universal House of Justice' as the legislative and administrative authority for the community. On 28 November 1921 'Abdu'l-Bahá passed away. The Bahá'í community had grown to approximately 100,000 followers by the time of his death.

Shoghí Effendí as the Guardian stepped away from a public role to embark on certain projects which included the development of the World Centre, the translation and interpretation of Bahá'i teachings, and the expansion of the Universal House of Justice. Between 1951 and 1957 he appointed several people to the position of 'Hands of the Cause of God' to teach the faith and protect its various institutions.

In November 1957, Shoghí Effendí died without naming a successor as Guardian. The Universal House of Justice was in a position to assume leadership, but the composition of the body had to be elected. Shoghí Effendí had died part way through a ten-year plan; the Hands of the Cause of God became stewards to complete the plan, and then would have elections to the Universal House of Justice in 1963, an election from which the Hands recused themselves from standing in. Since that time the Universal House of Justice has been responsible for the leadership of the Bahá'í community, which currently numbers between five and eight million members.

Message

The message of Baha'í can be summed up under three categories:

- The unity of God.
- The unity of humanity including the unity of religion.
- The achievement of world peace.

The unity of God will be explored in the next section (Nature of God); the latter two are summarised by Bahá'u'lláh:

> The fundamental purpose animating the Faith of God and His Religion is to safeguard the interests and promote the unity of the human race, and to foster the spirit of love and fellowship amongst men (*Proclamation of Bahá'u'lláh*, pp. 112–13).

Bahá'í

The unity of humanity and the unity of religion will necessarily lead to world peace.

The Unity of Religion
A fundamental principle of the Bahá'í religion is the unity of all religions. In the Bahá'í worldview, most, if not all, religions are part of the same history and revelation of God. Throughout history individuals have been inspired by God to teach part of the same message. Each individual, or Manifestation of God (see below: Nature of God), reflected the qualities of God and rejuvenated the spiritual and temporal activity of humanity, and the society to which they were sent. Each religion is seen to be rays of the same light, and the difference in expression may be down to the time and context within which the revelation was received. In a similar way, the faces of a prism receive light from the same source, but the faces (the context of the time) reflect the light in ways that are the same, but different.

In some ways, this view of the revelation of religion can be seen to be evolutionary in nature, that as history progressed and new messengers were sent they developed, or built upon, the message that is at the core the same for all humanity. This culminated in the revelation of Bahá'u'lláh:

> The Faith of Bahá'u'lláh should indeed be regarded ... as the culmination of a cycle, the final stage in a series of successive, of preliminary and progressive revelations (Effendí , The World Order of Bahá'u'lláh, p. 103).

The purpose of this revelation is to unite humanity. If a religion causes division then it is not fulfilling its purpose, and Bahá'ís feel that it would be better to live without a religion, than belong to a religion that sows discord in human relationships:

> If religion becomes a cause of dislike, hatred and division, it were better to be without it, and to withdraw from such a religion would be a truly religious act ... Any religion which is not a cause of love and unity is no religion ('Abdu'l-Bahá, *Paris Talks*, p. 130).

It is important to note an accusation that has often been made of the Bahá'í faith is that it is syncretic, reflecting the belief that Bahá'u'lláh is seen by Bahá'ís to be a successor to prior Manifestations of God including Zoroaster, Abraham, Moses, Jesus, Muhammad, Krishna and Buddha. This leads to the accusation that he merely appropriated aspects of their teachings into a syncretic belief system. Bah'áís and Bahá'í writings reject this and see the revelation of Bahá'u'lláh to be independent, though related to the teachings of the other religious figures. As a result, the teachings of Bahá'í are a fulfilment and supercession of all other faiths.

The unity of religions is not just something that exists in the past, or in their origination, but is a responsibility of all religions in the present and in the future. In 2002 the Universal House of Justice sent a *Letter to the World's Religious Leaders.* In this letter the Universal House of Justice outlined the commonality of religions, and argued that at heart they all worship the same God, and that service to humanity is the core principle of each. The letter further outlined that religious prejudice and division was the last of all prejudices, as all other forms were now seen to be wrong. It argued further that it is the duty of religious leaders to put aside any desire for power, and to unite in inter-faith activities that would draw people of all religions together under the same God and ultimately achieve world peace. This was followed by a further publication in 2005, *One Common Faith*, which reflected the teaching of Bahá'u'lláh:

> The utterance of God is a lamp, whose light is these words: Ye are the fruits of one tree, and the leaves of one branch. Deal ye one with another with the utmost love and harmony, with friendliness and fellowship (*Gleanings From the Writings of Bahá'u'lláh*, p. 288).

This unity of religion is part of the unity of the entire human family, towards which all Bahá'ís are working.

Peace
With the advancement and evolution of society, Bahá'ís believe that

Bahá'í

we stand on the cusp of a new age. An age that has been promised throughout history:

> They will beat their swords into plowshares and their spears into pruning hooks. Nation will not take up sword against nation, nor will they train for war anymore (Isaiah 2:4).
>
> ... a day in which the oneness of humankind shall uplift its standard and international peace, like the true morning, flood the world with its light ('Abdu'l-Bahá, *The Promulgation of Universal Peace*).

To usher in this age of peace, Bahá'u'lláh taught of two types of peace: the lesser peace, and the Most Great Peace. The lesser peace is a process wherein nations work together in a system of co-operation and protection of one another; this in turn will lead to the cessation of hostilities among nations. This is something that Bahá'ís believe is occurring through the influence of God, and upon which individual Bahá'ís can have little impact.

The Most Great Peace is the ultimate goal, and is the uniting of the entire human family. This was to be done under the guidance of Bahá'u'lláh. As this was unable to be fulfilled immediately as not all people accepted his teaching, the lesser peace was seen to be a precursor to the initiation of the Most Great Peace. This Most Great Peace was addressed in a letter from the Universal House of Justice in 1985, entitled *The Promise of World Peace*. In this letter, the Universal House of Justice recognised the scientific, technological and political developments of society as being evidence of the world moving towards a shared concern and a unity necessary for the establishment of peace. The League of Nations, and its 'successor', the United Nations are two such examples that are used.

These signs of the lesser peace are not enough; their existence without a spiritual component means that they are flawed:

> "The winds of despair", Bahá'u'lláh wrote, "are, alas, blowing from every direction, and the strife that divides and afflicts the human race is daily increasing. The signs of impending convulsions and chaos

can now be discerned, inasmuch as the prevailing order appears to be lamentably defective" (*The Promise of World Peace*, p. 2).

The removal of weapons, and co-operation of nations, are important steps to the establishment of peace, but they do little to address the causes of war in the hearts of people. The Letter outlines that secular philosophies such as materialism and capitalism have failed to produce a new world order founded on the principles of peace. Only a movement that breaks down all barriers can hope to unite humanity and establish peace:

> In the Bahá'í view, recognition of the oneness of mankind "calls for no less than the reconstruction and the demilitarization of the whole civilized world – a world organically unified in all the essential aspects of its life, its political machinery, its spiritual aspiration, its trade and finance, its script and language, and yet infinite in the diversity of the national characteristics of its federated units (*The Promise of World Peace*, p. 10).

The letter outlines the diverse nature of the united Bahá'í community as an example of how peace and unity can be discovered, and offers a hopeful view of the nature of humanity in seeking to establish this Most Great Peace:

> In contemplating the supreme importance of the task now challenging the entire world, we bow our heads in humility before the awesome majesty of the divine Creator, Who out of His infinite love has created all humanity from the same stock; exalted the gem-like reality of man; honoured it with intellect and wisdom, nobility and immortality; and conferred upon man the "unique distinction and capacity to know Him and to love Him", a capacity that "must needs be regarded as the generating impulse and the primary purpose underlying the whole of creation" (*The Promise of World Peace*, p. 14).

Until the people of the world unite in this era of peace, it is the responsibility of individual Bahá'í and the community of Bahá'ís to exemplify the unity of all races, genders, religions and nations.

Through their actions they believe that they can have an impact on individuals and society.

The advancement of society, in the Bahá'í view, is moving towards the end goal of an age of peace. This can only be achieved as barriers and divisions are removed from society and from people's hearts.

Nature of God

Bahá'ís believe in one God who is the creator of the universe and everything within it. Bahá'u'lláh taught of the pre-eminence of God:

> All-praise to the unity of God, and all-honour to Him, the sovereign Lord, the incomparable and all-glorious Ruler of the universe, Who, out of utter nothingness, hath created the reality of all things, Who, from naught, hath brought into being the most refined and subtle elements of His creation, and Who, rescuing His creatures from the abasement of remoteness and the perils of ultimate extinction, hath received them into His kingdom of incorruptible glory. Nothing short of His all-encompassing grace, His all-pervading mercy, could have possibly achieved it (*Gleanings From the Writings of Bahá'u'lláh*, pp. 64–65).

God is also a personal deity in the sense that he is concerned with his creation, and while not needing a personal relationship with his creation, it is possible for humans to develop a close, personal relationship with him through devotion, prayer, study and service. Yet within Bahá'í teaching the nature of God is unknowable, he is beyond all comprehension. Shoghí Effendí outlines that the Bahá'í religion

> proclaims unequivocally the existence and oneness of a personal God, unknowable, inaccessible, the source of all Revelation, eternal, omniscient, omnipresent and almighty (*God Passes By*, p. 139).

While humanity have striven to understand God and articulate his nature, these attempts all fall short of a full comprehension, and are seen by Bahá'ís to be struggles of the human imagination. Each description of God by the world's religions can be seen to have some validity within Bahá'í teaching, yet all conceptions of God as pantheistic or anthropomorphic in any way are rejected. Throughout the scriptures of Bahá'í there are various descriptions of the characteristics of God such as him being All-Knowing, Almighty, All-Compassionate and more, yet the best way to recognise his attributes are through his creation:

> Every created thing in the whole universe is but a door leading into His knowledge, a sign of His sovereignty, a revelation of His names, a symbol of His majesty, a token of His power, a means of admittance into His straight Path ... (Bahá'u'lláh, *Gleanings From the Writings of Bahá'u'lláh*, p. 160).

The most effective of these doors leading to knowledge of God's attributes are the Manifestations of God. They are considered to be mirrors of God's attributes, and can be seen to be theophanies rather than incarnations of him. In an analogy describing the relationship between God and the Manifestations, God is "likened to the sun because his is the unique source of life" in a similar way to the sun being the source of all life of this earth: "the spirit and attributes of God are the rays of this sun, and the individual Manifestation is like a perfect mirror" (Hatcher and Martin, 1998, p. 120). The diverse Manifestations are different to one another because of the individual positioning of the mirrors in reflecting the glory and attributes of God.

Through the Manifestations of God people are able to receive knowledge of, and from, God, and they are seen by Bahá'ís to represent the divine presence on the earth. They strive to bring unity to the people they teach "giving them peace, courage and certitude" (Smith, 2000, p. 231). The Manifestations of God are not limited to Bahá'í figures; though they are seen to deliver a message that has a common core that is revealed to humanity. Examples of Manifestations of God within Bahá'í teaching include Abraham, Krishna, Zoroaster, Moses, Buddha, Jesus Christ, Muhammad, the Báb and Bahá'u'lláh. Each of these was sent to rejuvenate a spiritual decline among humanity, their manifestation providing a new impetus among creation:

> ... when the Holy Manifestation of God, Who is the sun of the world of His creation, shines upon the worlds of spirits, of thoughts and of

Bahá'í

hearts, then the spiritual spring and new life appear, the power of the wonderful springtime becomes visible, and marvelous benefits are apparent. As you have observed, at the time of the appearance of each Manifestation of God extraordinary progress has occurred in the world of minds, thoughts and spirits. For example, in this divine age see what development has been attained in the world of minds and thoughts, and it is now only the beginning of its dawn. Before long you will see that new bounties and divine teachings will illuminate this dark world and will transform these sad regions into the paradise of Eden ('Abdu'l-Bahá, *Some Answered Questions*, p. 163).

Bahá'u'lláh taught that there would be future Manifestations of God, as there would again be a spiritual decline, but that this Manifestation would not come for at least a thousand years.

Within Bahá'í teaching there is also a subsidiary set of prophets who are followers and dependent on the Manifestations of God. These are important as "They are like the moon, which is not luminous and radiant in and of itself but which receives its light from the sun" ('Abdu'l-Bahá, *Some Answered Questions*, p. 164). Examples include Solomon, David, Isaiah, Jeremiah and Ezekiel. Thus, the attributes of God can be seen more clearly in these prophets than other humans.

In the person of 'Abdu'l-Bahá, the son and successor of Bahá'u'lláh, there seems to arise a third category of human. He seems not to be either a manifestation of God, nor a contingent prophet:

> He, by virtue of the station ordained for Him through the Covenant of Bahá'u'lláh, forms together with them [Bahá'u'lláh and the Báb] what may be termed the Three Central Figures of a Faith that stands unapproached in the world's spiritual history. He towers, in conjunction with them, above the destinies of this infant Faith of God from a level to which no individual or body ministering to its needs after Him, and for no less a period than a full thousand years, can ever hope to rise ... That 'Abdu'l-Bahá is not a Manifestation of God, that, though the successor of His Father, He does not occupy a cognate station, that no one else except the Báb and Bahá'u'lláh can ever lay claim to such a station before the expiration of a full thousand years — are verities which lie embedded in the specific utterances of both the Founder of our Faith

and the Interpreter of His teachings (Shoghí Effendí, *The World Order of Bahá'u'lláh*, p. 60).

Nature of humanity

In Bahá'í teaching humanity is a creation of God, and contains the divine with them:

> With the hands of power I made thee and with the fingers of strength I created thee; and within thee have I placed the essence of My light (Bahá'u'lláh, *The Hidden Words*, #12).

Human life, for Bahá'ís, begins at the moment of conception – the soul is a part of the body from the moment life begins, it does not 'enter' the body, it just 'is': "The soul of man is the sun by which his body is illumined, and from which it draweth its sustenance, and should be so regarded" (*Gleanings from the Writings of Bahá'u'lláh*, LXXX). The soul is the part of a human that reflects and contains thought, reasoning, understanding and imagination; it is through the soul that humans can rise within themselves, and gain an understanding of existence, and help society progress.

However, it is only with the help of God that spiritual understanding, which is the ultimate goal, can be gained:

> the human spirit, unless assisted by the spirit of faith, does not become acquainted with the divine secrets and the heavenly realities. It is like a mirror which, although clear, polished and brilliant, is still in need of light. Until a ray of the sun reflects upon it, it cannot discover the heavenly secrets ('Abdu'l-Bahá, *Some Answered Questions*, pp. 208–209).

Although, Manifestations of God, are more perfect mirrors of the divine, humanity is best among all of creation at reflecting the attributes of God. Each individual human can reflect the attributes in such a way that they are able to clean the mirrors that are within their hearts. This cleansing, or development of attributes takes place through prayer, through study of the scriptures, and through a living of Bahá'í principles. As Bahá'ís transform themselves they are able to transform society. This belief is reflective of the greater responsibility to love; to love God and to love others. Through a living of Bahá'í principles, they are able to exemplify that love for all of God's creation.

Recognising the divine and special nature of humanity does not make humans purely good. Rather, Bahá'u'lláh taught:

> In man there are two natures; his spiritual or higher nature and his material or lower nature. In one he approaches God, in the other he lives for the world alone. Signs of both these natures are to be found in men (*Paris Talks*, p. 60).

Human experience is to overcome the material nature and to approach God. They do this by acquiring the attributes of God that include: kindness, justice, truthfulness, trustworthiness, attraction to beauty, and thirst for knowledge. There is no such thing as evil, or an evil power, in Bahá'í. Rather it is the choices that people make that draw them closer to, or further away from, God.

Death is not the end; rather, in Bahá'í teaching it is the setting free of the soul. 'Abdu'l-Bahá taught:

> To consider that after the death of the body the spirit perishes, is like imagining that a bird in a cage will be destroyed if the cage is broken, though the bird has nothing to fear from the destruction of the cage. Our body is like the cage, and the spirit is like the bird ... if the cage becomes broken, the bird will continue and exist. Its feelings will be even more powerful, its perceptions greater, and its happiness increased ... (*Some Answered Questions*, p. 228).

Those attributes and experiences that are developed during this life are a part of the soul that lives on. The nature of the afterlife as a heaven/hell dichotomy is rejected, but is described in terms of a nearness to God where the soul continues its development of the perfections of attributes.

The purpose of this life, then, seems to be to draw closer to God by developing his attributes, a work that will continue after death.

Scripture
Bahá'í understandings of scripture build on their understanding of the

Manifestations of God. The writings of the Báb and Bahá'u'lláh are seen to be revelations from God and recognised as scripture. Though the writings of the Báb are seen to be used for inspiration, in matters of law and practice they have been superseded by the writings of Bahá'u'lláh, in particular the *Kitáb-i-Aqdas* (The Most Holy Book) and the *Kitáb-i-Íqán* (The Book of Certitude). Bahá'u'lláh wrote many books, and gave numerous talks that are seen as authoritative within Bahá'í. Those which have been translated into English include:

- The *Kitáb-i-Aqdas* – The Most Holy Book.
- The *Kitáb-i-Íqán* – The Book of Certitude.
- The Call of the Divine Beloved.
- Days of Remembrance.
- Epistle to the Son of the Wolf.
- Gems of Divine Mysteries – Javáhiru'l-Asrár.
- Gleanings from the Writings of Bahá'u'lláh.
- The Hidden Words.
- Prayers and Meditations by Bahá'u'lláh.
- The Seven Valleys and the Four Valleys.
- The Summons of the Lord of Hosts.
- The Tabernacle of Unity.
- Tablets of Bahá'u'lláh.

The *Kitáb-i-Aqdas* was written in Arabic in 1873 (approximately) and first translated into English in 1992. In its introduction by Shoghí Effendí it is described as "the most signal act of His ministry"; it is different to other books of scripture in the religions of the world because it contains directly the words of the Manifestation of God. Effendí describes further that it is "the principal repository of that Law which the Prophet Isaiah had anticipated" containing "the basic laws and ordinances on which the fabric of His future World Order must rest".

The *Kitáb-i-Íqán* is a collection of writings that seeks to answer questions posed to Bahá'u'lláh and written in Baghdad in 1861–1862. It was translated by Shoghí Effendí and first published in English in 1931.

Bahá'í

The writings of Shoghí Effendí and 'Abdu'l-Bahá are seen to be authoritative interpretation of the writings of the Báb and Bahá'u'lláh. The writings of the Universal House of Justice are seen as authoritative in terms of legislation.

Other books of scripture about/revealed by Manifestations of God also hold a degree of respect and authority within Bahá'í teaching. Smith (2000) outlines that books such as the Bible are seen to be "substantially authentic", while the Qur'an is "recognised as fully authoritative". Other books such as those found within Buddhism, Hinduism and Zoroastrianism were inspired revelation, but "doubt" is expressed about the validity of the modern day expressions (p. 307).

Religious expression
In response to requests from his followers, Bahá'u'lláh wrote the *Kitáb-i-Aqdas*, which is a book of law. Although it outlined various aspects of law, adherence to the laws are seen to be subject to an individual Bahá'í's conscience, reasoning and choice. The laws, if followed, provide a way of happiness, and the motivation behind following them should be "attraction to Bahá'u'lláh, combined with the fear of God" (Smith, 2000, p. 224). This means that "With the exception of behaviour that is criminal or liable to bring the Bahá'í community into disrepute, compliance is a matter of individual conscience" (Smith, 2000, p. 224). Each aspect of the law seeks to draw a person closer to God and to Bahá'u'lláh.

Prayer
There are three obligatory prayers (Salat) within the Bahá'í faith; one of these should be repeated each day. These prayers are obligatory for Bahá'ís from the age of fifteen to seventy; the young, old, and ill are excused, as are women who are menstruating (they will repeat 'Glorified be God, the Lord of Splendour and Beauty' ninety-five times).

An important feature of the prayers is that they are individual rather than communal. They do not have to be said in private, but are an expression of an individual's relationship with God and their spiritual state.

The obligatory prayers are the Short (to be recited at noon), the Medium (to be recited in the morning, at noon, and in the evening), and the Long Prayer (to be recited once in twenty-four hours). The Short Prayer is:

> I bear witness, O my God, that Thou hast created me to know Thee and to worship Thee. I testify, at this moment, to my powerlessness and to Thy might, to my poverty and to Thy wealth. There is none other God but Thee, the Help in Peril, the Self-Subsisting. Short obligatory prayer, to be recited once in twenty-four hours, at noon (*Prayers and Meditations by Bahá'u'lláh*, p. 314).

The other prayers are found on the following pages of the *Prayers and Meditations by Bahá'u'lláh*. Each is designed to show humility before, and reliance on, God. There are ritual actions associated with the obligatory prayers, for example in the Long Prayer the following instruction is given:

> Let him then raise his hands, and repeat three times the Greatest Name [Alláh-u-Abhá]. Let him then bend down with hands resting on the knees before God – blessed and exalted be He – and say: Thou seest, O my God, how my spirit hath been stirred up within my limbs and members, in its longing to worship Thee, and in its yearning to remember Thee and extol Thee (*Prayers and Meditations by Bahá'u'lláh*, p. 319).

The ritual actions within the three optional prayers are limited in number, and indicative of a deeper spiritual truth, being symbolic of the desired attitude of the worshipper. One example is the turning towards the qiblah which symbolises the turning of the person to the teachings and example of Bahá'u'lláh.

In addition to these three prayers a Bahá'í should repeat the 'Greatest Name' in an act of remembrance (dhikr) ninety-five times during the day. The Greatest Name is Alláh-u-Abhá. The number is chosen because of a teaching of the Báb which indicated that it is the numerical value of God. This recitation combines a remembrance of God, but also recognises the importance of Manifestations of God. These two beliefs are inseparable within the Bahá'í faith.

Each prayer is preceded by ablutions, washings of the hands and face, that are made in the direction of the tomb of Bahá'u'lláh in Bahjí (this is known as the qiblah).

> They must precede the offering of the three Obligatory Prayers, the daily recitation of "Alláh-u-Abhá" ninety-five times, and the recital of the verse prescribed as an alternative to obligatory prayer and fasting for women in their courses. The prescribed ablutions consist of washing the hands and the face in preparation for prayer. In the case of the medium Obligatory Prayer, this is accompanied by the recitation of certain verses. That ablutions have a significance beyond washing may be seen from the fact that even should one have bathed oneself immediately before reciting the Obligatory Prayer, it would still be necessary to perform ablutions (*Kitáb-i-Aqdas*, Notes, pp. 180–81).

The symbolic nature of the ablutions is to do with standing before God in a state of purity and cleanliness. This is the state to which all Bahá'ís aspire to in the afterlife.

Outside of the obligatory prayers Bahá'ís are encouraged to pray frequently to:

- Bring people closer to God and Bahá'u'lláh.
- Help them to purify their own conduct.
- Express the individual's love for God.
- Affect their individual spiritual state (Smith, 2000, p. 274).

These prayers can be offered in groups as they help the individual and the group turn towards God. When praying on their own, a Bahá'í should be focussed and free from distractions.

As has been noted all of the different expressions of prayer are focussed on bringing people closer to God and Bahá'u'lláh. Each of the ritual actions and prescribed words remind the worshipper of such; the individual general prayers should be offered in this attitude.

Fasting

The Báb instituted a new calendar known as the Badí' (wondrous) Calendar (it is sometimes known as the Bahá'í Calendar). The solar year is split into nineteen periods of nineteen days. This calendar requires a number of the intercalary (additional) days which are determined to make sure that the year ends on the day before the next vernal equinox. The names for each month were adopted from an expression of Shi'a Islam, and are said to refer to some of the characteristics of God; names include:

- Bahá (splendour).
- Jalál (glory).
- Jamál (beauty).
- 'Aẓamat (grandeur).
- Núr (light).

The Báb introduced this calendar, and outlined that it was subject to the acceptance of the messianic figure who was to come. Bahá'u'lláh accepted this calendar.

The final month of the Bahá'í calendar, the time between the intercalary days and the new year shown in the vernal equinox is a period of fasting during the daylight hours of the nineteen days (in areas of the world where daylight lasts for most of the day the times for fasting are set by the clock rather than the rising and setting of the sun). During this time a Bahá'í between the ages of fifteen and seventy should abstain from food, drink and smoking.

Although the life of an ascetic as an ideal is rejected within Bahá'í, this time of fasting is seen as a time of renewal of faith and a person's relationship with God:

> [T]his material fast is an outer token of the spiritual fast; it is a symbol of self-restraint, the withholding of oneself from all appetites of the self, taking on the characteristics of the spirit, being carried away by the breathings of heaven and catching fire from the love of God (*Selections from the Writings of 'Abdu'l-Bahá*, #35).

The month becomes a period of prayer, meditation and spiritual rejuvenation for the individual Bahá'í as they turn away from selfish desire and focus on what is truly important:

> [Fasting] is the cause of awakening man. The heart becomes tender and the spirituality of man increases. This is produced by the fact that man's thoughts will be confined to the commemoration of God, and through this awakening and stimulation surely ideal advancements follow ('Abdu'l-Bahá, cited in *Star of the West*, vol. 3 [1912], p. 305).

There are some people who are exempt from fasting in addition to the young and aged: the sick, pregnant, women who are menstruating, nursing mothers, those involved in heavy labour, and those on a journey (nine hours or more, unless it is by foot and then it is two hours). Those who are excused should eat little and in private as appropriate.

In a similar way to prayer, fasting is a time where a person can draw close to God and Bahá'u'lláh. Their minds should be unencumbered from the carnal appetites to which they are normally subject, and around which days are often structured.

Marriage and family life

Within the Baha'í faith, marriage, while not compulsory, is strongly encouraged:

> ... And when He desired to manifest grace and beneficence to men, and to set the world in order, He revealed observances and created laws; among them He established the law of marriage, made it as a fortress for well-being and salvation, and enjoined it upon us in that which was sent down out of the heaven of sanctity in His Most Holy Book. He saith, great is His glory: "Marry, O people, that from you may appear he who will remember Me amongst My servants; this is one of My commandments unto you; obey it as assistance to yourselves" (Bahá'u'lláh in *Bahá'í Prayers*, 1954, p. 187).

Marriage meets the spiritual and physical needs of the couple. It is important within the Bahá'í faith for the couple to be of the same faith, so that each can help the other on their spiritual journey. It is not prescribed and Bahá'ís are free to marry people from other faiths. There are some conditions that need to be met for a marriage to be acceptable:

- Marriage is between a man and a woman.
- Both sets of parents should approve of the marriage (this does not mean that they arrange the marriage, rather that they give their consent for the marriage of their child).
- The marriage should be conducted within three months of the announcement of the intention to marriage (engagement).

A Bahá'í should take great care in choosing their future spouse; there should be time to get to know each other, the different personalities, likes, habits and spiritual practices. Central to Bahá'í teaching is that sexual activity is restricted to married couples and, as such, premarital sex is forbidden (as is adultery).

> The Bahá'í teachings on sexual morality centre on marriage and the family as the bedrock of the whole structure of human society and are designed to protect and strengthen that divine institution. Bahá'í law thus restricts permissible sexual intercourse to that between a man and the woman to whom he is married (*The Kitáb-i-Aqdas*, Notes Section, Note 134, p. 223).

This prohibition also extends to the forbidding of homosexual relationships of any kind. Shoghí Effendí outlined the forbidden nature of such:

> No matter how devoted and fine the love may be between people of the same sex, to let it find expression in sexual acts is wrong. To say that it is ideal is no excuse. Immorality of every sort is really forbidden by Bahá'u'lláh, and homosexual relationships He looks upon as such, besides being against nature (*Kitáb-i-Aqdas*, Note 134, p. 223).

Part of the background to these beliefs is that one of the purposes of marriage is to have children and to raise them to follow the laws and teachings of Bahá'í. In this way society will be strengthened as there will be more people seeking to reflect the characteristics of God and build a just society; these will, in turn, have an effect on the people whom they live around.

If a couple are considering a divorce, while it is allowable, it is not a decision to be taken lightly. Bahá'u'lláh teaches in the *Kitáb-i-Aqdas*:

> Truly, the Lord loveth union and harmony and abhorreth separation and divorce (*Kitáb-i-Aqdas*, p. 44).

Every effort should be made to overcome the disharmony; advice should be sought from family members and the local Bahá'í community, but if the determination remains then divorce is permissible:

> Should resentment or antipathy arise between husband and wife, he is not to divorce her but to bide in patience throughout the course of one whole year, that perchance the fragrance of affection may be renewed between them. If, upon the completion of this period, their love hath not returned, it is permissible for divorce to take place (*Kitáb-i-Aqdas* p. 43).

This period of a year of patience should be attested to by two witnesses, and should also be started again if sexual relations occur between the couple.

Backbiting and Gossip

'Abdu'l-Bahá taught that:

> The worst human quality and the most great sin is backbiting, more especially when it emanates from the tongues of the believers of God. If some means were devised so that the doors of backbiting could be shut eternally, and each one of the believers of God unsealed his lips in praise of others, then the teachings of His Holiness Bahá'u'lláh would be spread, the hearts illumined, the spirits glorified, and the human world would attain to everlasting felicity (in Esslemont, 1980, p. 83).

The prohibition against backbiting and gossip is one of the aspects of the law found in the *Kitáb-i-Aqdas*. Bahá'ís are taught to restrain themselves in their criticism of others; they should focus on the positive and avoid speaking of the negative. The impact that this approach to others has on individuals and communities is immeasurable. It has a negative impact on the heart and soul of those who engage in such behaviour. This also reflects the belief that all people are on their own spiritual journey and have imperfections; as such they should not point out the imperfections of others. Such an approach in life will also build understanding and love in relationships. If the goals of life are to reflect the qualities of God, and to create a society built on peace, then positive relationships between individuals are imperative.

Alcohol, Drugs and Tobacco

The use of narcotics and alcohol is strictly forbidden in the Bahá'í faith. Their use harms both physical and mental faculties, causing impairment to a person's spiritual development:

> It is inadmissible that man, who hath been endowed with reason, should consume that which stealeth it away. Nay, rather it behoveth him to comport himself in a manner worthy of the human station, and not in accordance with the misdeeds of every heedless and wavering soul (Bahá'u'lláh, *Kitáb-i-Aqdas*, para. 119).

If life is about drawing close to God, for Bahá'ís this is only possible if one is able to strive to be unencumbered by things that will cloud the mind. This prohibition extends to the use of alcohol in foods. The only time that narcotics can be used is when prescribed by medical professionals for the treatment of illness, pain and disease.

Aside from the negative impact they have on the spiritual development of the individual, Bahá'ís would also recognise the weakening and addictive effect they can have on individuals, and the problems that drugs and alcohol can cause within society. There cannot be hope for peace in society when people act irrationally and violently while under the influence of such substances.

Although not forbidden, the use of tobacco is strongly discouraged. Both Bahá'u'lláh and 'Abdu'l-Bahá spoke of its inadvisability:

> But there are other forbidden things which do not cause immediate harm, and the injurious effects of which are only gradually produced:

such acts are also repugnant to the Lord, and blameworthy in His sight, and repellent. The absolute unlawfulness of these, however, hath not been expressly set forth in the Text, but their avoidance is necessary to purity, cleanliness, the preservation of health, and freedom from addiction. Among these latter is smoking tobacco, which is dirty, smelly, offensive—an evil habit, and one the harmfulness of which gradually becometh apparent to all ('Abdu'l-Bahá, *Selections From the Writings of 'Abdu'l-Bahá*, p. 147-48).

It would seem that it is not forbidden because it does not cloud the mind, but reading such quotes will affect the use of tobacco by Bahá'ís.

Huqúqu'lláh

Huqúqu'lláh, or the 'Right of God', is the claim that God makes on the capital wealth of an individual. Reflecting the belief that God is the source of everything Bahá'ís should pay one-nineteenth of their wealth in excess of nineteen mithqáls (2.2246 ounces or 69 grammes) of gold. The capital wealth of a person is calculated following the deduction of essentials such as property and furnishings of households and businesses. The payment of Huqúqu'lláh should be done willingly and with joy; no one should be forced to pay, and neither should it be requested. It is a free gift offering, giving to God what is his due. The collected funds are used to support the work of Bahá'ís worldwide, and to support charitable projects. Of all the donations that a Bahá'í might make, this is the most important.

Nineteen Day Feasts

On the first day of each nineteen-day month a gathering is held of the local Bahá'í community. Their purpose has been outlined by Shoghí Effendí:

> Also regarding the Nineteen Day Feasts: these are not strictly obligatory, but the believers should endeavour to regularly attend them, mainly for the following two reasons: first, because they foster the spirit of service and fellowship in the community and secondly, in view of the fact that they afford the believers a splendid opportunity to fully discuss the affairs of the Cause and to find ways and means for continued

improvement in the conduct of Bahá'í activities (in a letter written on behalf of Shoghí Effendí, 30 November 1936 to an individual believer).

These services are important for the maintenance of the community and the strengthening of the individual. Although attendance is not obligatory, it is encouraged for the reasons already outlined. The feasts themselves are usually structured with three distinct sections:

- An initial devotional section with prayers and readings from Bahá'u'lláh, the Báb and 'Abdu'l Bahá.
- An administrative section where reports from the assembly are discussed and there is consultation with the community.
- A social section where all people are in fellowship with each other. Refreshments will be served by the host even if all they can offer is water.

There is considerable freedom for the local assembly in their conduct of these meetings, though only Bahá'ís can attend the administrative section. The meetings reflect Bahá'í beliefs in the sense that they are seen to provide fellowship between believers, Bahá'u'lláh, God, and each other.

Pilgrimage

Pilgrimage is seen to be spiritually rejuvenating for individual Bahá'ís and is also a way of connecting Bahá'ís from around the world with the Universal House of Justice. Bahá'u'lláh identified two places of pilgrimage:

- The House of Bahá'u'lláh in Baghdad (the Most Great House).
- The House of the Báb in Shiraz.

For each of these he prescribed certain rites that should be observed at each. There is a responsibility for completing this pilgrimage "if one can afford it and is able to do so, and if no obstacle stands in one's way" (*Kitáb-i-Aqdas*, Notes, p. 191). A third place of pilgrimage was added by 'Abdu'l-Bahá.

- The Shrine of Bahá'u'lláh at Bahjí (for which no rites are prescribed).

Bahá'í

The recognition that it is only incumbent on Bahá'ís "if no obstacle stands in one's way" has proved to be especially appropriate as access to each of the sites designated by Bahá'u'lláh for Bahá'ís is currently impossible:

- The House of Bahá'u'lláh in Baghdad was confiscated by Shi'a authorities in 1922, and despite support for Bahá'í claims to the house, it was destroyed in June 2013.
- The House of the Báb in Shiraz suffered damage by arson in the early 1940s and was destroyed in 1955. Despite a restoration it was destroyed again during the Iranian Revolution of 1979.

The Shrine of Bahá'u'lláh at Bahjí where his body is interred, as well as being the qiblah for Bahá'ís, is, in conjunction with various sites at the Bahá'í World Centre, the focus of Bahá'í pilgrimage. There is still a hope that the other two sites can be restored, and they can become a place of pilgrimage again.

Bahá'ís are able to apply to the World Centre to participate in a nine-day pilgrimage which is facilitated by staff from the centre. During the pilgrimage Bahá'ís will visit:

- Bahjí
    - *Shrine of Bahá'u'lláh* where Bahá'u'lláh's body is interred.
    - *Mansion of Bahjí* where Bahá'u'lláh lived and died. The shrine is situated next to this house.
- Haifa
- *Shrine of the Báb:* After his death in 1850 followers of the Báb are believed to have moved his body on various occasions so that it was not defiled; in 1909 the Báb was interred at this site. Following his death in 1921 'Abdu'l-Bahá was buried here. 'Abdu'l-Bahá was responsible for the design and building of the shrine, with its location being designated by Bahá'u'lláh.
- *Bahá'í Terraces*: also known as the Hanging Gardens of Haifa. There are eighteen to represent the original disciples of the Báb.
- *Arc* is a number of buildings at the World Centre that include:
    - *Seat of the Universal House of Justice.*
    - *Seat of the International Teaching Centre.*

- o *Centre for the Study of the Sacred Texts.*
  - o *International Archives.*
- *Monument Gardens* at the World Centre that contain the graves of Bahá'u'lláh's son Mirzá Mihdí; Bahá'u'lláh's first wife, Ásiyih Khánum; Bahá'u'lláh's daughter, Bahíyyih Khánum; and Abdu'l-Bahá's wife, Munirih Khánum.
- *Site of the future House of Worship.*
- *House of `Abdu'l-Bahá.*
- *Resting place of Amatu'l-Bahá Rúhíyyih Khanum* the wife of Shoghí Effendí
- *Pilgrim Houses:*
  - o *Eastern Pilgrim House.*
  - o *10 Haparsim Street.*
  - o *4 Haparsim Street.*
- Akká:
  - o *Garden of Ridván, Akká* where Bahá'u'lláh enjoyed spending time.
  - o *House of `Abbúd* is the house that was first rented when Bahá'u'lláh was released from prison.
  - o *House of `Abdu'lláh Páshá* is a house used by Bahá'u'lláh's family.
  - o *Mazra'ih* is a house used by Bahá'u'lláh.

Each of these places is particularly focussed on the Manifestations of God and their successors. In reflecting the light of God, places associated with them enable Bahá'ís to reflect on the history and qualities of these people, and draw closer to them and God. 'Abdu'l-Bahá suggested that these

> Holy Places are undoubtedly centres of the outpouring of Divine grace, because on entering the illumined sites associated with martyrs and holy souls, and by observing reverence, both physical and spiritual, one's heart is moved with great tenderness ('Abdu'l-Bahá, *Synopsis and Codification of the Kitáb-i-Aqdas*, p. 61).

Ideas for the RE Classroom
Bahá'ís describe themselves as one of the newer manifestations of

Bahá'í

Table 8.1 – Bahá'u'lláh and the characteristics of religious experiences.

	Characteristic	Evidence
William James	**Passive** (the person having the experience does not initiate it. They feel 'done to' rather than proactive)	
	Transient (the experience is fleeting, comes and goes, cannot be retained or prolonged by their own effort)	
	Noetic (mystical experience generates knowledge, leaves people feeling sure in new ways, establishes personal certainty)	
	Inexpressible (there are no words which adequately or completely make sense of the mystical: it is beyond description)	
Rudolph Otto	**Numinous dread/awe (*Mysterium tremendum*)**	
	A feeling of **stupor**, a "blank wonder, an astonishment that strikes us dumb, amazement absolute" (1958, p. 26).	
	"The '**shudder**' reappears in a form ennobled beyond measure where the soul, held speechless, trembles inwardly to the farthest fibre of its being ... it implies that the mysterious is beginning to loom before the mind, to touch the feelings." (1958, p. 17).	
	Leading to what Otto calls "'**creature-consciousness**' or creature-feeling. It is the emotion of a creature, submerged and overwhelmed by its own nothingness in contrast to that which is supreme above all creatures" (1958, p. 10).	
	Otto develops this further to the person feeling unworthy and in a sense tainting the "holiness" by our presence. We thus need to "cover" ourselves to make ourselves able to approach the holy one (see 1958, p. 54).	

a 'world religion' and the movement is growing. As a result, there will be more community members found within classrooms around the UK in the future. Although Bahá'í is not mentioned on any examination specifications, it is becoming more prevalent in Agreed

Beyond the Big Six Religions

Syllabi around the country, as its influence on communities increases. Within all aspects of the RE curriculum there are opportunities for the exploration of Bahá'í beliefs and practices.

- The life of Bahá'u'lláh can be used at different stages throughout school. In a discussion of founders of religions, it may be a legitimate use of the story to illustrate religions that may have been founded in more recent times. For older groups the story, particularly his vision of the Maid of Heaven, could also be used to explore the nature of religious experiences. It could be linked with William James and Rudolph Otto and Table 8.1 might help pupils to categorise aspects of his experience. This exercise, used in conjunction with Table 3.1 (see p. 60), might help pupils to understand the arguments of James and Otto that religious experiences have shared characteristics.
- A simpler exploration of the life of Bahá'u'lláh could use a fortune line, where twelve events from his life are plotted, and children

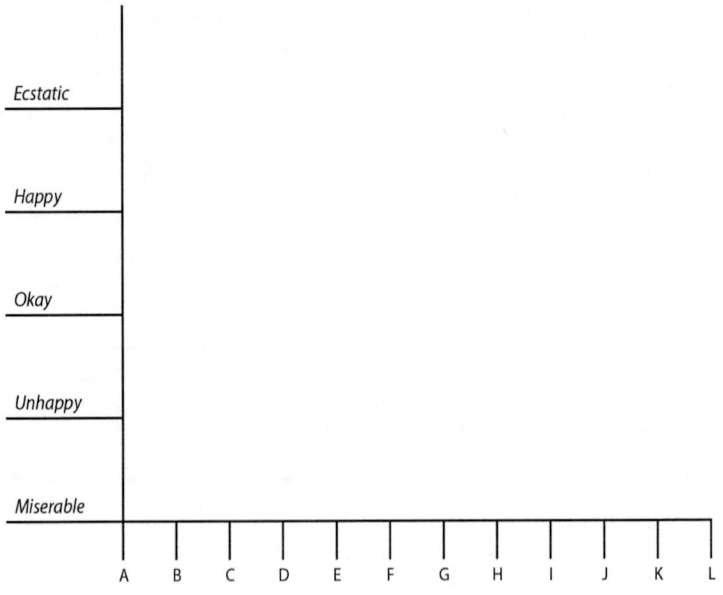

Figure 8.1 – Life of Bahá'u'lláh Fortune Line.

would be asked to explain how he would have felt at those points. After doing so, the children could suggest different words that would explain his feelings in a better way. [should this be a bullet point?]
- There are many opportunities within the RE curriculum to explore practices such as rites of passage and pilgrimage from a Bahá'í perspective. This may be only appropriate when there is a Bahá'í child in the class, or a community close by, but the inclusion of such will broaden the experiences of children.
- The concept within Bahá'í of people reflecting the characteristics of God, can be used in many different activities to explore the differences between God and humanity, and whether living a life reflecting his characteristics is possible.
- The practice of avoiding backbiting and gossip could be linked with discussions of Personal, Social, Health and Economic Education (PSHE); this is an eternal problem in schools and being able to reflect on other people's beliefs to consider different practices is an important part of RE.

Useful websites
www.bahai.org
https://bicentenary.bahai.org/

References
Bahá'í Prayers: A selection of the prayers revealed by Bahá'u'lláh, the Báb, and 'Abdu'l-Bahá. (Wilmette, IL: Bahá'í Publishing Trust, 1954).
Esslemont, J. E. (1980). *Bahá'u'lláh and the new era.* Wilmette, IL: Bahá'í Publishing Trust
Hatcher, W. S., & Martin, J. D. (1998). *The Bahá'í faith: The emerging global religion.* Wilmette, Illinois, USA: Bahá'í Publishing Trust.
Smith, Peter (2000). *A concise encyclopedia of the Bahá'í faith.* Oxford, UK: Oneworld Publications.
Star of the West (1912, 12 March). Vol. 3. Retrieved from https://s3.amazonaws.com/starofthewest/SW_Volume3.pdf

Writings of Bahá'u'lláh, 'Abdu'l-Bahá, Shoghí Effendí, and the Universal House of Justice used in this chapter are taken from publications reproduced on www.bahai.org/library/ and are used by permission © Bahá'í International Community. The publications are:

Bahá'u'lláh
Proclamation of Bahá'u'lláh
Gleanings From the Writings of Bahá'u'lláh
The Hidden Words
Kitáb-i-Aqdas
Kitáb-i-Iqan
Prayers and Meditations by Bahá'u'lláh

'Abdu'l-Bahá
Paris Talks
The Promulgation of Universal Peace
Some Answered Questions
Selections from the Writings of 'Abdu'l-Bahá,
Synopsis and Codification of the Kitáb-i-Aqdas

Shoghí Effendí
God Passes By
The World Order of Bahá'u'lláh
A letter written on behalf of Shoghí Effendí, 30 November 1936 to an individual believer quoted in Research Department of the Universal House of Justice, *Compilation of Compilations*: Volume 1, Section 5. Mona Vale, Australia: Bahá'í Publications.

The Universal House of Justice
The Promise of World Peace (1985)

CHAPTER 9

HUMANISM

Chapter Outline
What is Humanism?
Message
Nature of God
Nature of humanity
Sources of authority
Expression

What is Humanism?

In the 2011 Census of England and Wales, over fourteen million people identified as non-religious (25.1%), second only to Christianity. Non-religious worldviews are varied and we cannot be precise with the numbers of those identifying as non-religious who are Humanist (though those identifying as such on the 2011 Census was 15,607). While it is possible to suggest that a tenet of Humanist is atheism, this does not mean that all atheists are Humanists, though undoubtedly the majority would share some of Humanism's ideas and values.

Before going further, it is important to explore the term Humanism in relation to the possibility of religious Humanists. For example, Christian Humanism is a Christian worldview that recognises the value of human life and the importance of human endeavour. Indeed, Martin Spence (2016), has suggested that alongside the view of Humanism as non-religious, rational and atheistic it is:

> Informed by that, it approaches religion not as a problem or an enemy, but as an inevitable and recurrent human reality. This humanism underpins the academic concept of the "humanities", referring to disciplines such as anthropology, history, linguistics and philosophy. And this humanism has many variants – the revolutionary humanism of Marx, the pragmatic humanism of Schiller and James, the Christian

humanism of Bonhoeffer or Cupitt, the existential humanism of Sartre, to name a few.

Indeed, Humanism can be seen to be a word that was adopted in the early twentieth century by people such as E. M. Forster to describe a particular worldview. In so doing, a word was chosen that already had prior meaning. The Humanism of today is rooted in the historical tradition and can be seen to be an inheritor, or an evolution, of existing Humanist thought. Religious people may still have historical Humanist thought, but they, for the purpose of categorisation and understanding, are not Humanists. The definition of Humanism used in this book is the same as that used by organisations such as Humanists UK and Humanists International. Humanists International state in the IHEU (International Humanist and Ethical Union) *Minimum Statement on Humanism*:

> Humanism is a democratic and ethical life stance that affirms that human beings have the right and responsibility to give meaning and shape to their own lives. Humanism stands for the building of a more humane society through an ethics based on human and other natural values in a spirit of reason and free inquiry through human capabilities. Humanism is not theistic, and it does not accept supernatural views of reality (Humanists International, 1996).

Andrew Copson (2015) has defined the words humanism and humanist to "denote a non-religious, non-theistic, and naturalistic approach to life" (p. 4). He further recognises that within this type of worldview there are those humanists who will regard their views as "merely common sense", while for others it will be "a fully worked out and personally explicit worldview, recognised by its possessor as 'humanist', which may also be a self-identity" (p. 5). This reinforces the problem of homogenising humanism and humanists, in the same way as recognising only one form of expression and belief associated with a religion. People may construct a worldview that is humanist, or may only apply that term latterly.

It is sometimes tempting for observers of Humanism, and perhaps some Humanists, to define it in distinction to religions. This is not the approach of this book. Humanism is not a list of 'things we don't believe'; rather it is a vibrant approach to life that can affect the choices, actions and worldview of those who would describe themselves as Humanist. Humanism is much more than not religious and atheist.

Message

The message of Humanism is one of rationality and links with every aspect of their worldview. This rationality can be seen to be based on the scientific method:

> Science is always open to challenge and refutation, faith is not. Reason must be rigorously tested by its own lights (Grayling, 2015, p. 91).

In utilising science and observation as a basis for rationality, there is also a humility in the knowledge of existence. For example, in discussing the origins of the universe, Humanists would recognise that currently the evidence points towards the Big Bang; at the same time they recognise that there are many questions left unanswered in the science of how the universe came into being. In a medieval worldview, and perhaps in elements of worldviews today, this space in human understanding was filled by a concept that has been referred to as the 'god of the gaps'. In the progression of human history, it would be argued that humanity has moved beyond the need to fill in these gaps of knowledge with ideas of the supernatural. Humans now recognise that there is a humility in not having all the answers. There are always opportunities to learn new things, and possibly disprove accepted ways of thinking. This knowledge is within reach, but should be explored through rationality and testing. This message is reflected in Humanist writings about the nature of God and the nature of humanity.

Nature of God

In short, Humanists are atheist. Rationality suggests that the existence of anything supernatural is impossible. Tolstoy (1940) suggests in *A Confession*:

> Rational knowledge presented by the learned and wise, denies the meaning of life, but the enormous masses of men, the whole of mankind receive that meaning in irrational knowledge. And that irrational knowledge is faith, that very thing which I could not but reject. It is God, One in Three; the creation in six days; the devils and angels, and all the rest that I cannot accept as long as I retain my reason (Tolstoy, 1940, p. 47).

There may be many reasons for a belief in God, but in exploring the sociological and psychological writings of people such as Marx and Freud, it may appear evident that the creation and perpetuation of God and the influence of religion is to fill a need either within the self or within society. The philosopher Feuerbach suggested that what people call God is a reflection of humanity's own most desirable characteristics made large, a view that could be termed a Feuerbachian mirror, an idea also used by Nietzsche in discussing the creation of an idea of a 'superman'. Humanists could use the writings of David Hume to recognise the function and future of theism. Firstly, Hume posits a development of religion from polytheistic to monotheistic:

> It seems certain, that, according to the natural progress of human thought, the ignorant multitude must first entertain some grovelling and familiar notion of superior powers, before they stretch their conception to that perfect being, who bestowed order on the whole frame of nature (Hume, 1993, p. 135).

He then points forward to an atheism, which is the natural development of human thought, when people rely on rationality:

> While they confine themselves to the notion of a perfect being, the creator of the world, they coincide, by chance, with the principles of reason and true philosophy; though they are guided to that notion, not by reason, of which they are in a great measure incapable but by the adulation and fears of the most vulgar superstition (Hume, 1993, p. 155).

People are unwilling to look beyond God because of it being ingrained in their psyche. Rather, those who rely on reason also rely on evidence and verification. Karl Popper argued that scientists try to prove hypotheses wrong – it was in doing this that scientists could verify a hypothesis (Popper, 2002 [1959], pp. 85–86). Anthony Flew was influenced by this and developed the Falsification Principle for language. He argued that religious people refused the possibility that their beliefs and statements could be falsified; because the possibility that it can be proved false is not entertained, religious language is meaningless. No matter what evidence is presented to contradict a belief the believer qualifies the statement (or moves the goalposts) in what Flew called the "death of a thousand qualifications" (Flew, 1968, p. 266). This is shown in Flew's adaptation of Wisdom's parable of the Gardener:

> Two explorers come across a clearing in the jungle. In the clearing many flowers and weeds are growing. One is convinced that a gardener comes and tends the flowers, while the other disagrees, pointing to the weeds as evidence that no gardener comes. They pitch their tents and set a watch. No gardener is ever seen. The believer wonders if there is an invisible gardener, so they patrol with bloodhounds but the bloodhounds never give a cry. Yet the believer remains unconvinced, and insists that the gardener is invisible, has no scent and gives no sound. The sceptic doesn't agree, and asks how a so-called invisible, intangible, elusive gardener differ from an imaginary gardener, or even no gardener at all (Flew 1968, p. 266).

The ultimate truth, if there is such a thing, can be seen to be Reason, in which there is a humility; that a person may be taken, but reason and rationality have combined to make a decision based on evidence, experience and probability.

Nature of humanity
To say that the nature of humanity is the essence of Humanism, or central to the Humanist outlook on life, might inaccurately present an egocentric view of Humanist beliefs. All human life is respected, and while the individual is important, one is no more or less important than another. Human life itself is the result of a biological processes,

and the development of the mind is the accumulation of knowledge and wisdom throughout the ages, and within the lifetime of the individual. One view of humanity is outlined in an online introduction of Humanism:

> We are made from matter. We are of this world and this world alone. When we leave it, we do not continue to exist in some other world, nor will we return to exist again in this one. We were not individually created by some supernatural power, but are rather the result of natural, purposeless, physical and biological processes. We are a product of both nature and nurture: the result of the genetic inheritance acquired from our parents and our ancestors dating back to the origin of life, but those genetic propensities are also influenced by the environment in which we grow. Our personalities are located in, and dependent on, our physical brains, not within anything immaterial, such as a spirit or soul (Humanists UK, n.d.d).

This view of humanity is rooted in the physicality of humanity; of the various influences that affect human and animal development. While humans are unique, Humanists would recognise that humanity has much in common with the rest of the animal world. It is possible to suggest negative connotations to the idea that humans are "just another animal"; Malik (2001), however, recognises the uniqueness among the natural world:

> We are biological beings, and under the purview of biological and physical laws. But we are also conscious beings with purpose and agency, traits the possession of which allow us to design ways of breaking the constraints of biological and physical laws. We are, in other words, both inside nature and outside of it (p. 14).

Humanist beliefs are very clear, however, that this life is the end, of both the body and the personality associated with it. The writings of Bertrand Russell highlights the end of life implications for Humanists:

> I believe when I die I shall rot, and nothing of my ego will survive. I am not young and I love life (in Knight, 1961, p. 142).

This does not mean, however, that human life has no purpose or value. Quite the reverse; Richard Dawkins in his book, *Unweaving the Rainbow*, outlined the value of human existence:

> We are going to die, and that makes us the lucky ones. Most people are never going to die because they are never going to be born. The potential people who could have been here in my place but who will in fact never see the light of day outnumber the sand grains of Sahara. Certainly those unborn ghosts include greater poets than Keats, scientists greater than Newton. We know this because the set of possible people allowed by our DNA so massively outnumbers the set of actual people. In the teeth of these stupefying odds it is you and I, in our ordinariness, that are here … Admittedly we didn't arrive by spaceship, we arrived by being born, and we didn't burst conscious into the world but accumulated awareness gradually through babyhood. The fact that we gradually apprehend our world, rather than suddenly discovering it, should not subtract from its wonder (Dawkins, 1999, p. 1ff.).

The wonder of life and existence for Humanists can motivate them to seek for the purpose of their own life. The purpose is not laid out for them, rather a search for discovery becomes pre-eminent. Albert Camus suggests:

> But what does life mean in such a universe? Nothing else for the moment but indifference to the future and a desire to use up everything that is given. Belief in the meaning of life always implies a scale of values, a choice, our preferences. Belief in the absurd, according to our definitions, teaches the contrary … if I admit that my freedom has no meaning except in relation to its limited fate, then I must say that what counts is not the best living but the most living (Camus, 1955, (pp. 98–99).

There is no restriction on the possible purpose. In the book, *What is Humanism? How Do You Live Without a God? And Other Big Questions for Kids* (Rosen and Young, 2017), there are a variety of responses to the purpose of life, and how choices are made in life. One person suggests the purpose of life is to do good, not harm the planet and enjoy existing;

another may suggest that it is encapsulated in the word 'love'. Phillip Pullman suggests:

> The only way we can judge what's useful and good, and what's crazy and cruel, is by stepping outside religion altogether, and just judging by human standards: which is a better way to live? Can we take what's useful and good, and leave what's crazy and cruel? (Pullman, 2015, p. 27).

Pullman's recognition of human rationality is important in a discussion of Humanism and links with the discussion above on the nature of God.

Humanism while celebrating humanity endeavour, thought and potential in all its various guises presents a worldview of which humans are not at the centre. The universe is not designed specifically for human life, rather humanity evolved to fit perfectly the environment which developed over billions of years. Humanity is not inherently good or bad, they just are with the potential that is attached to them through both their nature and through their nurture. While humans may be subject to inbuilt passions, they have the agency to choose for themselves how they will react in the various circumstances in which they find themselves. The questions Humanists may ask themselves are: "how do I fulfil my potential?" and "How do I become the best I can be?"

Malik suggested, as referenced earlier, that a defining characteristic of humans is that they are "conscious"; that there is a consciousness within humanity that stands distinct to the remainder of the animal world. The 'distinctiveness' of the consciousness may be in terms of degree rather than in existence. Humanists would generally suggest that animals are sentient and conscious, but that, within humanity, there is a heightened or more developed consciousness. This can be both positive and negative. Eric Ackroyd (2009) has suggested that:

> Knowing ourselves, our deepest needs and high aspirations, as well as any blockages we are harbouring – doubts, fears, feelings of guilt or inadequacy that may lead to slothfulness or depression and disable us

> from realising our positive creative potential – is at least as important as knowledge of the universe as space and time outside us (Ackroyd, 2009, p. 25).

This suggests that consciousness is a knowledge, not just of existence, but also of potential and appetites within oneself that are beyond the physical needs. A Humanist will strive to meet the needs of the internal and the external, the physical and immaterial; and will consider how they as an individual relate to themselves and also to the external, meaning other beings and the natural world. Jeananne Fowler (2015) argues that "the interaction of the environment and genetic make-up opens the door to the transcending of the genetic self in many ways" (p. 355). The consciousness "is ceaselessly dynamic, in constant and exquisitely sensitive dialogue with the outside world" (Greenfield, 2000, p. 91). This dynamic ensures that humans are not just concerned with themselves; the consciousness ensures that people are concerned with others:

> And, when we say that man [sic] is responsible for himself, we do not mean that he is responsible only for his own individuality, but that he is responsible for all men (Sartre, 1989, p. 350).

Sources of authority

In exploring sources of authority within Humanism it is important to recognise that for most Humanists there is not an accepted list of sources to which they might go; rather a set of principles and ideas that might help them identify on what to base their knowledge of truths. In the book, *Cloud Atlas*, there is a discussion about the nature of truth, which might be appropriate in establishing what Humanists mean when they speak of truth:

> I was anxin' 'bout summit next day, so in part to blind my mind, I asked Meronym if Abbess spoke true when she said the Hole World flies 'round the sun, or if the Men o' Hilo was true sayin' the sun flies round the Hole World.
> Abbess is quite correct, answered Meronym.
> Then the true is diff'rent to the seemin' true? Said I.

> Yay, an' it usually is, I mem'ry Meronym sayin', an' that's why true is presher'n'rarer'n diamonds (Mitchell, 2004, pp. 287–288).

This is an important distinction to make; in recognising truth and belief Humanists will recognise the difference between things that appear to be true, but may be subject to change, and truth which is irrefutable. The humility outlined earlier, suggests that there are only a small number of things that are irrefutably true but that these should be sought. These truths cannot be viewed from different perspectives.

There are generally three types of truth for Humanists:

1. Scientific – based upon observation, hypothesis, experiment and reasoned testing, e.g. the boiling point of water is 100°C.
2. Historical – based upon documentary and archaeological evidence. e.g. Henry VIII had six wives. This can also be seen to be truth that is based on the authority of others, because others have outlined this conclusion.
3. Moral – based upon abstract reasoning, e.g. killing is wrong.

In exploring each of these truths it is evident that there can be a level of subjectivity to each, but reason should be used to recognise and find the truth. Arguably the most important source of truth for Humanists is that which is based on scientific method. As outlined above this is an empirical method of establishing the truth of a hypothesis. A hypothesis is formed based on initial observations or experiences but it is only through a repeated testing that the truth can be established. Sometimes, there is a lack of availability of testing, and so all of the available evidence is weighed in order to present a hypothesis that seems to fit. Sometimes these theories are later proved to be true or false; or perhaps the 'truthfulness' of a hypothesis is still in abeyance. One example may be the movement of the planets, and especially the sun in relation to the earth. An initial hypothesis was developed that the sun orbited the earth, because to the naked eye, that is how it seemed to be. Only through the observation, and repeated observation of the same, by people such as Galileo, was the opposite shown to be true.

Humanism

One of the most important sources of truth or authority for a Humanist is their past experiences, but each of these is similarly subject to change. These experiences feed into human reason and rationality. Stephen Law (2015) suggests that reason or 'armchair' rationality would enable people to see the truth or rationality of a claim:

> … suppose an explorer claims to have discovered a four-sided triangle in some remote rainforest. Do we need to mount an expedition to check whether this claim is true? No, again we can establish its falsity by conceptual, armchair methods (Law, p. 57).

This may lead to what some have termed a 'scientism': "the idea that all meaningful questions can be answered by science" (Law, 2015, p. 68). This again refers back to the idea of the 'god of the gaps' – just because there is a vacuum of an unanswered question does not mean that an answer has to, or indeed can, be found. There are some questions on which Humanists are agnostic; whether that is a temporary or permanent state is unknowable. Richard Dawkins recognises that this agnosticism in certain areas is much stronger than in others; he speaks of a friend who:

> regards God as no more probable than the tooth fairy. You can't disprove either hypothesis, and both are equally improbable. He is an a-theist to exactly the same large extent that he is an a-fairyist. And agnostic about both, to the same small extent (Dawkins, 2006, p. 52).

These questions can often be described as 'ultimate questions' and 'questions of morality'. As Carl Sagan has suggested: "It's OK to reserve judgement until the evidence is in" (1997, p. 169).

As for moral truth, for Humanists, it is much harder to identify a process whereby it can be established. Maybe it can similarly be based on experience and reason, but in a Humanist worldview, morality has its source within humanity itself. A. C. Grayling suggests that a "life worth living" has two characteristics:

> That it feels good to live, and that it is more beneficial than not in its impact on others (Grayling, 2015, p. 92).

This may lead to a charge of moral relativism; that every person is free to determine their own morality. In some ways this is true, but it fails to recognise the importance of recognising the nature of a person as a social animal.

> ... we are naturally social beings; we live in communities; and life in any community, from the family outwards, is much happier, and fuller, and richer if the members are friendly and co-operative than if they are hostile and resentful. (Knight, 1961, p. 49).

When considering morality, humans are not only responsible to themselves for the choices that they make, but also to others. This is not to suggest that there is necessarily a common morality that is shared by all Humanists; indeed, the use of a person's reason may lead them to different ways of living. One example could be surrounding issues such as abortion. The debate about the value of an unborn life will find Humanists on both sides; however, Humanists would be likely to allow people their own choice rather than impose their own views.

There are, perhaps, many aspects of morality that could be seen to have universal application. One such might be the prohibition against murder. This could be seen to affect more than the person committing the act; the rejection of murder is necessary for the effective relationships between people and the maintenance of an orderly society. It is not necessary to have a prophet or religious leader to declare things to be right or wrong, rather a societal and individual sense of morality is important. It is perhaps unsurprising that Humanists have been involved in movements that have sought change to the rights, which have been denied to certain individuals. One such example is that of LGBTQ+ issues; with the dignity of the human and the right of each human to be who they are, and to live as they choose (without negative impacts on the structure of society), it is easy to see why Humanists would lend their voices to such causes.

A further example, which may not be as straightforward is the issue of euthanasia. Most Humanists will support the right of the individual to choose their time and nature of passing when faced with a terminal illness. This can be seen to be the expression of a person's rational decision, it can also be seen to have no negative impact on society. There will be a number of Humanists who would oppose this, not for reason of the individual, but for the reason that it might be a first step in society that might then be seen to not value human life, and debate the appropriateness of further actions that might take away the rights of the individual.

There will, in this subjective morality, be people who value the individual over the communal. These could be seen to be reacting to evolutionary and biological forces within themselves. They may be genetically predisposed to certain actions. This kind of approach to decision making should not be overlooked. In some cases, such a view is seen to be incredibly valuable. Historically, homosexuality was seen to be 'against nature', but most people would now accept that generally sexuality is a part of a person, and that people are born with their sexualities. This has meant that barbaric acts, such as electric shock aversion therapy, have been largely seen to be ineffective and not something that should be used. There are still, however, actions that might be explained by reference to genetics or as result of human nature. Consider, the person who retaliates violently when feeling threatened – does the fight response absolve them of responsibility for the harm caused to another person and to potentially innocent bystanders?

It is at this point that human rationality and empathy can fill, what Norman calls, 'the motivational gap':

> Rather, the point is that if people are not sufficiently motivated by good moral reasons, then the only way to fill the motivational gap is for them to become more deeply aware of the reasons themselves. In the case of other-regarding values such as compassion, justice or honesty, that means becoming more aware of what it is like to be the victim of cruelty or injustice, what it is like to be cheated or betrayed, exploited or enslaved. This greater awareness is generated most powerfully by stories – accounts, whether historical or fictional, of particular individuals, which bring to life the felt experience of suffering and the

experience of having that sufferng met by good actions (Norman, 2016, 113-14).

When people are given the opportunity for empathy then this can also serve as a source for morality. If a person considers their impact on society and others then they are less likely to do something that will cause harm to either. This may be an expression of the Hedonistic Calculus, which is the idea that when seeking to decide whether to perform an action, the person should weigh up the potential pleasure and pain involved. This is not just based on the pleasure and pain for the individual, but on the effect it has more widely. The seven considerations that Jeremy Bentham outlined in this Calculus are:

1. Intensity: The strength of the pleasure.
2. Duration: The length of the pleasure.
3. Certainty or uncertainty: The likelihood of the pleasure.
4. Propinquity or remoteness: The immediacy of the pleasure.
5. Fecundity: Will it lead to similar pleasures as a consequence?
6. Purity: Will it be pleasurable, or followed by opposite feelings?
7. Extent: How many people it affects.

This calculus of consequences for the individual and others is a part of a utilitarian approach to ethics. Bentham summarised utility thus:

> By the principle of utility is meant that principle which approves or disapproves of every action whatsoever according to the tendency it appears to have to augment or diminish the happiness of the party whose interest is in question: or, what is the same thing in other words to promote or to oppose that happiness. I say of every action whatsoever, and therefore not only of every action of a private individual, but of every measure of government (Bentham, 2009, p. 1).

Further, an act should be performed only when it produces the most happiness for the largest number of people.

Morality thus contains two considerations: the individual and the communal. Caricatures of Humanism sometimes suggest the idea that a Humanistic approach leads inexorably to a hedonistic approach to life. This is based on the premise that only religion can give people a sense of morality. This is patently not the case, as Humanists utilise their rationality and consciousness to make moral choices, based not only on the best outcome for them, but also for others.

Contrary to the other chapters in this book this section has not identified authoritative books. In Humanism there is no canon of works that should be read. Rather, individuals use an eclectic range of sources to construct their worldview. This is not to suggest that this is why they read certain books, rather humans are the result of all of their experiences and it is possible to suggest that every person is changed because of each book they have read, film they have watched, and piece of music they have listened to. There are voices within Humanism who are seen to articulate a Humanist approach to life well, but they are by no means authoritative. Writers and broadcasters include: A. C. Grayling; Philip Pullman; Stephen Fry; Sandi Toksvig; Bertrand Russell; and Francesca Stavrakopoulou.

Expression

Ceremonies
Within Humanism there are various ceremonies that are offered within the community. These ceremonies seek to meet the needs of individuals, couples and families for whom religious services would feel inappropriate – they are not limited to Humanists but they are founded on Humanist principles and views of life. Humanists UK offers celebrants to officiate at naming ceremonies, weddings and funerals. These are times in people's lives where people often come together to celebrate.

Naming Ceremonies
> For many of us a religious service isn't appropriate but it is still important to bring our friends and family together to mark such a special occasion. A humanist naming ceremony gives you the opportunity to reflect and acknowledge the joy, wonder and responsibility of bringing a child into the world in a way that is not religious (Humanists UK, n.d.b).

These ceremonies celebrate the wonder of life, and the joy that that birth/adoption of a new child brings to a family. These ceremonies are informal, personal and can take place at a venue to suit the family. The family works with the celebrant to organise the service. A typical service may include:

- Welcome.
- Readings (these could be prose or poetry).
- Words about the child and their arrival, personality, etc.
- The celebrant, or others, discuss the importance of parenting.
- Parents make promises to the child.
- Involvement and promises by the extended family as appropriate.
- Appointment of guideparents/oddparents/guardians (the nomenclature is at the parents' discretion).
- Guideparents/oddparents/guardians make promises.
- Explanation of the choice of name.
- The naming.

The family may also choose to mark the occasion with activities such as planting a tree, signing a certificate or writing in a wish book. Nothing is mandatory and the celebration of a new life is paramount throughout.

Weddings

Humanist weddings are recognised as legal in Northern Ireland and Scotland, but as of 2019 are not yet legal in England and Wales. As such, Humanists in these countries may have a registry office/civil service first and then have a Humanist celebration. It may seem odd to some for people to have a Humanist ceremony, where a non-religious ceremony can be held in venues such as registry offices, and many Humanists may 'just' have this legal ceremony followed by a reception. However, Humanist ceremonies can be seen to be more personal and flexible to the needs of the couple, rather than the fairly restrictive nature of some other services that are available to them.

> Humanist weddings give you the flexibility to create an occasion that celebrates your marriage your way. You can get to know the person

who will be conducting your wedding, choose your own words and marry where and when you like. Every one of our humanist weddings is unique. No two people are the same and so no two ceremonies are the same either. Our weddings are inclusive and designed to be meaningful and poignant to everyone present, whatever their beliefs. Fun or romantic, traditional or deeply personal, you can set whatever tone you like (Humanists UK, n.d.c).

Humanist celebrants will work with the couple to provide a service that meets their needs and hopes. A service may include:

- The couple arrive (separately or together).
- Welcome.
- Comments about love and commitment.
- Music.
- Readings (these could be prose or poetry).
- How the couple met and their hopes for the future.
- The meaning of marriage for the couple.
- Guest encouragement.
- Promises made by the couple.
- Handfasting or similar action.
- Exchange of rings.
- Pronouncement of the couple's marriage.

A handfasting is a traditional practice, probably taken from contemporary Paganism, that may be used within a Humanist wedding. It is where a couple are united by having their hands bound together using ribbon. Words which are often read during the handfasting recognise the uniting of two people in love:

> These are the hands of your best friend, young and strong and full of love for you, that are holding yours on your wedding day, as you promise to love each other today, tomorrow, and forever. These are the hands that will work alongside yours, as together you build your future. These are the hands that will love you and cherish you through the years, and with the slightest touch, will comfort you like no other. These are the hands that will hold you when fear or grief fills your mind. These are the hands that will countless times wipe the tears from your eyes; tears of sorrow, and tears of joy. These are the hands that

will help you to hold your family as one. These are the hands that will give you strength when you need it. And lastly, these are the hands that even when wrinkled and aged will still be reaching for yours, still giving you the same unspoken tenderness with just a touch (Author unknown).

Humanist wedding ceremonies are thus a way to celebrate the individuals, their families, and most of all their commitment to one another.

Funerals

A funeral or memorial ceremony is an important time for family and friends to focus their thoughts on the person who has died. But for those who aren't religious, a church or other religious service can feel inappropriate. A humanist funeral brings people together to express and share sadness but also to celebrate the life lived in a way that is simple and sincere (Humanists UK, n.d.a).

Most funerals are performed with some element of religious belief and, as outlined in the passage above, this may be at odds with the Humanist beliefs that were held by the deceased. Celebrants will work with the family to ensure that the funeral service is both personal and appropriate. Services may include:

- Welcome.
- Music.
- Non-religious thoughts about life and death.
- Readings (these could be prose or poetry).
- A eulogy celebrating the life of the deceased.
- Readings of poetry and prose.
- A time of silence to think about the deceased and the associated memories.
- The committal – when the curtains are closed in a crematorium or coffin lowered into a grave.

One example of a reading used at a Humanist funeral is the writing from *Unweaving the Rainbow* that it outlined above (see Nature of humanity). The funeral, while a time of loss, is also a celebration of the unique contribution of the deceased to all who knew them and the wider world.

Moral Issues

In exploring the actions of Humanists it is difficult to identify practices that are common to many Humanists. With the use of reason and a weighing up of the consequences of potential actions there is no one approach to many of the issues and practices that are seen within religious expression. This is noted in the above discussion of ceremonies, in the sense that each one will be incredibly personal for the participants. What is clear is that Humanism does teach ethical responsibility, and the idea that only religion can provide a basis for morality is thoroughly rejected within Humanism. Within moral issues such as the 'rightness' of war; the use of abortion and euthanasia; there are various viewpoints within Humanism. Though Humanists may tend towards one view, these decisions are personal and are influenced by the individual and the context. There are certain examples that can be seen to evidence Humanist approaches to life and three such examples used below are the treatment of the Environment, the Family and Prejudice/Discrimination.

The Environment

Philip Pullman, writing in *The Independent*, highlighted the importance of environmental issues for Humanists:

> The threat of climate change is the biggest potential danger we face, and we seem to have no idea either how important it is or how to stop doing the things that are causing it (Pullman, 2015).

Although speaking only of climate change, this attitude in recognising that there are threats to the environment that need addressing reflects the general approach of Humanists. The world is beautiful, it sustains life and should continue to do so for generations. Utilising aspects of a Humanist approach to ethics, it can be seen that the way to produce the greatest good for the largest number of people is to sustain the world for future generations. It is not just a utilitarian altruism that guides Humanists, however. The world is beautiful and is a source of awe and wonder for all people; the things that humanity is doing to it will affect the quality of life for individuals in this generation. Although technological advances have had a part to play in the pollution of the world, scientific advances and understandings can help provide the solution to the problems facing the world.

Climate change for many, including Humanists, is a settled scientific fact. This scientific rationalism and the acceptance of what science is saying will enable humanity as a whole to move forward in finding ways to 'save' the planet. When the scientific findings are rejected, then this rejection becomes a stumbling block to progress. Listening to the scientific reality, both of the state of the planet and also of the various solutions that can be offered will help a Humanist move forward with confidence in the care of the planet. Colin Blakemore has suggested that "the rightful place of science is at the heart of policy for a threatened world. The oceans are already rising. Either we sink, separately, or swim, together" (Blakemore, 2009). Recognising the importance of science as part of the solution means that Humanists might be seen to be adopting a rational approach to the environment; they will recognise both the danger and promise of technological and scientific solutions to the problems that face the earth. There will be a balancing of advancements and protection. Sometimes others may be prone to one or the other and within a Humanistic worldview, there is opportunity for both.

The treatment of animals as a part of environmental ethics is, however, an issue with a broader spectrum of attitudes than may be evident in issues of climate change and care for the natural world. Humanists would generally extend the recognition of rights to the animal world; evolution and survival of the fittest show that animals are capable of feelings such as fear or the experiencing of pain. As such animals should be cared for. How this is shown in the lives of Humanists will differ. Some will oppose the use of zoos and aquariums, whereas for others they serve a vital service in the protection of species, and perhaps in the gaining of a greater understanding of the world. Some will be vegetarian, arguing that there are alternative resources that can be used to gain the nutrients necessary to a healthy lifestyle. Others will eat meat, but will ensure that it is ethically sourced.

In distinction to some forms of religion, there is no stated position that all Humanists should accept to be considered a practising Humanist. Rather the principles that underpin a Humanist outlook enable a person to develop their own responses to questions concerning a variety of environmental issues. Humanists will tend to explore all of the arguments and evidence and draw the implications for their lifestyle for themselves.

Marriage and the Family

The family has developed throughout the ages to meet the needs of individuals and society. Donnellan has suggested that:

> Anthropologists believe human beings evolved to survive in large family groups or tribes. Human beings are social animals, and we are dependent on each other for food, shelter, protection, and help with raising children. Today, however, the growing complexity of human society means we are increasingly dependent on people who we do not know personally for many of our basic needs. We have delegated many of the tasks that would originally have been done by the family. Often our houses are built, our food is farmed, our property is protected, and our children are educated and cared for by the state or by people with whom we have no close personal relationship (Donnellan, 2016b, p. 2).

This is an important element of Humanist attitudes, in the sense that the concept and function of family is fluid. It is an important aspect of human society and personal identity, but remaining fixed on one concept of what constitutes a family would be seen to be short-sighted. There are many different types of family: nuclear, reconstituted, extended, single-parent, adoptive, cohabiting parents, and the list could go on. Each of these families are of great importance for the people who live in them. From a Humanist perspective, it is not the responsibility of others to suggest how a family should be composed.

The composition of a family is, therefore, at the discretion of those involved as long as it does not hurt others. If people wish to marry, then that is fine; if they choose not to then that is also fine. This extends to sexual relationships also, if people have reached the age of responsibility and maturity then they are free to make sexual and marital decisions for themselves. As such, Humanists were at the forefront of marriage equality campaigns in many countries.

A family is important, but only in the sense that it helps those who are part of that family. If a relationship is toxic then it should be avoided. As society spreads and patterns of family life change it is important for Humanists to provide the support and help that families have traditionally provided. In this sense the whole of humanity is a family, as they have responsibility for one another's well-being.

These principles extend to all areas of family life: the allowance of adoption by same sex couples who have met the criteria as adoptive parents; the acceptability of divorce as a means to avoid unhappiness for the different parties. It is also possible for Humanists to have many children, or choose to be childless. There will be different feelings and demands in the lives of individuals and it is their responsibility to make choices that are, at the same time, best for themselves and for others.

In the raising of children it is important that their rights are similarly respected, and as such parents should be mindful of the influence that they exert. Richard Dawkins has suggested that:

> Natural selection builds child brains with a tendency to believe whatever their parents and tribal elders tell them. Such trusting obedience is valuable for survival: the analogue of steering by the moon for a moth. But the flip side of trusting obedience is slavish gullibility (Dawkins, 2006, p. 176).

In a fairly hyperbolic statement, he continues:

> Even without physical abduction, isn't it always a form of child abuse to label children as possessors of beliefs that they are too young to have thought about? (Dawkins, 2006, p. 315).

Humanism

The suggestion is that the labelling of any child as a particular worldview or faith is wrong. They should, in a Humanist approach, be taught the value of human life and be encouraged to develop the qualities that question and use evidence to draw conclusions. Only when they are old enough, can they begin to draw conclusions about ways of living for themselves. Most Humanists may not use the language of Dawkins, but the implication that children should not be labelled or unduly influenced is certainly in evidence.

Human responsibility is paramount in areas of family and relationships for Humanists. There is no dogma that insists on the correctness of a particular approach, but there is a freedom of expression that is crucial to all Humanist practice.

Prejudice and Discrimination

For a worldview that is based on the premise that all human life is of worth, then it naturally follows that all forms of prejudice and discrimination should be rejected. As a result of the shared human identity reflected in an evolutionary worldview, Donnellan (2016a) argues:

> Human beings like to feel part of a group. Sometimes, in order to achieve this, they put up barriers to protect the group identity and keep outsiders out. All groups, tribes, and nations tend to do this. Human beings also tend to be afraid, or at least suspicious, of anything or anyone new or different. This may have had a survival advantage in our evolutionary past. It may be a natural instinct, but that doesn't mean it's morally acceptable or that human beings can't progress beyond these primitive emotions. Many humanists believe that our ability use empathy and reason allows us to see how everyone's life would be improved if we were more tolerant of our differences (Donnellan, 2016a, p. 2).

The differences that are used to separate are social constructs that should have no place in an 'enlightened' age. These differences may be influenced by race, culture, gender, sexuality or many other factors. None of these should be used as a justification for the harsh treatment of others. Many circumstances require elements of judgement to be made, but when judgements are based on identity rather than capability this does not reflect Humanist ideals.

One of the key solutions to the overcoming of prejudice and discrimination is through education. Education enables the artificial barriers, or the justifications that are used to perpetuate inequalities. Examples abound throughout history that can be seen to support the Humanist perspective. In the eighteenth and nineteenth centuries there were racial theories which suggested that non-white races were inferior in many different ways. Science, experience and education have all been used to discredit such theories so that racial equality can (or at least should) be universally accepted. In the twentieth century beliefs about sexuality being a preference led to 'conversion' therapies and discriminatory laws. In the latter part of the century science has shown that sexuality is genetic; as such education in such areas should lessen issues of homophobia and discrimination.

Humanists should strive in all of their interactions to evidence their belief that all humans are of inherent worth, and are all of the same species.

The Humanist ethicist Peter Singer has discussed discrimination on the basis of species (speciesism). He argues that much work has been done to eliminate discrimination and prejudice from all areas of society, except in the case of species. If all life is of equal worth, then some Humanists would argue that a superiority over animals should not lead to negative actions.

In a discussion of prejudice and discrimination it is possible to see different elements of a Humanist worldview coalesce. The view of humanity is linked with the importance of science in recognising the commonality of all living things.

Ideas for the RE Classroom
Of all of the religions and worldviews that have been explored in this book, potentially the most important for inclusion in the RE classroom is the inclusion of non-religious worldviews. As religion in the UK declines the number of children who identify as "nothing"

Humanism

(see Rudge, 1998) increases, and while these children will not all subscribe as Humanists, elements of Humanist ideas will permeate their worldviews. How could Humanism and its associated ideas and practices find expression in the RE classroom?

- An exploration of how life can have meaning without reference to a deity or religion. Sometimes it can appear that religious belief and expression is the norm, and the recognition that there are different ways to construct and express meaning is important.
- This will be built on at any stage of schooling to explore rites of passage that might exist outside of a religious framework. If a class is exploring birth rituals or marriages then it is important for non-religious practices to be included.
- In exploring sources of authority and how people make decisions, the inclusion of reason, the scientific method, intellect and compassion are important sources. To explore issues of rationality is an important part of a Humanist worldview that can be explored at different stages.
- Ethical and philosophical issues. Although GCSEs in England and Wales stipulate the exploration of non-religious (including Humanist) worldviews, it is not necessary to limit them just to GCSE courses. There are areas throughout the school where ethical and philosophical issues are explored. It is also important that while these issues can be used as a counter-argument to certain religious views, Humanist views of life can stand independent and can be explored for themselves rather than only as a comparison.
- Humanist influence in the arts. There are many Humanist artists, authors and actors can be used to explore Humanist issues. The most famous of them is potentially Philip Pullman, and *His Dark Materials* series of books explores issues, in a fictional world, that can help this understanding of Humanism for pupils.
- Understanding Humanism is a website that has been specifically designed for use by teachers to support the teaching of Humanist ideas in schools. Their resources cover all of the suggestions developed above, and throughout this chapter.

Useful websites
Understanding Humanism – www.understandinghumanism.org.uk
Humanists UK – www.humanism.org.uk
Humanists International – www.humanists.international

References
Ackroyd, Eric (2009). *Divinity in things: Religion without myth*. Eastbourne, UK: Sussex Academic Press.
Bentham, Jeremy (2009). *An introduction to the principles of morals and legislation*. Dover Philosophical Classics. Oxford, UK: Clarendon Press.
Blakemore, Colin (2009, 19 December). This marked a turning point in human nature. *The Guardian: Comment is free*. Retrieved from https://www.theguardian.com/commentisfree/2009/dec/19/copenhagen-summit-colin-blakemore
Camus, Albert (1955). *The myth of Sisyphus and other essays* (Justin O'Brien, Trans.). London, UK: Hamish Hamilton.
Copson, Andrew (2015). What is Humanism? In Andrew Copson, & A. C. Grayling (Eds.), *The Wiley Blackwell handbook of Humanism* (pp. 1–33). Chichester, UK: Wiley Blackwell.
Copson, Andrew, & Grayling, A. C. (Eds.). (2015). *The Wiley Blackwell handbook of Humanism*. Chichester, UK: Wiley Blackwell.
Dawkins, R. (1999). *Unweaving the rainbow*. Boston, MA: Houghton Mifflin.
Dawkins, Richard (2006). *The God delusion* New York, NY: Bantam.
Donnellan, Luke (2016a). Understanding Humanism. Humanist perspective: Discrimination and prejudice. Retrieved from https://understandinghumanism.org.uk/wp-content/uploads/2016/09/Discrimination-and-Prejudice-Humanist-Perspective.docx
Donnellan, Luke (2016b). Understanding Humanism. Humanist perspective: Families and relationships. Retrieved from https://understandinghumanism.org.uk/wp-content/uploads/2016/08/Families-and-relationships-Humanist-Perspective.docx
Flew, Antony (1968). Theology and falsification. In Joel Feinberg, (Ed.), *Reason and responsibility: Readings in some basic problems of philosophy*, (pp. 48-49). Belmont, CA: Dickenson Publishing Company, Inc.). Retrieved from http://www.stephenjaygould.org/ctrl/flew_falsification.html

Fowler, Jeananne (2015). Spirituality. In Andrew Copson, & A. C. Grayling (Eds.), *The Wiley Blackwell handbook of Humanism* (pp. 347–73). Chichester, UK: Wiley Blackwell.

Grayling, A. C. (2015). The good and worthwhile life. In Andrew Copson, & A. C. Grayling, (Eds.), *The Wiley Blackwell handbook of Humanism* (pp. 87–93). Chichester, UK: Wiley Blackwell.

Greenfield, Susan (2000). *Brain story: Why do we think and feel as we do?* London UK: BBC Worldwide.

Humanists International (1996). 'HEU minimum statement on Humanism. Humanists International, General Assembly, 1996. Retrieved from https://humanists.international/policy/iheu-minimum-statement-on-humanism/

Humanists UK (n.d.a). Humanist ceremonies: Funerals. Bringing people together to say goodbye and celebrate the life lived. Retrieved from https://humanism.org.uk/wp-content/uploads/Humanist-Ceremonies-Clients-DL-Leaflet-Funeral.pdf

Humanists UK (n.d.b). Humanist ceremonies: Namings. The perfect welcome. Retrieved from https://humanism.org.uk/wp-content/uploads/Humanist-Ceremonies-Clients-DL-Leaflet-Naming.pdf

Humanists UK (n.d.c). Humanist ceremonies: Weddings. Your wedding, your way. Retrieved from https://humanism.org.uk/wp-content/uploads/Humanist-Ceremonies-Clients-DL-Leaflet-Wedding.pdf

Humanists UK (n.d.d). What is a human being? In *Introducing Humanism: Non-religious approaches to life*. London, UK: Future Learn. Retrieved from https://www.futurelearn.com/corses/introducing-humanism/5/steps/441450

Hume, David (1993). *Dialogues and natural history of religion* (World's Classics) Oxford, UK: Oxford University Press.

Knight, M. (1961). *Morals without religion and other essays*. London, UK: Dennis Dobson.

Knight, Margaret (Ed.) (1995). *The Humanist anthology*, (Rev. ed.). London: Rationalist Press Association, 1995).

Law, Stephen (2015). Science, reason and scepticism. In Andrew Copson, & A. C. Grayling (Eds.), *The Wiley Blackwell handbook of Humanism* (pp. 55–71). Chichester, UK: Wiley Blackwell.

Malik, Kenan (2001). *What is it to be human? What science can and cannot tell us*. London, UK: Academy of Ideas.

Mitchell, David (2004). *Cloud Atlas*. London, UK: Sceptre.
Norman, Richard (2016). Ethics and values: How much common ground? In Anthony Carroll, (Ed.), *Religion and atheism*. Abingdon, UK: Routledge.
Popper, Karl (2002). [1959]. *The logic of scientific discovery*. Abingdon, UK: Routledge.
Pullman, Philip (2015, 31 January). If I were Prime Minister: I would privatise religion, *The Independent*. Retrieved from https://www.independent.co.uk/voices/comment/if-i-were-prime-minister-i-would-privatise-religion-10060100.html
Rosen, Michael, & Young, AnneMarie (2017). *What is Humanism? How do you live without a god? And other big questions for kids*. London, UK: Wayland.
Rudge, Linda (1998). 'I am nothing' – does it matter? A critique of current religious education policy and practice in England on behalf of the silent majority. *British Journal of Religious Education, 20*(3), 155–165.
Sagan, Carl (1997). *Science as a candle in the dark*. London, UK: Headline.
Sartre, J-P. (1989). Existentialism is a Humanism. In Walter Kaufman (Ed.), *Existentialism from Dostoyevsky to Sartre* (pp. 345–68). London, UK: Penguin.
Spence, Martin (2016, 30 March). What the Renaissance did for us, *New Humanist*. Retrieved from https://newhumanist.org.uk/articles/5010/what-the-renaissance-did-for-us
Tolstoy, Leo (1940). *A confession*. Oxford, UK: Oxford University Press.

CHAPTER 10

JAINISM

Chapter Outline
What is Jainism?
Message
Nature of God
Nature of humanity
Scripture
Religious expression

What is Jainism?
Jainism is an ancient religion with its origins in India. In the 2011 Census for England and Wales there were just over 20,000 people who identified as Jain, whereas in India the figure was approximately 4.5 million. There is debate about the origins of Jainism – some scholars see it as having its roots in Vedic religions that were the precursor to Hinduism, whereas others suggest that it developed from other pre-existing religions and beliefs. Its history is tied up with Hinduism, in the sense that it developed in the same area and there are beliefs that seem to overlap. To some Jainism is an offshoot of Hinduism, but in actuality it is an Indian religion that may have been associated with Hinduism from a Western viewpoint but is distinct in its practices. It is a religion that is characterised by ahimsa (the principle of not harming any living thing) and the desire to care for all living things, but could also be considered to be a religion without God/gods. It is important for teachers to recognise Jainism as a separate world faith.

For Jains, Jainism is an eternal religion that is as old as the universe, which it is believed has no beginning. The truths found in Jainism are believed to be revealed by tirthankaras or Jinas. Tirthankara literally means 'ford maker' in Sanskrit, while Jina means 'victor'. The concept of a tirthankara is someone who has crossed the stream of rebirth and has provided a pathway for others to follow. By following the teaching of a tirthankara, a person is able to find their way across the stream.

Jains believe that in this half of the current time cycle there have been twenty-four tirthankaras. The first was called Adinatha/Rishabhanatha (Adinatha is a title that means 'First Lord'). Adinatha lived millions of years ago (16,310,000,000,000,000,000,000,000,000,000,000,000,000,000,000,000,000,000,000,000,000,000,000,000,000,000,000,000,000,000) and is believed to be the first person who brought Jainism to India – in so doing he also helped with the development of culture and society, including the establishment of caste.

The most recent Tirthankara is Mahavira (Great Hero), also known as Vardhamana, who lived in the sixth century BCE. He is often seen to be the founder of Jainism, but this designation would be rejected by Jains, as he is the latest in the line of tirthankaras. With some similarities in his life story with that of the Buddha, historically commentators have often conflated the two figures, but it is now accepted that they are two distinct individuals. His life and teachings can serve as an example and inspiration to Jains on their way across the stream.

Mahavira was born in 599 BCE with the birth name Vardhamana to royal parents who were the followers of the twenty-third Tirthankara, Parashwanatha. His mother, Queen Trishala's pregnancy with Vardhamana was auspicious in the sense that she had fourteen dreams indicating that her unborn child was destined for greatness.

As a child, Vardhamana led a simple life, but displayed great courage at different times. At his parents' behest, while young, he married Princess Yashoda, and the couple had a daughter, Priyadarshana. Digambara Jains teach that Vardhamana refused to get married.

Following the passing of his parents when he was twenty-eight, at the age of thirty he left the palace to live a life free from worldly attachments. He gave everything away, placed a single piece of cloth on his body as clothing and said "Namo Siddhanam" (I bow down to the liberated souls), living the life of a renunciate.

For the next twelve and a half years as a renunciate he strove to overcome his basic desires and emotions. He lived a life full of hardships, and one that rejected any form of harm towards any living being. In addition to the usual hardships associated with the life of extreme renunciation he eschewed clothes, observed fasts, often slept for only three hours a day and travelled widely through Bihar, Bengal, Orissa and Uttar Pradesh.

After twelve or so years he experienced a series of ten dreams. These dreams and their meanings are explained in Jain writings:

1. He defeated a lion which symbolises the destruction of attachment to the world (moha).
2. He was followed by a bird with white feathers. This symbolises the purity of mind that he was to attain.
3. He saw a bird with multi-coloured feathers. This symbolises the attainment of the different forms and facets of knowledge.
4. He saw two gem strings – symbolising the preaching of a way of life that addresses the needs of a monk's life and those of an ordinary person.
5. He saw a herd of white cows symbolising the service of his devoted followers.
6. He saw open lotuses on a pond symbolising the heavenly spirits that will help develop and spread the message.
7. He swam across a waxy ocean symbolising freedom from the cycle of death and rebirth.
8. He saw the rays of the sun spreading in different directions symbolising the attainment of Kevala Jnana (Omniscience).
9. A mountain was encircled with his bluish intestines symbolising the knowledge that will be given to all the universe.
10. He sat on a throne at the top of Mount Meru which symbolised the people who would revere Mahavira and would be taught by him.

Each of these dreams taught Mahavira about his identity and purpose; in similar ways they can be used by individual Jains to reflect on his identity but also on the purpose of their lives.

In 557 BCE Mahavira attained Kevala Jnana (Omniscience) while he sat under a Sal tree on the banks of the river Rijuvaluka (now Barakar). He gained perfect knowledge and bliss and became a Jina, one who has overcome attachment. This omniscience is often described by using the tale of the blind men and the elephant. Each person in this life only understands the part of life that they experience, but Kevala Jnana enables a person to see the truth of the whole of existence (the entirety of the elephant) and recognise the interconnectedness of life, and the reality of existence.

Following the attainment of Kevala Jnana, Mahavira established a Samavasarana (Refuge to All) which is a teaching hall for the Tirthankara, believed to be built by heavenly beings. His first attempt to hold a Samavasarana and share his knowledge with all people was not successful; following this 'failed' attempt he held a second Samavasarana in the garden of Mahasena in Pava. The events of the first Tirthankara's Samavasarana are described by Champat Rain Jain (1929a):

> The Discourse Divine was like a shower of amrita (ambrosia), so tranquilising, so cooling, so satisfying was it to all! The voice of the Lord could be heard distinctly all round, and it was also being rendered into different spoken tongues by the devas, in different parts of the Great Hall ... Those who were there were filled. Their questions were answered there and then ... (pp. 134–35).

Jains see similar events and architecture accompanying Mahavira's Samavasarana. Jain also described the layout of the Samavasarana built by the devas (heavenly beings) as follows:

- It was above ground.
- It was at least 12 square kilometres.
- There was a row of gold pillars with crocodile heads on top. These had strings of pearls in their mouths.
- It had a border of different coloured crushed gems which led to a rainbow effect when touched by the sun.
- Four wide roads led to the centre.

Jainism

- Four large pillars stood on gold platforms, with banners and flags flying from the top.
- The gold platforms were surrounded by areas of precious metals.
- There were four lakes of crystal water.
- A moat encircled the lakes.
- A forest stood on the other side of the moat, containing raised platforms.
- The forest was encircled by a wall of gold and precious stones, with four gates.
- In the centre was the throne on a raised platform. The Tirthankara was seated on this (without touching it – rather he was seated two inches above it), seeming to look in all four directions.
- The various peoples were sat in specific orders: firstly, the gandhars sat around the throne, followed by ascetics, the first class of female devas, nuns and laywomen, three other classes of deva ladies, the four classes of devas, men, and animals.

At Mahavira's second Samavasarana, the people responded positively and to his preaching, and eleven Brahmins chose to become Jains, and these Brahmins were the eleven chief disciples (gandhars):

- Achalbhadra.
- Agnibhuti.
- Akampita.
- Indrabhuti.
- Mandikata.
- Mauryaputra.
- Metarya.
- Prabhasa.
- Sudharma.
- Vayubhuti.
- Vyakta.

These gandhars brought their followers into Jainism, a total of about 4,400. Mahavira taught his gandhars the Three Pronouncements (Tripadi Knowledge): Upaneiva (Emergence), Vigameiva (Destruction) and Dhuveiva (Permanence). These will be explored in detail in the Message section.

One of the characteristics of the message of Jainism, and of Mahavira, was that it was preached so that all could understand. Rather than using the traditional Sanskrit, that was accessible only to the highest in society, Mahavira taught in the vernacular. The remainder of his life was spent in teaching his Kevala Jnana. His final preaching lasted for forty-eight hours and was delivered at Pavapuri. Soon after this sermon he attained moksha (freedom from the cycle of death and rebirth) in 527 BCE at the age of seventy-two.

Mahavira was succeeded as leader of the Jain community by one of his disciples, Sudharma Svami who in turn was succeeded by Jambuswami. Both of these leaders are said to have achieved Kevala Jnana (the last known people to have done so). Jambuswami was followed in turn by five sutrakevalis (those who are knowledgeable). The last of these was Bhadrabahu who moved south to Karnataka during a famine. During this move, Sthulabhadra, a follower of Bhadrabahu, stayed in Magadha. When followers of Bhadrabahu returned from the south, the resulting clash led to the splitting of the community. Those who stayed behind clothed themselves in white, and those who had gone south found such clothing inappropriate and remained naked, in following what they saw as the example of Mahavira. These remain the two main groups within Jainism: Digambara (sky clad) and Svetambara (white clad) sect. Each of these has different expressions which generally accept the main teachings and practices of Jainism. Where there is divergence, it will be explored in the appropriate section below.

Message

Mahavira is seen to have established the Jain 'ford'; this language helps people to understand the underlying message of Jainism. Referring back to the idea of a Tirthankara as a 'ford-maker', Jain has suggested that:

> The Tirthankaras show the 'fordable' path across the sea of interminable births and deaths. They may be called Teaching Gods. They alone are to

Jainism

be followed, for They alone possess the practical knowledge and have no motives to mislead anyone (1930, p. 3).

The message of Jainism is clear and unequivocal as a way to escape the cycle of birth, death and rebirth. An important principle is that this should be taught clearly and not by allegory. This approach, when it has been tried, has caused confusion, and thus Jainism relies on the clear message and example of the Tirthankaras, especially Mahavira.

The message of the Tirthankaras is that karmic atoms hold or bind souls to the cycle of reincarnation. These karmic atoms are accumulated, or attached to the soul, through good or deeds. A person becomes trapped in karmic delusion as they seek happiness from the world in which they live rather than seeking the knowledge of the reality of existence. In seeking this happiness outside of themselves, people accumulate more karma. The goal of Jainism is self-realisation of the difference between the soul and matter. This knowledge and freedom from the material or physical aspects of existence enables a living being to rid themselves of all their acquired karma, and thus attain liberation from the cycle of birth and rebirth. Within Jainism the karma attaches itself to the soul and grounds the self in the continual cycle of birth, death and rebirth.

These truths of Jainism are seen to be encapsulated in the Three Pronouncements (Tripadi) and the Three Gems (Ratnatrya).

Tripadi
The Tripadi are:

- Upaneiva (Emergence): the emergence of a new phase of matter.
- Vigameiva (Destruction): the old mode of matter disappears.
- Dhuveiva (Permanence): the qualities of the matter remain constant.

Within Jainism everything is subject to change and these three phases/qualities refer to all living beings, and also to all that is matter. Throughout existence, the three events are constantly occurring, even at the most minute level; a new form is being created, while an old form is being destroyed. Yet even during this process, the inherent quality does not change. An example that is often given is of the use of gold by goldsmith. The goldsmith takes a gold bangle and makes it into a chain; the bangle has been destroyed as the chain is created, but through all of this the inherent quality of the gold remains the same. The bangle and the chain are transient forms (Paryava), but the gold is the matter.

When one thing is 'destroyed' it is not really so; it passes on to a different form. Although the example of the gold seem very concrete examples, within a Jain philosophy this can happen at a micro level, possibly even sub-atomic – because it is the qualities that combine to form objects and beings. At the end they disperse, but then combine with other particles to form new things. The number of substances is the same throughout the universe's history; it never decreases or increases, but their constructions and combinations do change. It is this process to which all matter and existence is subject.

This then describes the inherent quality of the soul. As it moves from one life to the next, the life is being destroyed, emerging in a new form, yet the inherent quality (Guna) remains the same. Some of the qualities that the soul has are knowledge (Jnan), bliss (Ananda) and energy (Virya); they remain an inherent part of the soul, but these qualities can increase. The application of Tripadi is for humans to use this understanding to know how to develop these permanent aspects of the soul, and detaching the karma that attaches itself to it.

From a Jain perspective it is possible to see how this truth, and its three parts, found expression in the Trimurti of Hinduism (Brahma, Vishnu and Shiva). This would link with the allegorical and symbolic expressions of truths that Jains reject. These symbols could be seen to have become more important than the truth they represent. As such, Jains avoid the personification of their deeply held beliefs as they may cause a distraction from the search for Kevala Jnana.

The Three Gems
The Three Gems are:
- Right faith.

Jainism

- Right knowledge.
- Right conduct.

It is important in Jainism that these are not individual paths, rather they work together as the path to moksha/liberation.

Right faith

Right faith is described in the *Tattvarthsutra* as:

> Belief in substances ascertained as they are right in faith (Jain, 2011, p. 2).

There are seen to be several substances, or attvas, that constitute reality:

- *Jiva* – the soul which has consciousness, knowledge and perception. The soul is the reality expressed in a living thing, and the body is that which houses it.
- *Ajva* – these are the non-living aspects of the universe which include:
    - Matter (pugdala). Matter can be solid, liquid, gas, etc. There is matter at its smallest level which is known as Paramanu (an indivisible particle of matter).
    - Medium of Motion (Dharma-tattva) which is the force that controls motion throughout the universe.
    - Medium of Rest (Adharma-tattva) which is the force that controls rest throughout the universe.
    - Space (akasa).
    - Time (kala).
- *Asrava* – this is the influx of karmic matter into the soul. There are two kinds of karma that flow into, and attach to the soul. The first kind attaches itself to the soul as a result of passions driving the actions performed. The second results from actions that are not driven by passions; these can be seen to be positive and help reduce the time in the cycle of reincarnation.
- *Bandha* (bondage) – this is the attachment of the karma to the soul following asrava. The causes of bandha or the karmic bondage, can in some ways be described as the bonding of the karmas to the soul are outlined in the Tattvarthsutra:

    > Wrong belief, non-abstinence, negligence, passions, and activities are the causes of bondage. The individual self

attracts particles of matter which are fit to turn into karma, as the self is actuated by passions. This is bondage. Bondage is of four kinds according to the nature or species of karma, duration of karma, fruition of karma, and the quantity of space-points of karma (Jain, 2011, p. 114).

Yoga is the vibrations of the soul, and the intermingling of karma with yoga determines the bondage of karma.

- *Samvara* (stoppage) – this stops the flow of karmic matter into the soul. This is accomplished through freedom from attachment to and self-control over the passions of life. The vows of Jainism, along with the self-control of living the dharma and controlling the pashas, enables no more karmic matter to attach itself to the soul.
- *Nirjara* – this is the gradual removal of the karmic matter that is already attached to the soul. This occurs naturally over time as the fruits of the karma are exhausted. There is a possibility of removing the karma before this time, this is accomplished through penance. These penances include: fasting, restricting certain foods, sleeping in a lonely place, practising solitude. Other more 'internal' penances include the practising of politeness, serving others without expectation of reward and the letting go of passions. The most important is the practice of Dhyana meditation. The Three Gems of Jainism are a positive start to the seeking of nirjara.
- *Moksha* (liberation) – the complete destruction of all karmic matter that is bound to the soul, resulting in complete freedom from the cycle of birth, death and rebirth. The Tattvarthsutra outlines this fact:
> Owing to the absence of the cause of bondage and with the functioning of the dissociation of karmas the annihilation of all karmas is liberation (Jain, 2011, p. 146).

It is described in various ways throughout Jainism. One example is that the soul is a mirror on which dust accumulates, to which it adheres. Through samvara and Nirjara it is possible to stop more dust accumulating and remove the dust that is already there. When the dust is removed, the mirror is clear and shining, and the soul is liberated from all karma that binds it to the cycle of rebirths. Those souls who achieve moksha are known as siddha and are perfect in their Right Faith, Right Knowledge and Right Conduct:

Jainism

> No longer subject to the *de-pressing* influence of matter, He rises up immediately to the topmost part of the universe to reside there, forever, in the enjoyment of all those divine attributes which many of us have never even dreamt of. A conqueror in the true sense of the word, He now enjoys, to the full, the fruit of His unflinching fight with His own lower nature. Pure intelligence in essence, He now becomes an embodiment of knowledge by bursting his bonds (Jain, 1917, p. 121).

The overall message of Right Faith Jainism is the attainment of moksha; the freedom from all attachments both at a physical and metaphysical level. Existence is about the removal of karmic matter which binds the soul to the cycle of reincarnation. Only through following the example and teachings of the Tirthankara can a soul hope for this liberation.

Right Knowledge

One of the most important aspects of knowledge to be accepted by Jains is known as anekantavada. This reflects the idea developed in the story of the blind men and the elephant. The knowledge of truth, except the omniscience developed in Kevala Jnana, is many sided. Indeed, anekantavada can mean many-sidedness, or non-onesidedness. It is a humility and recognition that truth is multi-faceted and there can be many different interpretations. Language is used to express truth of experience and existence, but it can only manage to capture it partially. In this way Jains would exercise epistemological humility in every aspect of their lives, and in the different types of knowledge.

The Tattvarthsutra outlines five types of knowledge:

> Knowledge is of five kinds – sensory knowledge, scriptural knowledge, clairvoyance, telepathy and omniscience. These (five kinds of knowledge) are the two types of pramana (valid knowledge). The first two (kinds of knowledge) are indirect (knowledge). The remaining three constitute direct (knowledge) (Jain, 2011, pp. 5–6).

These five types of knowledge should be sought by a Jain:

- *Sensory knowledge (mati-jnana)* – utilising sense perception to acquire knowledge of surroundings, environment and events. Generally

seen to have four stages: First observation (Avagraha); Curiosity (Iha); Confirmation (Apaya); and Impression (Dharana). All living beings have this knowledge.
- *Scriptural knowledge (srutajnana)* – this is knowledge acquired through an understanding of what is written, though it should be noted that the scriptures themselves, without understanding, do not equate as having knowledge:

> Scripture is not knowledge because scripture does not comprehend anything. Therefore, knowledge is one thing and scripture another; this has been proclaimed by the Omniscient Lord (Jain, 2012, p. 184).

Beings that have five senses have the capability of this knowledge.
- *Clairvoyance (avadhi-jnana)* – this is knowledge outside of the five senses which beings in heaven have naturally. Humans can develop this knowledge through specific practices although it is rare.
- *Telepathy (manahparyayajnana)* – the ability to read other people's minds or to communicate through the mind. Only highly advanced humans have this type of knowledge.
- *Omniscience (kevala-jnana)* – this is all knowledge, the type of knowledge that was attained by Mahavira, and only Jinas have acquired this level of knowledge.

Knowledge seems to be a continuum within Jainism that a soul is able to develop. Through the development of this knowledge, in concert with Right Faith and Right Conduct, a soul is able to attain moksha.

Right Conduct

Jain's (1917) *Practical Path* outlines two aspects to right conduct; the spiritual path and the observance of vows:

> Right conduct which includes:
> a) five kinds of spiritual purity –
>   i. equanimity
>   ii. penalties for faults arising from inadvertence, or negligence, on account of which one loses equanimity,
>   iii. refraining from himsa [violent acts]
>   iv. control of passions, and

Jainism

    v. contemplation of one's own atman [soul]; and
 b) observance of vows – ahimsa, truthfulness, non-stealing, celibacy, and non-attachment to the objects of sense (p. 57).

The vows outlined by Jain above are also known as the five Mahavrata (Great Vows):

- Ahimsa (non-violence).
- Satya (truth).
- Asteya (not stealing).
- Brahmacharya (chastity).
- Aparigraha (lack of attachment).

Each of these will be explored in greater detail below (see: Religious expression on p. 251). There are also seven supplementary vows (the first three are Gunavratas, Merit vows and the last four are Siksavratas, Disciplinary vows):

- Digvrata (restriction of movement).
- Bhogopabhogaparimana (limiting use of consumables and non-consumables).
- Anartha-dandaviramana (avoiding harmful occupations and activities).
- Samakiya (meditation).
- Desavrata (restricting movement to certain places for a period of time).
- Upvas (fasting regularly).
- Atihti samvibhag (offering food to those in need).

This conduct can be practised in different ways and by different people. However, the important aspect of Right Conduct, is that it is only efficacious on the path to liberation if combined with Right Knowledge and Right Faith. This path provides the disciple of Jainism a way across the river that has been crossed by Mahavira.

Nature of God

Jainism is a religion that does not have a concept of God; indeed, Acharya Hemacandra in the twelfth century outlined the operation of the universe in his book, Yogasastra:

> This universe is not created nor sustained by anyone;
> It is self-sustaining, without any base or support (Bothara, & Gopani, 1989, p. 106).

In the Mahapurana, the eternality of the universe is confirmed and the existence of God is questioned:

> Some foolish men declare that creator made the world. The doctrine that the world was created is ill advised and should be rejected. If God created the world, where was he before the creation? If you say he was transcendent then and needed no support, where is he now? How could God have made this world without any raw material? If you say that he made this first, and then the world, you are faced with an endless regression ... If God created the world by an act of his own will, without any raw material, then it is just his will and nothing else – and who will believe this silly nonsense? ... If he is ever perfect and complete, how could the will to create have arisen in him? If, on the other hand, he is not perfect, he could no more create the universe than a potter could ... If he were transcendent he would not create, for he would be free: Nor if involved in transmigration, for then he would not be almighty. Thus the doctrine that the world was created by God makes no sense at all. And God commits great sin in slaying the children whom he himself created. If you say that he slays only to destroy evil beings, why did he create such beings in the first place? Good men should combat the believer in divine creation, maddened by an evil doctrine. Know that the world is uncreated, as time itself is, without beginning or end, and is based on the principles, life and rest. Uncreated and indestructible, it endures under the compulsion of its own nature.

The existence of a deity in control of the universe and of people's lives is thus rejected in Jainism. This does not mean, however, that there is no concept of a focus for worship. Within Jainism there are five categories of beings, the Pancha Paramesthi (five supreme beings) in a hierarchy that are worthy of veneration. They are:

1. Arihant.
2. Siddha.
3. Acharya.

Jainism

4. Upadhyaya.
5. Muni.

It is these beings who can be the object of Jain prayer or worship. By focussing on one of these they are praying for the qualities that they exemplify. They are the beings that light the way across the river of reincarnation. They can be referred to as a bhagwan – a being that gives guidance on the spiritual path.

An arihant (also known as jina meaning 'victor') is a soul who has attained keval gyan (supreme/complete wisdom/understanding) or possibly omniscience. The story of the wise men and the elephant is often used to exemplify the knowledge and wisdom gained by arihants. In the normal course of existence a soul is only able to comprehend the existence and reality that they are currently experiencing. An arihant is able to step back and recognise the truth of all existence and the whole elephant, comprehending every aspect of existence and being free of the chains of the limitations placed upon the soul by the inner passions and enemies. The twenty-four tirthankaras would be examples of arihants; these arihants establish/re-establish Jainism. Whereas Sāmānya are concerned and focussed on their own liberation, and while they may help others through guidance, their role in the world was less expansive than that of the tirthankaras.

A siddha is a liberated soul and this is the ultimate aim and existence of all Jains. A siddha is a being who has attained final and complete liberation, living in the realm of liberated beings known as Siddhashila. The Acharanga Sutra 1.197 describes siddhas thus:

> The siddha perceives and knows all, yet is beyond comparison. Its essence is without form; there is no condition of the unconditioned. It is not sound, not colour, not smell, not taste, not touch or anything of that kind.

They have attained eight supreme qualities, which are the focus of emulation for all Jains who pray to them.

1. Infinite knowledge (ananta jnana).
2. Infinite vision or wisdom (ananta darshana).

3. Infinite power (ananta labdhi).
4. Infinite bliss (ananta sukha).
5. Without name (akshaya sthiti).
6. Without association to any caste (being vitaraga).
7. Infinite life span (being arupa).
8. Without any change (aguruladhutaa).

An Acharya and an Upadhyaya are the leader and the second highest leader of Jain ascetic orders. In Digambara Jainism they are seen to exemplify many virtues needed for liberation. The final category of being worthy of veneration is a muni, which is a Jain monk or nun. All of these beings are not God, but are able to assist in the journey of a soul and thus, maybe worthy of veneration.

Nature of humanity

As is evident from the discussion of the Three Gems above, every human has a soul (jiva) that is part of the cycle of birth, death and rebirth. The soul is unique, but it is also connected with every other living thing; Jainism also has the view that the soul is constructed of matter – sub-atomic matter – but it is not the non-spatial soul that others might suggest:

> ... a soul is exactly coterminous with the body of its current state of bondage (svadehaparimana). Even a fully liberated soul (siddha), having completely transcended contact with the material realm, is said by the Jainas to retain the shape and size of that body which it occupied at the time moksa was attained (Padmanabh, 1980, p. 219).

There are different levels of the soul, based on the consciousness of the body that it has. At the bottom of the hierarchy are those beings with only one sense, working up to those with five senses (such as lion); then to humans and then to the divine/Jinas who have extra sensory knowledge. The soul regresses or progresses based on the karmic matter that is binding it; the soul's natural direction is upwards, while the karmic matter drags it down. The number of rebirths is not known, however Ajivikas (who are now part of the Digambara community) suggested that there are:

... definite limits to samsara, with each soul passing through exactly 8,400,000 mahakal - pas ("great aeons") before reaching moksa (Padmanabh, 1980, p. 228).

There is also the belief that within the cycle of birth, death and rebirth there are souls that will never attain moksha (these are known as abhavya) because of "some shockingly evil act" (Padmanabh, 1980, p. 225).

In the progression through existence, there is a debate among Jains about the possibility of moksha for both genders. Some Jains suggest that moksha is only available to men. For most Jains, however, the status of the soul is defined by its characteristics:

The fourteen spiritual stages (gunasthana) are outlined as:

1. Mithyadrsti – deluded.
2. Sasadanasamyagdrsti – downfall.
3. Samyagmithyadrsti – mixed right and wrong belief.
4. Asamyatasamyagdrsti – vowless right belief.
5. Samyatasamyata – partial vows.
6. Pramattasamyata – imperfect vows.
7. Apramattasamyata – perfect vows.
8. Apurvakarana – new thought-activity.
9. Anivrttibadara-sdmpardya – advanced thought-activity.
10. Suksmasamparaya – slightest delusion.
11. Upasanta-kasaya – subsided delusion.
12. Ksina-kasaya – destroyed delusion.
13. Sayogakevali – omniscient with vibration.
14. Ayogakevali – non-vibratory Omniscient (Jain, 2014, pp. 13–14).

The soul's progression begins with the development of right faith/belief that enables a soul to begin to develop actions and practices that can lead to the removal of karmic matter from the soul. Every person will be somewhere in this continuum of spiritual progression. The ultimate goal, as mentioned throughout the chapter is that of liberation.

The symbol of Jainism shown in Figure 10.1 (overleaf) helps to bring together all of the beliefs outlined so far, and finding expression particularly in the nature of the soul.

Beyond the Big Six Religions

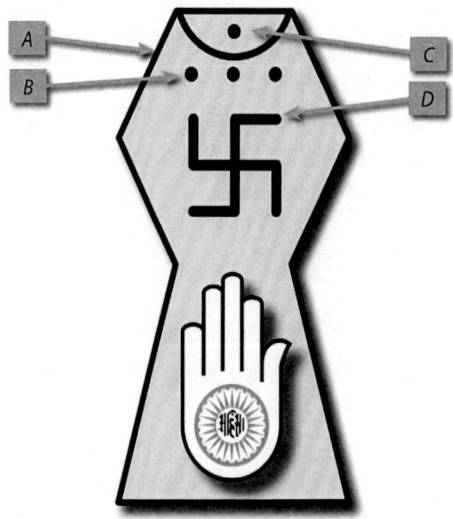

Figure 10.1 – Jain symbol.

A: The shape of the symbol represents the shape of the universe. The bottom part of the shape is hell, the middle part is the earth, the very top is the heavens.

B: The three dots remind Jains of the Three Gems of Jainism through which liberation is found.

C: The semi-circle shape symbolises the place where siddhas/Jinas (those who have achieved moksha) abide. The single dot represents a siddha.

D: The swastika represents reincarnation into one of the four realms:
- Heavenly beings (who will be reborn).
- Human beings.
- Animals.
- Hellish beings.

Scripture

Although the source of Jain scripture is held to be the same by Svetambara and Digambara, their understanding of its current expression differs somewhat. The scriptures originated from Mahavira when he was in his omniscient state, and contained teachings from earlier tirthankaras. His immediate disciples (ganadharas) at once memorised the sounds and words that came from Mahavira, and these were passed down through an oral tradition for approximately 300 years. In approximately 300 BCE there was a famine in northern India, in which many people perished, and there was another group (the Digambara) who migrated southwards. It is at this point that the authenticity of the traditions begins to be questioned by the other. As they developed independently there is a question about which teachings were remembered correctly; as a result of these disagreements Digambara Jains have a smaller corpus of scripture than Svetambara Jains.

The scriptures when uttered by Mahavira, and passed down by the ganadharas, are known as the Agamas which contained three main branches:

- The Purvas which explored Jain philosophy and cosmology. These contained elements of the teachings of the twenty-third tirthankara, Parsvanatha.
- The Anga which contains laws for ascetics, doctrines and conduct guidelines; it also contained elements of the Purvas preserved in its last section, the Drstivada.
- The Angnahya which includes teachings on the soul, the first Tirthankara of this age, time cycles, monastic discipline, and lectures around a variety of moral themes. It includes a text called the Prajnapana, which Sventambara Jains believe contains the essence of the Purvas.

For Sventambara Jains, while the Purvas have disappeared, the others have survived and were collected together first of all, at the first council of Pataliputra under Sthulibhadra (fourth century BCE), but then recompiled in the fifth century CE at the Vallabhi council under the leadership of Acharya Shraman Devardhigani. This text of the Vallabhi council is rejected by Digambara Jains.

For Digambara, although the majority of these teachings are lost, the Drstivada and elements of other teachings are preserved in the Satkhandagama and Kasayaprabhrta. The Satkhandagama is believed to have had its origin in the first century CE and Acharya Dharasena. He summoned Pushpadanta and Bhutabali, two Jain monks, to a cave, known as the Moon Cave. He taught them all that he remembered of Mahavira's teachings that had been passed down and the two monks wrote down the teachings on palm leaves. The work has six sections:

1. Jiva Sthana (Categories of Living Beings).
2. Kshudraka Bandha (Minutiae of Bondage).
3. Bandhasvamitva (Ownership of Bondage).
4. Vedana (Perception).
5. Vargana (Divisions of Karmas).
6. Mahabandha (Great Bondage).

The Kasayaprabhrta has its origins in the remembrances of Acharya Gunadhara (first century CE). Within the Digambara community the two texts are known as the first and second agamas respectively.

A further scripture of Jainism is the Tattvartha-sutra (full name: Tattvarthadhigama-sutra, translated as Aphorisms on the Sense of Principles Aphorisms on the Understanding of Principles). This is accepted by both Sventambara and Digambara groups, but they do have slightly different versions. It was compiled by Umasvati (an acharya: head of a monastic order) in the second century CE. He produced a volume that brought together the teachings in existence from Mahavira into one Jain philosophy. The ten chapters contained therein are titled:

1. The Categories of Truth.
2. The Nature of the Soul.
3. The Lower and Middle Regions.
4. The Gods.
5. Substances.
6. The Inflow of Karma.
7. The Vows.
8. Karmic Bondage.
9. Inhibiting and Wearing of Karma.
10. Liberation.

Jainism

It is seen to be an authoritative source of Jain teaching and philosophy and an important exercise within Jainism for commentaries to be written to help individuals and communities.

In 1974 the major groups of Jainism came together and composed the Saman Suttam which contains writings of Jainism that are accepted by all Jains.

Religious expression

The Five Great Vows are an important expression of Jain identity and will be explored in this section, before other elements of Jain practice will be touched upon. The Five 'Great' Vows are enjoined upon monks, whereas the 'ordinary' Jain followers are subject to them as the anuvrata (or minor vows) which are the same except with less strictness.

Ahimsa (Non-violence)

In the Jain symbol (see above: Nature of humanity) the hand at the bottom of the image represents a reminder for a Jain to 'stop' and think before they act. The word in the middle is 'Ahimsa' which suggests that a Jain should think about the principle of ahimsa first and foremost in anything that they do. Although common in other karmic religions, Gandhi has suggested that the principle of ahimsa is best expressed in Jainism:

> No religion in the World has explained the principle of Ahimsa so deeply and systematically as is discussed with its applicability in every human life in Jainism. As and when the benevolent principle of Ahimsa or non-violence will be ascribed for practice by the people of the world to achieve their end of life in this world and beyond. Jainism is sure to have the uppermost status and Lord Mahavira is sure to be respected as the greatest authority on Ahimsa. In Jainism Himsa [violence: the opposite of ahimsa] is subdivided into bhava-himsa and dravya-himsa or violence in thought and violence in physical action. Jain thinkers have classified violence into 108 varieties so that an aspirant can detect even the minutest form of violence (in Joseph, 1998, p. 50).

For a Jain monk/mendicant there is adherence to a rigorous ahimsa; in every action they perform they have to be aware of ahimsa and the possibility of killing minute life forms. Practices differ between the schools of Jainism, but examples of actions that are performed to avoid harming living beings include gently brushing the ground before they step to ensure that insects are not hurt as they place their foot down. Others wear a small mask to avoid breathing in tiny insects. Jain monks adopt the habit of samti (carefulness) which includes the taking of care in five actions:

(a) walking, so as not to injure any living being;
(b) speech, so as not to cause pain to anyone by offensive, disagreeable language, or by a careless use of words having a tendency to incite others to violent deeds;
(c) eating, so as not to cause injury to any living being;
(d) handling things – the water gourd, books and the feather whisk, with which there is a great danger of injury to small insects; and
(e) evacuation and disposal of faeces, urine, and the like (Jain, 1929b, p. 29).

This reflects the belief that an action, regardless of intention, has the possibility of attaching karmic matter to the soul.

For a Jain who has not taken the Great Vows it would be impossible to follow the law of ahimsa to the same extent as an ascetic. Rather, they adopt a lifestyle where they vow not to kill without a purpose and intention. It would be impossible to avoid killing minute forms of life during the acts of daily living, working and cooking. They will avoid intentionally causing harm; this can extend to not just overt actions such as causing physical harm or overburdening an animal, but also actions which deny animals and living things of rights such as food and drink. While the minor vow is important in the life of a Jain, it will inevitably cause some karmic matter to bind to the soul, and liberation is only possible with the living of the Major Vows.

Jains will adopt a strict vegetarian diet, and will also avoid, where possible, the use of leather and other goods that are made from the killing of living things. Plants are one sense (ekindriya) and so are acceptable to eat, as the least developed form of life. For some Jains they will avoid root vegetables and bulbs (onion and garlic) as in the process of digging them up, many insects may be harmed. Mushrooms are similarly forbidden as there may be other life forms in and around them. There is also the belief that root and bulb vegetables, while being one form have infinite lives within them, whereas other plants have either single, or countable number of lives.

Some very strict Jains will also avoid dairy products as taking them from the animal will have inevitably have caused harm. The leaving out of food could potentially mean that it could not be eaten, as bacteria and microorganisms would accumulate and then be harmed in the eating.

Ahimsa will also affect the career that a lay Jain pursues. They will choose jobs that do not cause harm. The Jain belief of the jiva being within every living thing perhaps finds its greatest expression in the vow of ahimsa. The motivations behind the lifestyles that are adopted, can be seen to reflect these Jain beliefs to the extent that harm can be avoided. During the festival of Paryushana, lay Jains will try and live the five Major Vows, and in particular avoid causing harm to any living thing. This festival is also a time to seek forgiveness for any harm to living beings during the day of Samvatsari. They do this by saying: *Micchami Dukkadam* or *Khamat Khamna* to others which means, "If I have offended you in any way, knowingly or unknowingly, in thought, word or action, then I seek your forgiveness."

Satya (Truth)
This is the vow to always tell the truth, to not lie and not encourage others to do the same. One reason for this is that the underlying cause is passion such as hatred or embarrassment, and the lie will cause harm. Even when it appears that telling the truth will cause harm, monks and nuns will either tell the truth or say nothing. This is, perhaps, the major difference between the monks and the laity; lay Jains are permitted to say something false if it is said to prevent harm to another living thing.

Asteya (Not stealing)

The avoidance of stealing in thought, word, or action is the third of the Jain vows. The *Sarvarthasiddhi* outlines five ways that the vow can be broken:

> Prompting a person to steal, or prompting him through another or approving of the theft, is the first transgression. The second is receiving stolen goods from a person, whose action has neither been prompted nor approved by the recipient. Receiving or buying goods otherwise than by lawful and just means is an irregularity or a transgression. An attempt to buy precious things very cheaply in a disordered state is the third transgression. Cheating others by the use of false weights and measures in order to obtain more from others and give less to others, is the fourth transgression. Deceiving others with artificial gold, synthetic diamonds and so on, is the fifth transgression. These five are the transgressions of the vow of non-stealing (Jain, 2012, p. 208).

For a mendicant they also extend these five prohibitions to include suggesting to someone that they would prefer something different to that which is being offered. For lay Jains the minor vow is described as being honest in all of their dealings, which would embrace the five ways outlined by the *Sarvarthasiddhi* above. In some ways this can be seen to be a further expression of ahimsa, and avoiding acting motivated by passions which will cause the soul to be further bound to the cycle of rebirth.

Brahmacharya (Celibacy/Chastity)

As one of the five Major Vows, Brahmacharya is a vow of celibacy and sexual restraint. This includes all sexual activity and also sexual thoughts. These are usually driven by passion and as such will attach karmic matter to the soul. Jain mendicants will not only avoid all purposeful sexual activity and thought, but also will avoid situations where sexual thoughts or responses may occur inadvertently. Many Jain mendicants will live in single sex communities, and may avoid touching a person of the opposite sex.

Jainism

When a monk or a nun comes into contact with other people, usually when seeking alms (Jain mendicants will usually receive alms once or twice a day) a mendicant will take care to keep interaction and certainly any physical contact to a minimum to stop inadvertent sexual thoughts or feelings. In different forms of Jainism rituals have developed around the giving of alms that reduce the opportunity for such thoughts or responses. In some groups only a person of the same gender can offer food; in all forms with food offered there will be little opportunity for inadvertent touching of any kind.

For the lay Jain, Brahmacharya will often mean chastity to different extents. For all Jains it will include no sexual activity before marriage, and with anyone who is not their spouse. This vow of chastity may also be extended to include refraining from sexual activity during marriage for festival times to improve the karmic merit. For others, it may mean that they limit sexual activity to acts with the specific purpose of procreation. There will be some Jains who become a brahmacari (m) or brahmacarini (f) which means a celibate lay person. They may wear simple white clothes similar to those worn by Sventambara mendicants (Digambara mendicants are naked). A lay Jain who adopts this vow of celibacy can be seen to be on the sixth stage of progress outlined earlier: pramattasamyata – imperfect vows. In this stage a lay Jain may make additional vows, and as they develop these vows they are making 'progress' to the stage where they may move from the laity to becoming a mendicant. A lay Jain is under no responsibility adopt all of the stages (pratima). The pratima are

1. Darshan Pratima (right perspective): the following of the way of the Tirthankara, not gambling, eating meat, being chaste, no stealing, hunting or drinking wine.
2. Vrat Pratima: observing the twelve vows (the Five Vows, the Gunavratas and the Siksavratas).
3. Samayak Pratima: regular meditation.
4. Proshadhopvas Pratima: regular fasting usually four times in a month.

5. Sachitta Tyaga Pratima: avoiding the eating of vegetables which are able to grow again.
6. Ratribhukti Tyaga Pratima: abstaining from eating at night, and sexual intercourse at night.
7. Brahmacharya Pratima (celibacy): abstaining from all sexual activity.
8. Arambha Tyaga Pratima: not performing any activity to earn a living.
9. Parigraha Tyaga Pratima: giving up possessions.
10. Anurnati Tyaga Pratima: not giving orders or consent within family relationships.
11. Uddishta Tyaga Pratima: living the life of a mendicant.

Aparigraha (Lack of attachment)

Aparigraha is the complete giving up of worldly possessions for a mendicant. Attachment to possessions is what can lead to passions, which in turn lead to actions which bind karmic matter to the soul. For a monk or a nun this includes two categories of possessions:

- Physical possessions: this refers to any kind of property or possessions. For this reason a mendicant of the Digambara tradition will wander and have no attachment to anything, including, as the name suggests, any clothing. They will have a water pot for toileting, and a broom made of peacock feathers which a bird has shed. In the Svetambara tradition they may be resident in a community, and will wear a simple white robe and have possessions such as an alms bowl and a broom. For each tradition these items, are not possessions, rather they are freely given alms to which the mendicant has no attachment.
- Mental or psychic possessions: these are possessions such as emotions, likes, dislikes and any form of attachment. A monk or nun should give up the four key passions of anger, ego, deceitfulness and greed. The other ten passions refer to wrong belief, three passions of sex, and disgust, fear, laughter, like, dislike and sorrow.

For a lay Jain, the way that this vow is interpreted is on a much more limited scale. The individual will own things that they need to live, such as clothes, furniture and land. They should not have things to

Jainism

excess, and should strive to avoid becoming attached to the possessions they own. This is very much an individual approach to life, and each Jain should consider what they need to live. They may also begin to develop habits that enable them to shed mental possessions.

The seven additional vows only adopted by mendicants (Gunavratas and Siksavratas) are:

- Digvrata (restriction of movement).
- Bhogopabhogaparimana (limiting use of consumables and non-consumables).
- Anartha-dandaviramana (avoiding harmful occupations and activities).
- Samakiya (meditation).
- Desavrata (restricting movement to certain places for a period of time).
- Upvas (fasting regularly).
- Atihti samvibhag (offering food to those in need).

Sallekhana

Sallekhana is a death or end of life vow within Jainism. It involves the gradual reduction of food and liquids to be consumed so that the person is able to die without any attachment, and this reduces the passions and karmic matter being attached to the soul. Once the vow is taken it can take years to prepare and implement.

It is a vow that can be taken by both lay and mendicant Jains. It is a controversial practice to observers as it can be seen to be a form of suicide, though Jains would reject this as it is a passionless act. The vow is broken if the person desires a positive rebirth as part of the process. Its use has been limited in modern times, though Jitendra Shah in a 2006 article in *The Indian Express* notes that:

> On an average, about 240 Jains (both Shewtambar and Digambar sects) attain Sallekhana, though most of it goes unnoticed and unrecorded

Worship

Within Jainism there are seen to be six practices that are performed by householders/lay Jains that could be seen to be worship, and these are:

1. Devapuja, worship of the Tirthankaras.
2. Guruupasti, venerating and listening to the teachers.
3. Svadhydya, study (of the scriptures).
4. Sarnyama, restraint (including observance of the mulagunas, the anuvratas, the gunavratas, and the first siksavrata, samayika.
5. Tapas, austerities (especially fasting on holy days, as in the second siksavrata).
6. Dana, charity (giving alms to mendicants) (Jaini, 1979, p. 190).

Devapuja is worship of Tirthankaras. This is an act of meditation (Samayika) and silent prayers performed in front of an image of a Siddha (usually a Tirthankara but it could be an Arihant). Samayika lasts for forty-eight minutes, it being a time of prayer and reflection. The purpose of the meditation is to seek the removal of karmic matter.

One prayer that is said each morning and evening, as well as prior to the beginning of any meditation is the Namaskara Mantra:

> I bow to the Arihants
> I bow to the Siddhas.
> I bow to the Acharyas.
> I bow to the Upadhyayas.
> I bow to all the Sadhus and Sadhvis.
> These five salutations completely destroy all the sins.
> Of all things, this prayer is foremost.

While it is being recited, the worshipper bows to the Panca-Parameshti (the Supreme Five) as outlined above (see Nature of God on p. 243):

1. Arihant.
2. Siddha.
3. Acharya.
4. Upadhyaya.
5. Muni.

Meditation is a form of bhavapuja (internal puja) where the intention and thought process behind the act underlies all meditation. The proper intention is the removal of karma and all attachments. Bhavapuja should be for worldly benefit or spiritual progression. Bhavapuja underpins all acts of devotion such as fasting or the offering of alms.

Jainism

The meditations of the day will also involve the prayer ritual of Pratikramana, which is a prayer for forgiveness. It is usually performed in the morning to ask for forgiveness of bad actions performed in the night, and in the evening to seek forgiveness for actions performed in the day. Part of the Pratikramana is:

> I forgive all living beings,
> May all living beings forgive me;
> All living beings are my friend,
> I have enmity with none.

Dravyapuja (external puja) is also performed and usually involves articles. One example is Astaprakari puja which is performed in some traditions of Svetambara Jains. It utilises eight substances:

- Purified water (to remind the worshipper of moksha).
- Sandalwood (as a cooling substance to remind the worshipper of getting rid of the heat/karma of this life).
- Flowers (a reminder of being free from desires and passions).
- Incense (to remove karmas).
- A lamp with camphor (a symbol of omniscience).
- Uncooked rice (something which does not decay; i.e. the attainment of moksha).
- Sweets (to represent freedom from greed).
- Fruit or nuts (to remind the worshipper of moksha).

Having bathed, dressed in clothes suitable for worship and covered their mouths with a cloth (to prevent impurities being breathed onto the image), a layperson approaches the image of the Tirthankara repeating the word nishi (it is abandoned) and circumambulates the image three times in a clockwise direction. The image is cleaned, and then anointed with the water. Sandalwood is dabbed on to the image; flowers are placed on the Tirthankara's lap, knees, shoulders and head, and a garland placed around the neck. The remaining offerings are placed before the Tirthankara. At this point incense and the lamp are waved in front of the image, and auspicious signs, such as the swastika, are made with the rice. Following this process, nishi is said once again and meditation is begun.

Every aspect of worship reminds the devotee of the purpose of life; to remove karmas and attain moksha. The seeking of freedom from karmas enables omniscience to be developed and a soul to become liberated.

Festivals

Jains celebrate many different festivals, though the adoption of festivals differs among the traditions. Some festivals include:

- *Mahavir Jayanti* celebrates the birth of Mahavira.
- *Akshaya Tritiya* remembers the first act of giving alms, following the example of the first Tirthankara, Rishabhanatha.
- *Paryushana/Dasa Laksana Parvan* is a time of austerity for lay and ascetic Jains, often including an eight-day fast, with just water being taken.
- *Diwali* celebrates the liberation of Mahavira and the enlightenment of Indrabhūti Gautama, one of Mahavira's ganadharas.
- *Ahimsa Day* is a British festival to focus attention on ahimsa.
- *Posh Dashami* celebrates the life of Parsvanatha, the twenty-third Tirthankara.

Most of these festivals will include devotions such as fasts. Other practices will differ according to location and the festival being celebrated. In Divali there will be an emphasis on community, celebration and meals. Although special and sacred times, the festivals are times to remind Jains of their path to liberation, and would not be considered times of excess.

Ideas for the RE Classroom

In the study of religions with an Eastern origin, Jainism is perhaps the one that receives least attention in the classroom. The main reason for this is the number of adherents in the UK and around the world. There are elements of Jainism that would be fruitful for study throughout the school.

Jainism

- The stories associated with the Tirthankaras and others enable pupils to understand some of the beliefs of Jainism. Hynson (2010) has collected together a book of Jain Tales which use Jain "stories to tell people about their ideas and beliefs. Stories make ideas more solid because they are about people and about the difficulties and the choices that they have to make" (p. 3). The stories associated with Mahavira are particularly important and can be used for pupils to identify beliefs or suggest meanings to stories. The Jain story of blind men and the elephant (which is also found in other faiths) is a story from which pupils can learn the importance of stepping back and observing the whole, while also being able to be used to discuss the Jain belief in Omniscience.
- The Jain belief in ahimsa, and the avoidance of himsa, is particularly evident and impactful for use in the classroom. As noted in the chapter, Jains are perhaps the most scrupulous in their adherence to the principle. The use of a Jain's dietary rules and daily rituals would engage pupils and help them to understand their impact on all living beings. As it is a belief that is found within Hinduism and Buddhism, a similarities and differences exercise could be undertaken, such as in Figure 10.2 (overleaf).
- The idea of karmic matter and its attachment to the soul, especially its binding and weighing down effect, contains links with aspects of science education. The scientific principles would be a useful experiment/introduction to a discussion of the impact of karma. This could also be linked to a design of the game of moksha chitram – which is essentially snakes and ladders. The teacher could design the board, or have children design it with specific features (the first thirty or so squares should have a number of different lifeforms in order); at about thirty-five the human should be put into the square. Ladders with positive actions which remove karmic matter noted can be placed, and snakes with bad actions are also added. Square 100 should be moksha. The instructions could be:

> This game is designed to show how a Jain believes in reincarnation and the belief that karma can affect a person's spiritual progress. The Jains believe that everything has a jiva (soul). This jiva travels through the cycle of life, death and rebirth until the soul escapes this cycle because of the removal of karmic matter from the soul.

Beyond the Big Six Religions

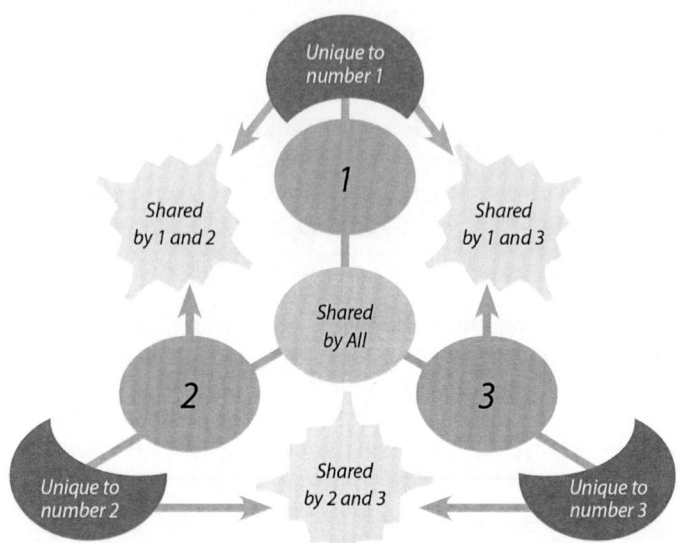

Figure 10.2 – Similar and different: Ahimsa.

Karmic actions have the potential to remove or add karmic matter to the soul. During the game you might make moves that lead to the attachment of karmic matter. (i.e. landing on a laziness or harming a living thing square); these will be at the top of the snakes. Actions which remove karmic matter such as the Five Great Vows will enable you to move up the board.

- Before you play the game you will need a piece of paper. As you play the game write down what happens to you, and why.
- Playing the game:
    - Choose a counter each and place this at the start position.
    - In turn roll the dice. The one with the highest score goes first and so on.
    - In turn roll the dice to see how many places you can move forward.
    - If you land on a square with a ladder in it you have made a good move and have shown that you have removed karma. You move up the ladder.

Jainism

- If you land on a square with a snake's head in it you have attached karmic matter to the soul. Therefore, you have to slide down the snake and be re-born as a lower animal.
- When you have finally made it as far as the human life form you know that you are doing well. Shake the dice to see how many squares you can jump forward.
- The first one to reach 'Moksha' is the winner.
  - Tasks
    - Write a diary of your game with the title 'The Journey of the Jiva'. You must remember to talk about karma and how the jiva shifts from one body to another.
    - How would these beliefs in karma and reincarnation affect the way a Jain would live their life? Explain your answer.
- The life of asceticism adopted by Jain mendicants could be explored in detail; or even the minor vows taken by householders. Each of these are reflective of Jain beliefs, but such a lifestyle could be seen to be counter-cultural and engagement with such practices are important for pupils to explore how different people find fulfilment in their lives.

Useful websites
www.jainpedia.org
www.learnjainism.org

Reference list
Bothara, Surendra (Ed.), & Gopani, A. S. (trans.) (1989). *Yogaśāstra (Sanskrit) of Ācārya Hemacandra*. Jaipur, India: Prakrit Bharti Academy.
Hynson, Colin (2010). *Jain tales*. London, UK: Institute of Jainology.
Jain, Champat Rai (1917). *The practical path*. The Central Arrah, India: Jaina Publishing House.
Jain, Champat Rain (1929a). *Risabha Deva. The founder of Jainism*. Allahabad, India: The Indian Press.
Jain, Champat Rai (1929b). *The Practical Dharma*, Allahabad, India: The Indian Press.
Jain, Champat Rai (1930). *Jainism, Christianity and science*, Allahabad: The Indian Press.

Jain, Vijay K. (Ed.) (2011). *Acharya Umasvami's Tattvārthsūtra*, Dehradun, India: Vikalp Printers.
Jain, Vijay K. (Ed.) (2012). *Acharya Kundkund's Samayasara*. Dehradun, India: Vikalp Printers.
Jain, Vijay K. (Ed.) (2014). *Ācārya Pujyapada's Istopadeśa – The golden discourse*. Dehradun, India: Vikalp Printers.
Joseph, Joson (1998). Nonviolence in the teachings of Mahavira and Mahatma and its relevance in the 21st century. In Janardhan Pandy (Ed.), *Gandhi and 21st century* (pp. 48–52). New Delhi, India: Concept Publishing.
Padmanabh, Jaini, (1979). *The Jaina path of purification*, Delhi, India: Motilal Banarsidass.
Padmanabh, Jaini (1980). Karma and the problem of rebirth in Jainism. In Wendy Doniger (Ed.), *Karma and rebirth in classical Indian traditions* (pp. 217–40). Berkeley, CA: University of California Press.
Shah, Jitendra (2006, 30 September). Over 200 Jains embrace death every year, *The India Express*, Retrieved from https://web.archive.org/web/20150714055021/http://expressindia.indianexpress.com/news/fullstory.php?newsid=74730

CHAPTER 11

PAGANISM

Chapter Outline
What is Paganism?
Message
Nature of God
Nature of humanity
Scripture
Religious expression

What is Paganism?
Paganism can be seen to be groups based on a reverence for nature. Those who consider themselves to be pagan draw on the traditional religions that were practised in ancient times. In some ways it could be more correct to define modern expressions of Paganism as neo-Paganism as they are a reclamation of ancient beliefs and practices. This is a contested point, as there are some Pagans who would see themselves as the inheritors of an ancient tradition that has been passed down, and this may have been in secret. The word pagan comes from the Latin *paganus*, one meaning of which is 'country dweller'; Joyce and River Higginbotham suggest that "It may have been a derogatory term created by city dwellers to describe 'those hicks out there,' much like the word 'redneck.' Because 'pagan' tended to have a negative meaning, it was later adopted as an insult" (2002, p. 6). The word pagan can be seen to have been reclaimed by modern self-identified Pagans who have strived to articulate what it means as an expression of belief. Pagans are of particular interest because of their place in the history of the UK, their ecological focus and their identification in Agreed Syllabi such as Cornwall.

Paganism is an umbrella term which covers different groups which could include, but are not limited to the following:

- *Wicca (also known as Witchcraft)* – which is perhaps the largest of the modern Pagan groups within the United Kingdom. There are different expressions of Wicca including: Gardnerian, Alexandrian, Traditional, Hereditary (Family), Dianic, Hedgewitch and Seax-Wicca. Various nuances of Wicca will form parts of this chapter. Witchcraft or Wicca has many different elements which focus on a communion with nature and the importance of love. This is the expression which is most associated with Paganism in the public psyche. It can be practised in groups or by a solitary practitioner. The general ethic of Wicca can be found in the aphorism "An it harm none, do what ye will" (Wiccan Rede, in Glass, 1973, p. 58).
- *Druidry* – which is seen as a renewal of the ancient tradition and practices of Britain. It creates a sacred link and relationship between the people and the land and nature. It is a deeply spiritual path that links people with the spirits of nature, their ancestors and the cultural heritage of the country and the land. Emma Restall Orr has defined Druidry as follows:

    > Druidry is exquisitely simple ... Druidry is the sacred relationship between the people and these islands. It is a religion wrapped in history, heritage, language, the beauty of these lands, the seas that shape them, the skies above, abundant greens, soft mists, summer storms, wild roses, the natural tides of living and dying (quoted in Jennings, 2002, p. 84).

    There are many reasons why an exploration of Druidry would be important within the classroom, but as a focus on the British Isles and its associated traditions, this perhaps becomes more important.
- *Shamanism* – which focuses around a Shaman, who is often seen in popular culture to be a 'medicine man' but this is a misrepresentation of who and what they are. Shamanism is a diverse path, with many different expressions, especially as it tends to be solitary. Shamans may well be sought at times of illness, but Shamanism teaches of the importance of communication with a spiritual realm. Shamans have the ability to go into trances and transcend the material world and the realm of the spirits seeking help and assistance. Joan Halifax has outlined elements of their practice and identity:

> Shamans are healers, seers, and visionaries. ... they are in communication with the world of gods and spirits. Their bodies can be left behind while they fly to unearthly realms. They are poets and singers. They dance and create works of art ... they are familiar with cosmic as well as physical geography; the ways of plants, animals, and the elements are known to them. They are psychologists, entertainers, and food finders. Above all, however, shamans are technicians of the sacred and masters of ecstasy (Halifax, 1979, pp. 3-4).

- *Asatru and the Northern Tradition, including Odinism* (sometimes found within the umbrella term of *Heathenry*) – which is a Pagan path that is focussed on the Nordic, Germanic and Icelandic deities. Asatru identifies 'Asa' as a collective name for these gods, and therefore Asatru has come into more common usage than heathenry which is a reclamation of the beliefs and practices of the countries that surround the North Sea which include those with a Scandinavian, Viking or Anglo-Saxon heritage. The main deities, that are also known in popular culture, include some from (Norse/Anglo Saxon) traditions:
    - Odin/Woden.
    - Thor/Thunor.
    - Tyr/Tiw.
    - Figga.
    - Balder.
    - Frey.
    - Freyja.

Asatru is also closely linked with the importance of nature; the two subdivisions of deities, the Aesir and the Vanir find their expression in nature and the landscape (the Vanir) and aspects of civilisation and agriculture (the Aesir). It is impossible to ignore the cultural importance of Asatru historically, and today, in literature and with the naming of the days and certain heritage of areas of the UK, such as their use of Stonehenge. Elements of such a belief system may be seen by some to belong to a bygone age, but it is important to recognise the value that such a system can bring to people's lives. It may be tempting for some to write the beliefs of such a system off as primitive mythology. It is important to recognise that although they are ancient beliefs, which are seemingly at odds with today's 'enlightened' society, in the lives of believers these have just as much validity as other belief systems. This is indicated in a conversation in the Marvel comics between Thor and Captain America where Thor suggests that Christian beliefs are based on the same amount of faith as those found in Odinism:

> *Thor:* Listen, I'm sorry about this. I really didn't want that to happen and I'm serious when I said I'd nothing to do with outing Banner. That said, I think I know who might have released those files.
> *Captain America:* Who?
> *Thor:* My evil half-brother, Loki. A messenger from Asgard came to warn me that he escaped from his bonds again and journeyed to Midgard to do everything he could to –
> Captain America: Thor, please.
> *Thor:* What?
> *Captain America:* Just shut up.
> *Thor:* You go to church every Sunday, Captain. What I've got to say's no stranger than that (Millar, & Hitch, 2005, p. 17).

- *Eclectic/Blended* – which is a path within Paganism upon which the adherent will choose the parts of Pagan tradition, and sometimes non-Pagan tradition, to combine them into a worldview and practice that is appropriate and important for them.
- *Hellenism* or *Hellenismos* – which is a reclamation of the beliefs and practices of those who worshipped the ancient Greek gods such as Zeus, Apollo, Hera and Athena. While there is little left in terms of records surrounding the practices of such, the recognition that the gods have an influence on people's lives, and are approachable forms a fundamental background to the beliefs and practices of those who follow the path of Hellenism.

In England and Wales there were over 50,000 Pagans according to the 2011 Census – this number may be an underestimation as there are other groups on the census such as Wicca (approximately 12,000), Druids (5,000) and Witchcraft (around 1,300) who would traditionally be seen as within Paganism, and others such as Shamanism (650) who could be included depending on the definition.

Paganism

The danger in a chapter as short as this in trying to explain the nuances of the different forms of Paganism is that it is impossible. It is important for any teacher who explores Paganism with their pupils to recognise the diversity within the spirituality and strive to be precise in their definitions and articulation. This chapter will necessarily paint with a broad brush, but will hopefully outline expressions of Paganism that will be recognisable and acceptable to many.

Message

As there are many different forms of Paganism, there are many messages that could be discussed. One common theme that may be seen as an identifying feature is the recognition of both the divine feminine and the divine masculine. There is a balance in all things; that extends the nature of the divine, and this will be discussed below (see: Nature of God on p. 271).

A further theme that can be identified is a deep reverence for, and the sacredness of, nature and the earth. Throughout the different forms of Paganism this is a central part of the belief system and practices. One such example that reflects this sacredness of nature is the idea of 'Awen' within Druidry. Awen is a Welsh word that generally means 'poetic spirit' or 'flowing inspiration'. It flows throughout everything, through humanity and also through all of the natural world. It is the inter-connectedness of everything; Joanna van der Hoeven has explored Awen and how it can find expression in life. She suggests that it is an awareness of the "entirety of existence" and as such:

> It is seeing the threads that connect us all. It is the deep well of inspiration that we drink from, to nurture our souls and our world and to give back in joy, in reverence, in wild abandon and in solemn ceremony (2014, p. 20).

This interconnectedness of all living things inspires a deep reverence for, and a desire to live in concert with, the natural world. Van der Hoeven provides a further example of how this might find expression in a Druid's consciousness:

> When out walking in the forest, we can lose our sense of self in order to become the forest. Once we are in the forest we are able to drink deeply from the flow of awen that is all life around us. We become the trees, the deer, the fox, the boulder, the streams and the badger. We can learn so much from this integration. When we are fully immersed in simply 'being', we are fully in the flow of awen. Our footsteps become lighter, our passage becomes barely noticeable (van der Hoeven, 2014, p. 21).

This reverence for, and oneness with, nature enables the Pagan to have a deep respect for every living thing. Awen also moves a person with compassion for all that they find around themselves and is a reflection of the awareness that imbues the flow of nature and the world.

This belief of Awen, while not articulated as such, can be seen to have links with principles and ideas that can be found in other paths of Paganism. Joyce and River Higginbotham (2002) identify the sanctity of nature being linked with three of Paganism's principles:

> Everything contains the spark of intelligence.
> Everything is sacred.
> Each part of the universe can communicate with each other part, and these parts often cooperate for specific ends (see pp. 134–135).

These stand in contrast to the mechanistic view of the universe, and to some extent, the commodification of the world and its resources so prevalent in the modern world. A speech attributed to Native American Chief Seattle in 1855 outlines the interconnectedness of all and the place of humanity in the world from a Pagan perspective:

> Teach your children
> What we have taught our children –
> That the earth is our mother.
> Whatever befalls the earth
> befalls the sons and daughters of the earth. If men spit upon the ground, they spit upon themselves.
> This we know.
> The earth does not belong to us;
> we belong to the earth.
> This we know.

Paganism

> All things are connected
> like the blood which unites one family. All things are connected.
> Whatever befalls the earth
> befalls the sons and daughters of the earth. We did not weave the web of life;
> We are merely a strand in it.
> Whatever we do to the web,
> we do to ourselves ... (Smith, 1887, p. 3).

Elements of all the Pagan paths outline the sacredness of nature. One enduring theme that can be found in Shamanism and Asatru is the concept of a 'world tree'. This tree is sacred, and is a symbol of how different worlds/realms are connected by this tree. In certain forms of Shamanism it is seen as symbolic of Mother Earth, and the health of the tree is transmitted to the rest of nature. In Asatru, Yggdrasil connects the known worlds. The branches and roots of Yggdrasil extend throughout the worlds. The interconnectedness and sacredness of trees as expressed in the myth of the world tree encapsulates the Pagan view of nature.

As the background for Pagan spirituality the sacredness of nature finds expression in some of its most deeply held beliefs and practices. The awareness of the self in relation to the natural world is key; it leads to an attitude that sees the importance of working in concert with it, rather than plundering it to fulfil the immediate and perhaps transitory needs of humanity. In embracing a place within the natural world that recognises an interdependence the flow of the world, the interconnectedness of the forces that appear in the world would be in harmony and balance. How this can be achieved, and how this is shown will be developed below in the sections about the Nature of God, the Nature of humanity and Expression. It is in nature that all three of these elements of Paganism intersect.

Nature of God

Trying to define a description of belief in God that would meet the needs of all Pagans is impossible. It is possible to suggest that Paganism does not teach of a God in the sense of the Abrahamic religion, but it would be possible to identify monotheism, polytheism, pantheism and animism within the traditions found within Paganism.

- *Monotheism*: This is the belief in one God, and while it is common in Abrahamic faiths, and with different understandings within Hinduism and Sikhism, this is not a common belief within Paganism as a whole, especially with a focus on the male and female aspects of the divine. It is possible to explore a concept of God within Paganism that is one deity but expressed in different forms.
- *Polytheism*: The belief in more than one deity. In some belief systems these deities form a pantheon which is a number of deities that are part of the same worldview/culture, e.g. the Greek Pantheon of gods.
- *Pantheism*: This belief suggests that the created world as one represents, and potentially is, deity. There are aspects of the divine within everything and as such all of the universe is God.
- *Animism*: This is the belief that everything in creation is filled with the divine soul. The deity is present everywhere in creation, but in distinction to pantheism where everything shares the same divinity/soul, animism recognises the distinctive nature of the individual soul.

A Pagan understanding of deity is personal and may differ even within traditions and may utilise various aspects of elements of the above. Higginbotham and Higginbotham (2002) identify the third principle of Paganism as: "You are responsible for deciding who or what Deity is for you, and forming a relationship with that Deity" (p. 40). The 'reality' of the deities is also answered in diverse ways within Paganism; for some the deities are real, in the sense that they exist as described, whereas for other Pagans the reality of the deities is with regard to their personification of various powers and forces that will help a person live in harmony.

If we explore a Wiccan approach to Deity, it is possible to recognise two main deities – the male and the female – the God and the Goddess. Although it is traditional to see elements of Wicca prioritising the Goddess, there will be some followers who prefer to focus on the male aspects of Deity. It is important within Wicca to recognise the balance that should be in the world and within everything. Raymond

Paganism

Buckland (2002) suggests that the universal force, the 'Ultimate Deity' is both masculine and feminine and only to make it understandable is it broken down into the masculine and the feminine. This is an important aspect of Wicca as all people contain aspects of both the masculine and the feminine and part of life is to find balance. Other forms of Gardnerian Wicca see the two deities as intermediaries with the Ultimate Deity, thus highlighting the diversity that is found in different forms of Wicca, which is then increased in the wider study and exploration of Paganism generally.

The Horned God/Sun God

The Horned God/Sun God has many qualities that are recognised. He is the ruler of the sun and is thus linked with fire and light. As the sun is seen to be the source of life, the Sun God is also linked with sex and procreation and, as such, is often represented by phallic symbols such as a spear, a sword, a wand, or an arrow. This is the masculine aspect of God and some Pagans will seek to focus on representation of the divine.

As the Horned God he is also depicted with horns as he shares a connection with the animals of the forest. It is this 'picture' of the deity which has most entered the public perception, as he is often portrayed with the head of a beast. This has led some to erroneously conflate elements of Paganism with the worship of Satan. This is untrue as there is nothing demonic about him. Rather, as the Horned God he rules wild animals.

There are various manifestations of the male deity within Wicca and it is possible to see, along with Buckland, that depending on the need of the person they will feel it appropriate to invoke the assistance of different manifestations of the deity. Many Pagans would also recognise the masculine aspect of deity whether it be Osiris, Pan or Cernnunos.

The Goddess

If the God, as the Sky Father, is the source of all life, the Goddess, as the Earth Mother, is the source that sustains life and allows it to flourish. As a nurturing and tending essence, she is also associated with domesticated animals. Her realm of influence includes the Earth and its oceans, as well as the Moon that creates the tide (Chamberlain, 2014, p. 33).

While the masculine aspect of the deity is represented by phallic symbols, the symbols of the divine feminine are usually receptive in kind, such as a cup or a cauldron. Oftentimes because of her link with nature, plants and flowers are used as symbols. The role of the Goddess is perhaps the most unique aspect of Wicca, and indeed of wider Paganism with their focus on the divine feminine. Some have seen this as one of the features that attract people to a Pagan way of life, as the masculine nature of God may been seen to be unfamiliar and unrelatable to some. It is important to note, however, that while a focus on the Goddess is important and for some will be the major feature of their worship, it does not exclude the masculine aspect of the divine:

> The symbolism of the Goddess is not a parallel structure to the symbolism of God the Father. The Goddess does not rule the world. She is the world. Manifest in each of us, *She can be known internally by every individual, in all her magnificent diversity* ... The importance of the Goddess symbol for women cannot be overstressed. The Image of the Goddess inspires women to see ourselves as divine, our bodies as sacred, the changing phases of our lives as holy, our aggression as healthy, our anger as purifying, and our power to nurture and create, but also to limit and destroy when necessary, as the very force that sustains all life. Through the goddess, we can discover our strength, enlighten our minds, own our bodies, and celebrate our emotions. We can move beyond narrow, constricting roles and become whole (Starhawk, 1999, p. 33, emphasis added).

There are often seen to be three aspects to the Goddess, with each related to the life cycle of the earth, and the earth and nature are explicitly linked with the Goddess. The three forms are the Maiden, the Mother, and the Crone, each in turn representing different phases of the moon, as well as the three phases of a woman's life.

Paganism

The Maiden

The Maiden represents the youthful aspect of the Goddess, where she is in the growth period of life. She is most closely associated with springtime, and innocence yet having the responsibilities of a mother. She has been associated and known by various names in different Pagan paths, including Artemis (the daughter of Zeus and Leto, the Goddess of forest, hills and fertility); Brigid (worshipped in Celtic traditions); Freya (Nordic); and Eostre (a Germanic Goddess). This aspect of the Goddess is associated with the waxing of the moon, as it moves towards fullness.

The Mother

The Mother represents the full moon as the Maiden becomes the Mother, and in so doing she gives birth to the fullness of nature. She is most closely associated with the summer and the time of the year where everything is grown and flourishing including the forests, the fields and animals. As such, she is closely associated with fertility, stability, power, life and the earth. The Mother is often seen as the strongest of the three aspects of the Goddess as she is the giver and nurturer of life. She has been, and is, known by different names including: Demeter (Greek); Selene (daughter of the Titans Hyperion and Theia); Gaia (the Earth herself); and Cerridwen (Celtic).

The Crone

The Crone, or the Hag, represents the waning moon and the final stage of a woman's life. She represents the time in a woman's life where child-bearing is at an end, and is linked with Autumn and Winter as the growing season is ending. She is the wisest aspect of the Goddess. Her roles link all of these areas, as she is closely associated with ageing, death, and rebirth as well as visions, prophecy and guidance. She serves an important role in reminding people that death is as much a part of the cycle of life as is birth. She has been known in different ways, such as Hecate (Greek), Baba Yaga (Russian) and Morrigan (Celtic).

In listing these three aspects of the Goddess, it should also be recognised that she is not limited to these representations. Buckland (2002) has suggested that:

> To these aspects we have given names. It would seem that by so doing we are limiting what is, by definition, limitless. But so long as you know, and keep always in the back of your mind, that "It" is limitless, you will find that this is the easiest path to follow. After all, it is pretty difficult to pray to a "Thing'" a Supreme Power, without being able to picture someone in your mind (p. 21).

Druidry and the Northern Tradition

Within Druidry and the Northern Tradition, the concept of 'God' is at the same time polytheistic and animistic. Reflecting their connection with the land and nature it is possible to identify rivers, the sun, oceans, seas, fire, lightning, cold and mountains among others as deities. To imagine them as deities from a Judeo-Christian perspective would be erroneous; rather these are elements and forces in nature with which it is possible to have a connection.

> So ... the forests [are] understood to be gods – and the rivers and the moorlands, the tundra and the desert, deep caverns of gems and fossils, the seas, the planet's atmosphere, the very earth herself. Life is sacred, and each ecosystem is dependent on a delicate balance of life. To mess with that balance is to dishonour the deity the place embodies (Restall Orr, 2004, p. 103).

This is not to discount a universal force that is within everything for both understandings are possible within a Druidic approach to life as Druids seek to reverence the divine.

There are perceptions that could be seen to personify these forces, for example, the Green Man who is the god of growth and vegetation. Further examples from Celtic Druidry are described as follows:

- *Rhiannon* is a figure in Welsh mythology who is seen to be both a horse goddess, but later as a protector of the king as a goddess of sovereignty. There are tales of her in the Mabinogi.
- *Arianrhod* is a figure in the Mabinogi and is seen to be the goddess of fertility, rebirth and the weaving of time and fate.

- *Cerridwen* is associated with many different forces such as the moon and fertility. A tale tells the story of her creation of a potion in a cauldron to transform her son Morfan into a wise boy.
- *Bran* is a giant and a king in Irish mythology. For some, he is associated with the Fisher King of Arthurian legend.
- *Lugh* is a god in Irish mythology who is a warrior and a king. The tale is also told of his defeating an older king to gain knowledge of planting and the harvest.

From other cultures and traditions such as the Northern Tradition, the ancestral gods are personified as Odin, Freya, Loki and Thor from Viking culture. While these are seen as the 'traditional' gods of Druidry:

> It is of these ancestral gods that the myths are told. Still holding glimmers of clues as to the forces of nature that they originally held, the magical threads connecting the people with their energy run through these tales like invisible wires, shimmering with electricity. If we are able to tap into the flow, they offer glorious vistas of understanding, clarifying what feels like generations of relationship between our heritage and the land (Restall Orr, 2004, p. 135).

However, there is seen to be a danger within these tales that the depth that is inherent in them and the personifications of the gods is missed, and they become merely entertainment or inaccessible to others. One story from Asatru or Northern Druidry might help illustrate the dual possibilities in these traditions; the story of Odin and Yggdrasil can be seen as entertainment, or symbolic of deeper truths that can find expression in the Pagan paths. In the Havamai (sayings of the high one) Odin narrates a poem that tells of his search for wisdom in which he hung on Yggdrasil (in actuality the tree is not named but it is assumed to be the world tree) for nine nights with a spear stabbed into him:

> I know that I hung on a windswept tree
> nine long nights,
> wounded with a spear, dedicated to Odin,
> myself to myself,
> on that tree of which no man knows
> from where its roots run (Larrington, 2014, p. 32).

While on the tree he received no drink, but at the end of the ordeal he was able to gain possession of the runes, while screaming and then falling from the tree. Knowing the runes are of divine origin, places a mystical power from the gods in their use:

> The mystical and magical runes are also central to the Northern Traditions mysteries. These are chanted, inscribed as spells and copied in bodily posture, as well being used for divination. Sometimes three or more are combined together to make a bindrune spell ... Runes are a powerful tool, and should be treated as potentially dangerous; they are not merely to be played with (Jennings, 2002, pp. 96-97).

Understanding the efforts that Odin went through to gain knowledge of the runes, means that modern day Pagans are not merely entertained by the story, but also warned.

Shamanism

Gods within Shamanism would be subject to a similar diversity of beliefs. There will be some who focus on an Infinite Force who take on the form of spirits within the 'Otherworld'. While others would see the Otherworldly spirits to be ancestors associated with an area, these spirits are reached out to but not worshipped. MacLellan (1999) has noted that the 'gods' take different forms according to the Shaman. It is the responsibility of the individual Shaman to discover how the spirits manifest themselves. He further explains:

> The shaman stands in this world and the Otherworld. She moves between the two, her spirit family beside her, her community around her. Beneath her feet is the land, feeding her and shaping her flesh, and behind her stand the gods, encompassing mystery and passion to thrill the blood and release her from the world, carrying her beyond the edges of the Otherworld and into the spaces between the worlds. The domain of the Great Mystery stretches from the depths of the earth to the farthest reaches of the stars. The shaman's gods are the voice of the mystery in her life (p. 91).

It is evident from this brief discussion of Shamanism that trying to position an idea of god into more traditional understandings is impossible.

It is evident from the discussion of 'God' in three different expressions of Paganism that it is impossible to note an embracing philosophy that would be found within each expression. Underlying commonalities seem to indicate a reverence for nature and heritage (whether that is the heritage of the land or the individual). The outworking of this will be explored below (see Religious expression) but it indicates a deep connection with, and reverence for all aspects of nature, the world and the universe.

Nature of humanity
Earlier, words attributed to Chief Seattle were outlined, and an aspect of those words clarify the place of humanity in existence:

> We did not weave the web of life;
> We are merely a strand in it.
> (Smith, 1887, p. 3)

If nature and existence is seen as a web, then humanity is one strand within it. Not the most important strand, for no one strand is more important that another. All must work together to maintain the balance that is throughout existence and the natural world. Like all species and kinds of animals and plants, humanity can only be understood in relation to the rest of the natural world, not merely in the esoteric strands of the web of existence, but also in the shared DNA with much of the natural world, or how humanity is shaped by the environment around it. Nature and humanity have a symbiotic relationship, where humans are affected by her, and nature in turn is affected by human interaction with her.

As humans observe nature they can see the natural processes to which they themselves are subject. Just as in the symbolism of the Goddess which can be seen in the moon, so human life goes through a period of waxing, of growth and youthful vigour. This is followed by the full moon, where growth has potentially reached its apex and life flourishes in all its richness. Inevitably this is followed by a period of waning, where what was flourishing begins to lose its vigour, to eventually decay and die. The promise is that at the end of this process, the moon will rise again, and life in all its kinds will go through its various phases again. This is replicated in nature, whether it is the cycle of deciduous trees with the growth of spring, its flourishing in the summer to be followed by the shedding of its leaves in the autumn and winter. Everything is subject to change; humanity as a part of nature is no different.

What does this mean for the eternal nature of the human 'soul' or essence? There are many different views within Paganism. All of life returns to the earth that gave it life. The natural cycle of life means that the physical body becomes part of the natural world when it dies, either through cremation or burial. The possibility of an afterlife in some kind of heaven-like place, for some Pagans, is unnecessary as life is to be lived, and death is just a natural part of the process. In this view of the afterlife this does not negate the influence that people can have beyond the grave. Ancestors and connection with them is a very important part of different Pagan paths.

Within Shamanism the web that ties all of existence together does not just exist in the present, but also connects the present with the past and the future. The Shaman's visits to other worlds could also be encounters with the spirits of ancestors. This 'spirit' does not have to be literal, rather the link could be:

> ... the lingering awareness of past members of your family or society. The ancestors represent a store of the accumulated wisdom of a people, a legacy that the current generation can turn to for advice and guidance. A people survived because they did things in certain ways and it is in the interests of the tribe to maintain those survival traits. Easy contact is usually a feature of continuing traditions rather than broken ones (MacLellan, 1999, p. 64).

Within Druidry, there are three types of ancestors who are revered – the ancestors of the traditions that Druids now practise, the ancestors of the place where a person lives and the ancestors of 'the blood', which includes those from whom we are descended and also those to whom we are related in any way. With the consciousness that all of humanity is inter-related, past, present and future, this knowledge and interconnectedness helps people to develop a positive relationship with all of the people around them, and also an awareness of what they are leaving for future generations. When the ancestors of the place are considered, van der Hoeven suggests:

> Knowing that one day we will also be ancestors of place gives us a responsibility to maintain our human habitats to the best of our abilities. It means looking out not only for ourselves and our community but also the entire planet. Our future ancestors are, after all, the ones who will inherit (van der Hoeven, 2014, p. 34).

However, to view humanity as being only a part of the earth's cycle of birth, growth and death would be to miss aspects of Pagan beliefs. The process of this cycle could also find expression in the idea of reincarnation. The belief that everything has a soul could quite easily lead to a belief in reincarnation, where the soul or spirit of a being transmigrating to another life is certainly a possibility. Raymond Buckland, at different times a practitioner of Gardnerian Wicca and Seax-Wicca, suggests that this is "the most sensible, most logical explanation of much that is found in life" (Buckland, 2002, p. 26). Whether this is working towards a particular end point, or just to enjoy life in all of its varieties and experiences is unclear. One Pagan has suggested:

> As for me, after death I expect to spend a nice long restful time in the land of the Gods and ancestors. Eventually, I expect to be back in this world. I have many past life memories, and they don't lead me to think I'm close to being done ... whatever "done" means. Eventually, I expect to stop coming back and take a place in the great web of Life (Beckett, 2015).

There is also the idea of a heaven-like land that may be thought to be the destination of the soul; for Wiccans it may be Summerland; for Odinists, Valhalla; and for Druids Tir na nOg or Otherworld.

- Summerland is a concept of a plane of existence where spirits go between lives. This time could be short or long. They may be

'watchers' of events on earth, or guardians. It may also be that in the fullness of time when this period of reincarnations ends that all souls will be found there. This could also possibly be the 'place' from where the spirits that are found on earth during Samhain originate.
- Valhalla is a hall of Asgard ruled over by Odin. Half of those who die in battle will find themselves in Valhalla to aid Odin at Ragnarok. The other half find themselves in Fólkvangr, or Freya's field.
- The Otherworld/Tir na nOg (land of the young) is a realm in Celtic mythology of the gods and the dead. It is a place of everlasting youth. In Celtic mythology, Samhain and Beltane are festivals where contact with the Otherworld is possible.

In light of this diversity of belief about the nature of the soul and of humanity in particular, it is evident that there is a core of responsibility that gives a person a purpose in their life. The mythology of the past helps a person understand those characteristics that are most desirable. As part of the web of existence, while a person is free to chart their own course, they are also responsible to those who have come before, those who will come afterwards, and the whole of nature in the present.

Scripture
Unlike most other religious traditions, Pagans generally do not have scripture as is traditionally understood. This is not to say that writings are not important or of value, rather the belief is that there is no canonical work that is seen as authoritative in terms of belief or practice. There are many writings that provide inspiration and can help people find their path, but they are for the personal development of a person's understanding, rather than a dogmatic truth that must be accepted by all.

Within elements of Paganism there is a great reverence for mythology. A shared mythology can help a community come together, and form terms of reference for discussion. The things that are taken from this mythology will differ from person to person, but will form a tie that binds communities together. Mythologies that have been referred to in this chapter include Celtic, Druidic and Norse. Their use is not to suggest that they are historical narratives, rather that they have truths that might inform worldviews and rituals. The story of Yggdrasil may be seen to be particularly evocative; or the stories that are associated with the Green Man.

There have also been modern writers who have caught the imagination of Pagans, and who may be seen to be authoritative in their discussion of beliefs and practices. These include people like Gerald Gardner, Raymond Buckland, Ronald Hutton, Doreen Valiente, Emma Restall Orr, and Starhawk. Each of these would recognise that they are not the final voice in any expression of Paganism. Their writings can help a person, but in the end Paganism is an individual's relationship with nature. This truism is pithily outlined by Isaac Bonewits who when listing suggested reading about Druidry said:

> When in doubt, consult your nearest tree … (Bonewits, 2006, p. 398).

Nature and a person's relationship with her is the authority in life. Other books can help, and can assist with the carrying out of rituals but the written word is less important in Paganism than most other religions.

Religious expression
Magic/Magick[9]

Magic is perhaps the most recognisable aspect of Paganism, and especially Wicca, in the zeitgeist. The popularity of the Harry Potter series, as well as other books such as *The Discovery of Witches* has ensured that the magical aspect of witchcraft remains in the public eye. It is, however, different to that which is seen in films. Magic is a power, but it is much more about the power to control the forces of the universe:

> *"Magic"* is a word used for the phenomena that occur when people consciously participate in the co-creative forces of the Universe, by using the subtle energies of nature to cause desired change in their reality (Chamberlain, 2014, p. 60).

---

[9] Magick is synonymous with magic, but sometimes Pagans prefer to use 'magick' to differentiate it from the elaborate and sleight of hand stage magic.

This definition of magic is supported by Higginbotham and Higginbotham (2002) who suggest that it is:

> ... the actions of many consciousnesses voluntarily working together within an aware and interconnected universe to bring about one or more desired results (p. 164).

The powers of the universe are harnessed, maybe manipulated, to bring about a desired cause of action. Some witches would suggest that they work alongside nature to perform the magic, while others would suggest that they can command magic. In some ways the ideas of black and white magic are rejected, as magic is neither good nor bad except with regard to the purpose it is used for. A poppet doll can be used for positive or negative means.

Although spells and incantations are used, they are also often accompanied by rituals which enable witches to become receptive and in a state ready to perform magic. The first step might be to 'cast a circle'; a circle is a symbol of both the God and the Goddess (the sun and the moon), a symbol of protection (once cast the circle should not be broken until the ritual is complete) and can be seen to be a container for magic power. Within Wicca there are solitary practitioners and those who practise in covens. The process of casting a circle is similar in both, but coven Wiccans may suggest a greater power in there being a number of witches. The circle is cast as in a way such as this:

- The circle is drawn on the earth; this can be done with a natural material such as sea salt, or maybe candles, or rocks. Other magical objects filled with magical elements may also be used within the circle. As mentioned earlier, people should not leave the circle once it has been cast, without performing an action such as a circle cutting spell which provides a doorway that can be used.
- The designated witch will go to each of the four directions, and invoke the energy of a particular element such as earth, water, fire, etc., and also a deity if so desired. At the conclusion of this 'Calling the quarters". the circle is ready for the ritual to be performed.
- There are various actions that can also be performed to 'build up the power' of the circle. This may be through physical actions such as

dancing, or through the use of a tool. This will vary from ritual to ritual, and from group to group. It may also include the use of magic tools such as:
- A broom which may be used to clear the clutter from the space before the circle is cast; it symbolises purity and can be used to ward off negative energies.
- The altar, usually made of wood, on which the tools and objects used in the rituals are placed.
- A wand, as a straight line, can be used to direct the energy that is being used. Usually made of wood it represents the element of air, and harnesses the power of the God. It can also be used to draw the circle during the casting.
- The cauldron, a symbol of water, is used to contain magically charged herbs that will be used in a potion, or may just contain water for scrying (foretelling the future).
- A knife, which is usually used to draw images in the air and in the earth. It is not usually used to summon a deity, as it would be seen to be a threatening gesture to invoke a deity with a knife.
- A cup or chalice, which is usually placed on the altar containing wine to symbolise the Goddess.
- A pentacle, which may be worn or placed on the altar. It is an object that adds strength, and protects from negative energies.
- Candles, which represent the element of fire.
- Crystals, which as they come directly from the earth, can have magical properties that add energy and power.

- The ritual itself may include a casting of a spell, or it could also be utilised for a rite of passage such as handfasting. There are different ways of casting a spell, whether it is through an incantation; or through a tying of a cord. Buckland (2002) suggests a candle burning ritual to attract the love of another. A specifically coloured candle should be used to signify the qualities that the person desires in a loved one, and one candle to signify the person for whom the spell is cast. Specific words are said, before the candles are blown out. Each day the candles are moved closer to one another.

There are seen to be different types of magic that can be performed, as described below:

- *Imitative* is a kind of magic that re-enacts the desired action. This could be pictorially as in the drawing of a successful hunt on cave walls; or using actions, or possibly through the use of objects like poppet dolls. This ritual will enable the desired action to happen.
- *Transference* where positive or negative energy is transferred out or into one's self. Examples may be transferring an ailment into a degradable object which is placed in the ground to decompose. It may also be burning a piece of paper on which has been written something that needs to be forgotten.
- *Shamanic* is a trance state where other realms and spirits are visited. It could also be the sending of the spirit form of a person (a fetch) to another realm to heal or gain information.
- *Talismanic* involves the making and use of a talisman, to imbue it with magical power for a specific purpose.
- *Ceremonial* is magic that is generally ritualistic and performed in groups (though not always so). This repeats certain ritual actions to enact change for individuals and the universe.
- *Chaos* magic recognises that the forces around us are chaotic, and beginning from this premise the rituals are designed to bend and manipulate the chaos to their will.
- *Musical* magic as dance and music are seen as ways to build up magical power and energy
- *Divination* is the 'reading' of a person's future using objects such as Tarot cards, scrying, runes, or a crystal ball.
- *Sigil/Rune* is the use of symbols and letters to draw power for the desired magical effects. The use of a bind rune enables different runes to be used together to have different energy to the runes themselves. As an aside, the symbol for Bluetooth™ is a bind rune of the initials for the Norse King Harold Bluetooth, using his initials Hagall and Bjarkan. King Harold was known as a uniter; and so computer and wireless technologies are united through Bluetooth™.

The casting of spells, and the rituals associated with them, seem to be very different to the way they are presented in films. What is important is to recognise that magic is working in harmony with nature to effect change. While some will try to bend nature to their will, the majority of witches will work in harmony with nature to perform magic. This is not to say that there are not curses that are cast, there are.

Rites of Passage

As part of the rituals outlined above, the circle that has been cast may be used to celebrate events in the lives of Wiccans. This ritual could be an initiation, a marriage or handfasting, the welcoming of a child or the marking of a particular phase in the life of a person such as adolescence to recognise the cycle of life. The rituals mirror the cycle that is found throughout nature.

- *Baby naming/Welcoming* – There is a debate within Paganism about whether anyone should become a Pagan before the age of eighteen. Whatever someone's view, the welcoming of a baby can be performed to ask for protection for the child, and welcome it to the world. For this protection the child may be presented to the deities as a way of introducing it to the natural world. There may also be a request for the five elements (earth, air, fire, water and spirit) to protect the child. It is also an opportunity to welcome the child into the community that may offer support as the child grows.
- *Puberty* – The main rites of adolescence generally surround girls. There are not many rituals that mark the puberty of a boy, though they may be practised. Oftentimes this rite is used to recognise the first menstruation of a girl. This is done in way that recognises it as a natural and healthy part of life, rather than it being a taboo topic. This stands in contrast to some religions which do not allow menstruating women to be a part of ritual worship.
- *Initiation* – This will vary from path to path, and even within specific paths the rites will differ, and some will not have any. A number of paths keep their initiation rites secret, but they may include oaths, or a series of questions to which there are prepared and ritualistic answers. It may include the initiate bathing beforehand and being given a new robe. This process, whatever form it takes, is seen as a rebirth into a new way of life, and sometimes a new name is taken. This new name may have even been chosen at birth by Pagan parents but not revealed until the time of initiation.

- *Dedications* – These are similar to initiations, but are often completed by individuals for themselves where declarations are made about the path that the person has chosen to follow. There is debate about the efficacy of individual dedications, though most people would accept them.
- *Handfasting* – This is the marriage ceremony within Paganism; in the UK these are not recognised as legal ceremonies and so the participants may have a legal ceremony in addition to the handfasting; others are not concerned about the legal process and see handfasting as the sign of commitment that they need to make. This ceremony does not involve the 'giving away' of the bride as she is her own person and does not belong to anyone to be given. The handfasting utilises the loose tying the wrists of the couple before they jump over a broomstick, fire or candle. The couple will usually write their own vows. These vows can last for as long as the couple decide, and can be renewed at any time.
- *Handparting* – This ceremony is not always used, but a handparting could be engaged with to mark the divorce or separation of a couple. It is a time to remember what was had, seek healing and look forward. These ceremonies are linked with autumn, the time for letting go and reflecting on what has passed.
- *Croning/Saging* – The marking of the menopause for a woman and the entering of the final part of their life for a man (maybe on retirement). It involves a marking of celebration and marking of all that has come before, and looking forward to a time of rest where they can enjoy the fruits of all that has come before.
- *Funerals* – A Pagan funeral will usually involve an eco-friendly burial using coffins sometimes made from wicker. The death of a person is recognised as a natural part of the cycle of life and funerals will utilise aspects that celebrate the life and legacy of the deceased. In some forms of Paganism, a talking stick will be passed around for people to share their memories and the influence that the person has had.

Festivals

Among many Pagan paths, eight festivals are celebrated to mark the cycle of the solar and lunar year. The Pagan year tends to follow the seasonal calendar as the earth rotates around the sun. Four of the festivals take place at the winter and summer solstices, and the spring and autumn equinoxes. The other four 'earth' festivals take place near the mid-points, or cross-quarters between these other four festivals. There are various traditions that trace the customs associated with the celebration of these festivals to Celtic, Germanic or Anglo-Saxon traditions. The linking of the God and the Goddess within Wicca with the Sun and the Moon also provides reason to celebrate the different phases of the year that mark different elements of the divine. Starhawk (1999) has suggested that:

> The rituals of the eight solar holidays, the Sabbats, are derived from the myth of the Wheel of the Year. The Goddess reveals her threefold aspects: as Maiden, She is the virgin patroness of birth and initiation; as Nymph, She is the sexual temptress, lover, siren, seductress; as Crone, She is the dark face of life, which demands death and sacrifice. The God is son, brother, lover, who becomes his own father: the eternal sacrifice eternally reborn into new life (p. 53).

Although elements of the festivals are ancient, the combination into the wheel of eight cannot be traced back before the 1950s and today's celebrations will contain some more modern influences. The eight Sabbats, or festivals, are:

- Samhain, All Hallow's Eve, Hallowmas: 31 October or 1 November.
- Yule, Winter Solstice: 20, 21, 22 or 23 December.
- Imbolc, Brigid, Candlemas, Imbolg or Brigid's Day: 1 or 2 February.
- Eostre, Spring Equinox, Ostara, or Oestarra: 20, 21, 22 or 23 March.
- Beltane, May Eve, Beltaine, Bealtaine, or May Day: 30 April or 1 May.
- Litha, Mid-Summer Solstice, or Midsummer: 20, 21, 22 or 23 June.
- Lughnasad, Lughnasagh, Loafmas or Lammas: 1 August.
- Mabon, Autumn Equinox, or Harvest Home: 20, 21, 22, or 23 September.

Samhain
Samhain (pronounced Sow-un) is the end of the Pagan year and translated means 'Summer's end'. It symbolises the beginning of the

time of the year where the influence of the sun (the God) has receded and the moon (the Goddess) is pre-eminent. It marks the time in the year when agricultural societies are making decisions about how much produce to store, as it marks the end of harvest festival. It is a festival that remembers a person's ancestors, and others who are dead. During Samhain it is believed that the veil between the worlds is at its thinnest and the dead may return to visit. During the festival, in Pagan homes, a place at the table is set for any ancestors who may wish to join the family/community for the festivities. As an expression of the significance of ancestors within Paganism this is an important festival. Elements of the celebration may be rather solemn, as the dead are remembered and thanks are given for their lives and influence.

There are also opportunities to join in with the traditional Hallowe'en activities. Jack-o'-lanterns, for example, were originally carved to guide the spirits of those who had returned to the earth during the festival. Trick or treating developed from the old Pagan tradition of leaving food out for the ancestors who were to visit.

Yule

Yule is the Mid-Winter Solstice. This marks the mid-point of the dark part of the year, and from this point sunlight will increase until the Summer Solstice. In some traditions this is the time of year when the sun is reborn, and is seen to be a festival of light.

There are many traditions associated with Yule such as:

- The burning of a Yule log to symbolise the increasing of the light during the winter. Pagans may spread some of its ashes over the fields, or keep part of it to light the following year's Yule log.
- The use of Mistletoe as a symbol of fertility.
- The utilisation of evergreen leaves/trees, such as holly, remind Pagans of the promise that new life will come again in the spring.

All festivals in the Wheel of the Year symbolise, and remind Pagans of, the cycle of life to which all things are subject. The Wheel itself marks each point, but it helps people keep in mind the processes that the earth is going through, and also provides hope that the darkness will pass, and light will come. During the winter the earth is seen to rest, in preparation for the new life of the spring.

Imbolc

Imbolc is the mid-point between the Winter Solstice and the Spring Equinox and a time to remind Pagans that the light is growing. Many candles are lit in memory of the Celtic Goddess of fire, Brigid, and there may be candlelit processions or lighting of fires. As people reflect on the leaving behind of the winter, they may consider a major theme of the festival to be purification, a time to declutter, both mentally and spiritually, and prepare for the new life of the spring.

Coinciding with Imbolc is the north American tradition of Groundhog Day – a day that tests or foretells the coming of spring.

Eostre

At the Spring Equinox, the influence of the sun has grown to the point where the length of the day matches the length of the night. Light and darkness are completely balanced, and as such, it marks the beginning of the light half of the year. The new life that Spring brings is celebrated in this festival, as trees are beginning to bud and flowers have begun to bloom. Many of the traditions associated with the Spring Equinox celebrate new life, renewal of life and fertility. The most common symbol is that of an egg which reminds people of new life and fertility. It was also the symbol of the Anglo-Saxon goddess Eostre.

As with all of the festivals of Paganism it is important to recognise them within the Pagan tradition. The beliefs that they remember and express are Pagan, but it would be interesting as an aside to recognise the traditions that have survived into Christian celebrations, whether it is the eggs of Easter, or the lighting of candles at Candlemas (Imbolc) which is also the feast day of St Brigid. As a modern expression of Paganism it may also be of interest to look at the reciprocal interplay in the celebrations. The influence can be seen to work both ways (Cush, 2015).

Beltane
Also known as May Day, Beltaine finds its celebration between the Spring Equinox and the Summer Solstice.

> This is an exuberant holiday that celebrates sexuality, fertility, and the unfolding of spring. It is a time when the divine male and female energies come together in a union whose fruits are ourselves, the crops, and livestock. The month of May was set aside to honour this "divine marriage" (Higginbotham and Higginbotham, 2002, p. 21).

One symbol of this festival is the Maypole dance – the Maypole itself is a phallic symbol of fertility and of the masculine aspect of the divine. The streamers that are used by the two sets of dancers (who dance in opposite direction) weave together and symbolise the weaving together of life and death. Other traditions include the crowning of the May Queen who celebrates spring time and youth, and the wearing of flower crowns.

Litha
The Mid-Summer Solstice celebrates the time of year when the sun is at its strongest and marks the mid-point of the light half of the year. It is a celebration of strength, growth, creativity and abundance. The night before the solstice is known as Midsummer's Eve and is a night of strong magic; in some traditions it is believed that fairies are particularly free on this evening to move around the land. It is also a time to rest before the work of the harvest begins.

Lughnasagh
Lughnasagh takes place between the Summer Solstice and the Autumn Equinox. It is the first of the harvest festivals. It's alternative name 'Lammas' means 'Loaf mass' and celebrates the first grains of the harvest that are able to be baked as bread. The name used here, 'Lughnasagh', remembers the Celtic God Lugh who is said to have fought a much older god to gain the secrets of planting, growing and harvesting.

Paganism

There are many games and celebrations including the baking and sharing of bread. In some traditions the sacrifice of the Corn King is remembered as bread is broken up over the land. The Corn King was killed and his remains (corn) are spread across the land.

Mabon
The Autumn Equinox is known as Mabon and symbolises the ending of the light half of the year, and the beginning of the dark half. From this point onwards the nights will be longer than the days. Here the influence of the sun begins to wane, and the earth begins to rest after a period of growth and flourishing. It is the second harvest festival. This is often celebrated with a feast using the fruits of the earth which may include wine to remember the harvesting of the grapes. It is also a time for sorting and clearing out so that the mind is ready for a time of reflection and peace in the winter. Mabon himself is a Celtic figure in Arthurian mythology, and is linked to a divine mother and son.

Ideas for the RE Classroom
Jacqueline Bolton, in a Farmington Report into the teaching of Paganism in schools, suggested different ways to infuse elements into the classroom curriculum. These ideas seem to be a good start, but there are also other areas that could be suggested. Areas that could be explored in the classroom, outside of a systematic study of Paganism include the following:

- A unit of work that is focussed around pagan religions is a way to introduce the topics of "animism, magic, myths, totem poles, astrology, ... and divination" (Bolton, 1999, p. 9).
- Including myths and legends, especially with regard to creation, or British myths that have helped construct identity.
- The Wheel of the Year in any discussion of festivals. This would be particularly pertinent in exploring the Pagan roots of Hallowe'en or elements of the celebration of Christmas.
- An exploration of the meanings behind the days of the week, whether it is the day of Thor or Woden.

- Rites of passage are especially important if teaching children of Pagan families.
- Sacred sites throughout the UK that have links to ancient rites, rituals and events. There are in addition to stone circles:

    … holy wells and hills (Silbury Hill and Glastonbury Tor) chalk figures (Cerne Abbas and the white horses) and caves. In many older local churches, Pagan carvings such as green men can be found and visited (Bolton, 1999, p. 10).

- Environmental issues. This is perhaps the clearest place in which Paganism can contribute to the classroom at all ages. If the earth is a living entity and all living beings are connected, then what does this mean for environmental responsibility?
- The use of art to explore beliefs. Whether this is the symbology of runes, or Shamanic art that is used in a journey to the Otherworlds, each have rich symbolism that help enrich exploration of art and its spirituality.
- The exploration of the feminine aspect of the divine. This stands in contrast to aspects of many religions, and provides a good basis for issues of feminist and feminine spiritualities.
- The beliefs and history of the British Isles. In exploring the 'native' beliefs in the history of the British Isles, pupils will be able to see the impact that these beliefs and practices had, and continue to have.
- With many different expressions of Pagan pathways, it might be desirable to draw comparisons between them. For example, choosing three paths and their views of God will help pupils to crystallise the unique and common beliefs between paths. A way to do this is through a specifically designed outline (Figure 11.1), that can be edited to highlight the similarities and differences between any three things:

Useful websites
www.paganfed.org
www.wicca.com
www.druidry.org
www.shamanism.com
www.odinbrotherhood.com

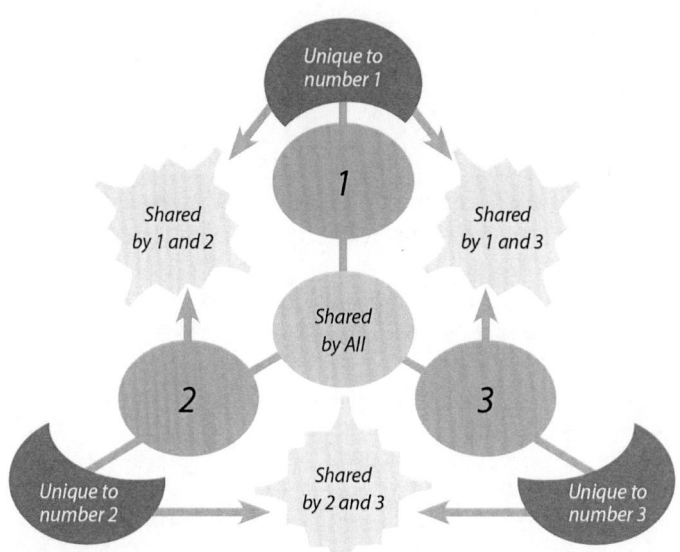

Figure 11.1 – Similar and different: Paganism and God.

Reference list

Beckett, John (2015). *Thoughts on death and afterlife*. Retrieved from https://www.patheos.com/blogs/johnbeckett/2015/10/pagan-thoughts-on-death-and-the-afterlife.html

Bolton, J. (1999). *An investigation into the place of paganism within RE: A teacher's guide. Farmington Fellows' reports on teaching and training*, TT33. Oxford, UK: Farmington Institute.

Bonewits, Isaac (2006). *Bonewits's essential guide to druidism*. New York, NY: Citadel Press.

Buckland, Raymond (2002) [1986]. *Buckland's complete book of witchcraft*. Woodbury, MN: Llewellyn Publications.

Carr-Gomm, Philip (1991). *The elements of the Druid tradition*. Shaftesbury, UK: Element Books.

Chamberlain, Lisa (2014). *Wicca for beginners. A guide to Wiccan beliefs, rituals, magic, and witchcraft*. UK: Chamberlain Publications.

Cush, Denise (Ed.) (2015). *Celebrating Planet Earth, a Pagan/Christian conversation: First steps in interfaith dialogue*. Winchester, UK; Washington USA: Moon Books.

Glass, Justine (1973). *Witchcraft: The sixth sense*. Chatsworth, CA: Wilshire Book Co.

Halifax, Joan (1979). *Shamanic voices*. New York, NY: E. P. Dutton.

Higginbotham, Joyce, & Higginbotham, River (2002). *Paganism: An introduction to earth-centered religions* (8th ed.). Woodbury, MN: Llewellyn Publications.

Jennings, Peter (2002). *Pagan paths*. London, UK: Random House.

Larrington, Carolyne (Trans.) (2014). *The Poetic Edda* (2nd ed.). Oxford, UK: Oxford World's Classics.

MacLellan, Gordon (1999). *Shamanism*. London, UK: Piatkus.

Millar, Mark, & Hitch, Bryan (2005). *The Ultimates 2, Volume 1: Gods and monsters*. New York, NY: Marvel.

Restall Orr, Emma (2004). *Living Druidry: Magical spirituality for the wild soul*. London, UK: Piatkus.

Smith, Henry A. (1887, 29 October). Early reminiscences. Number Ten. Scraps from a Diary. Chief Seattle – A gentleman by instinct – his native eloquence. Etc., Etc. *Seattle Sunday Star*, p. 3.

Starhawk (1999). *The spiral dance. 20th anniversary edition*. San Francisco, CA: Harper.

van der Hoeven, Joanna (2014). *Pagan portals – The Awen alone: Walking the path of the solitary Druid*. Alresford, UK: Moon Books.

CHAPTER 12

RASTAFARI

Chapter Outline
What is Rastafari?
Message
Nature of God
Nature of humanity
Scripture
Religious expression

What is Rastafari?
Within society, Rastafari[10] is defined by its place in popular culture. Symbols of Rasta identity will often be appropriated on T-shirts or by musicians, and the things that people know about Rastafari will usually be Bob Marley, dreadlocks, and the coloured hats of red, black, yellow and green. Indeed, this type of representation, along with a Jamaican accent, found its way on to children's television and the character of Rastamouse. The identity of Rastafari is sometimes stripped of its religiosity to a cultural expression. This approach to Rastafari is to divorce the practice from the belief, and produces a sterile picture that is unreflective of the depth of Rasta spirituality.

Rastas take their name from Tafari Makonnen, the pre-coronation name of Emperor Haile Selassie I of Ethiopia. Ras is a title that means

---

10 A note on the use of nomenclature. Although Rastafarianism is a term used by observers of the religion, and some practitioners it is seen by some to be a divisive term. Cashmore (2013) outlines that: "Almost every contemporary commentator on the movement has used this insensitive term without considering the discipline of doctrine and organisation it seems to connote … Ras Tafari most certainly does not warrant the attachment of 'ism' to its name" (p. 8). In light of this, and the fact that the terms Rastafari, Rasta and Rastafarian seem to be acceptable terms to all involved in the religion, this book avoids the term Rastafarianism.

'duke' or 'prince' and was put with Tafari's given name. It would be wrong to identify Haile Selassie as the founder of Rastafari, rather he is seen within the community to be the embodiment of Rasta principles.

Rastafari developed in Jamaica during the 1930s following the coronation of Haile Selassie as Emperor of Ethiopia. One of the first to preach a Rasta ideology was Leonard Howell who taught that Haile Selassie was the Second Coming of Jesus foretold by the Bible. Howell's message was rooted in Christianity, but was also seen to be anti-colonial in nature drawing on African ideas and identity, offering an approach different to the European Christianity that was found in Jamaica and surrounding islands. It was a message of black empowerment, and a policeman who witnessed Howell's first declaration of Haile Selassie in 1933 recorded:

> The Lion of Judah has broken the chain, and we of the black race are now free. George the Fifth is no more our King ... Ras Tafair [sic] is King of Kings and Lord of Lords. The Black people must not look to George the Fifth as their King anymore – Ras Tafair is their king (cited in Murrell et al., 1998, p. 38).

Howell wanted to formulate a spiritual practice that would give a political voice to Jamaica's poorest workers. He drew on the teachings of Marcus Garvey whose organisation, the Universal Negro Improvement Association (UNIA)'s, stated goal was to unite those of the African race with their homeland in Africa from which they had been forcibly removed. Garvey is revered as a prophet by some Rastas. In the *New York Times* of 3 August 1920:

> We shall organize the four hundred million Negroes of the world into a vast organization to plant the banner of freedom on the great continent of Africa ... If Europe is for Europeans, then Africa is for the black people of the world (Garvey, 3 August 1920).

Howell faced opposition from authorities and was imprisoned for sedition. On his release he organised a community in Pinnacle, this was to be a temporary home for those wishing to repatriate to Ethiopia.

It soon developed into a place for those in society who had little voice and few rights.

The identification of Howell as the 'First Rasta' is controversial; at the same time as Howell's teaching and establishment of community there were at least three other Rasta organisations in Jamaica. Stephen A. King highlighted that among differences, there were four shared beliefs:

> First, all four groups condemned Jamaica's colonial society. Second, all believed repatriation to Africa was the key to over-coming oppression. Third, all of these early groups advocated nonviolence. Finally, all four groups worshipped the divinity of Haile Selassie (King, 1998, p. 50).

This highlights the disparate nature and the lack of a central authority, that characterises Rastafari. Over the years, many different strands and expressions of Rasta have developed and it is difficult to tie all of the groups together. One example of this diversity is in the understanding of the relationship between Jesus Christ and Haile Selassie. As has been outlined, many believe that he is the Second Coming of Jesus Christ. As part of this, Selassie's removal from Ethiopia after the invasion of Italy in 1935, followed by his return in 1941 is related to the fulfilment of biblical prophecy:

> I saw heaven standing open and there before me was a white horse, whose rider is called Faithful and True. With justice he judges and wages war. His eyes are like blazing fire, and on his head are many crowns. He has a name written on him that no one knows but he himself. He is dressed in a robe dipped in blood, and his name is the Word of God. The armies of heaven were following him, riding on white horses and dressed in fine linen, white and clean. Coming out of his mouth is a sharp sword with which to strike down the nations. "He will rule them with an iron sceptre." He treads the winepress of the fury of the wrath of God Almighty. On his robe and on his thigh he has this name written: **king of kings and lord of lords**. And I saw an angel standing in the sun, who cried in a loud voice to all the birds flying in midair, "Come, gather together for the great supper of God ..." (Revelation 19:11–17 emphasis added)

Other Rastas see him as the second person of the Trinity, along with the Creator and the Holy Spirit; a further discussion of the place and identity of Haile Selassie I can be found below (see: Nature of God).

In striving to avoid emulating the structures of Babylon (see below: Message), hierarchies are avoided within Rastafari; though this approach is also reflective of the individualistic nature of religion that is advocated alongside the importance of IandI (see Nature of humanity on p. 307). There are groups/mansions that can be seen to have developed under the umbrella term of Rastafari. Some are listed below:

> *Twelve Tribes of Israel* is a group that was started by Vernon Carrington, a person who declared himself the reincarnation of the prophet Gad, in 1968. They can be seen to be the most 'Christian' of all of the various manifestations of Rastafari, believing Jesus to be the only Messiah. As such they are often described as 'Christian Rastas'. While Haile Selassie is important and a king by divine right, he is not regarded as the second coming of Jesus. Within the community there are twelve groups which are divided according to the month of the Hebrew calendar in which the person was born. Bedasse (2010) has suggested that it is the largest structured Rastafari group. They can be seen to be the least Afrocentric of Rasta groups, in the sense that their identity as the Twelve Tribes is pre-eminent, and as such people of other races can be found within the Twelve Tribes. Its most famous adherent was Bob Marley who was of the tribe of Joseph because he was born in February (though he also belonged to the Ethiopian Orthodox Church and got many of his teachings from Nyahbinghi). Each month/tribe has associated mental practice/function, colour and body part as detailed in Table 12.1.
>
> *Bobo Ashanti* (also *Bobo Dreads*) was founded in 1958 by Emanuel Edwards who was often addressed as Prince Emanuel I or King Emanuel I in recognition of his importance to the community. He established a commune in Bull Bay where different members assumed different roles in the community. Outside of these functional roles, male members are assigned as either priests (who conduct the religious rites) or prophets (who explore the principles of Rastafari in great depth). Since the death of Edwards, more Bobo Ashanti Rastas have lived outside of the commune (while regarding it as a place of pilgrimage). The supremacy

Rastafari

Table 12.1 – The Twelve Tribes and their associated mental practice/function, colour and body part.

Tribe	Month	Mental function	Colour	Body part
Reuben	April/Nisan	Strength	Silver	Eyes
Simeon	May/Iyar	Faith	Gold	Ears
Levi	June/Sivan	Will	Purple	Nose
Judah	July/Tammuz	Praise	Brown	Mouth and heart
Issachar	August/Av	Zeal	Yellow	Hands
Zebulun	September/Elus	Order and Compassion	Pink	Stomach
Dan	October/Tishri	Judgement	Blue	Back
Gad	November/Heshvan	Power	Red	Reproductive organs
Asher	December/Kislev	Understanding	Grey	Thighs
Naphtali	January/Tevet	Love	Green	Knees
Joseph	February/Shevat	Imagination	White	Calves
Benjamin	March/Adar	Elimination	Black	Feet

of Black Africans over white Europeans is an essential aspect of Bobo Ashanti, as is the identification of the Trinity: Haile Selassie I is God, Edwards is seen as Christ and Marcus Garvey is seen as a prophet. Followers of Bobo Ashanti are often identified by their long flowing robes and their wearing of turbans.

Nyabinghi is not a specific organisation but a loosely held grouping of Rastafari who tend to emphasise the teachings that originally developed in the 1940s. Cashmore (2013) has described their beginning:

> 1935 saw the appearance of Nyabinghi, a vehemently anti-white wing of the cult which had drawn inspiration from a misinformed article in the Jamaica Journal which told of a 'secret society to destroy whites' whose members afforded Haile Selassie messianic status (2013, p. 25).

They are, perhaps, the largest group of Rastafari and will wear dreadlocks alongside holding central the belief of Haile Selassie I as God and the second coming of Jesus.

The beliefs and practices articulated in this chapter will explore aspects that will generally be held in common by Rastafari, but a blanket statement is impossible in such a diverse and individual religious expression.

Message

There are many elements to the Rastafari message, which were explored in the introduction. It is a religion of black empowerment; it seeks to reclaim black identity in such a way as to throw off the shackles of what is seen to be white imperialism. In *The Promised Key*, a writing attributed to Leonard Howell (cited in Murrell et al., 1998), there is the suggestion that 'Anglo-Saxon' (meaning white) religious organisations are "a hypocritical political and religious system designed to keep the people in ignorance of their wicked course". The subjection of recent black history was because "King Alpha was wroth with us the Black people and had polluted our inheritance for 2,520 years and had given us into the hands of the Anglo-Saxon white people" (in Murrell et al., 1998, p. 367). The cultural and religious imperialism that Howell identified formed the basis for a religion that spoke, and speaks, to the reclamation of black identity.

Rastafari can also be seen to be a social movement. It sought the reclamation of black identity and the establishment of 'Black Supremacy' where the place of the downtrodden would be elevated. In discussing 'Black Supremacy' in *The Promised Key* the indication seems to be that it is about the raising of the status of the African rather than the subjugation and rejection of the white race. Howell suggests that "Black Supremacy will promote the mortals of every shade according to our power to go" (in Murrell et al., 1998, p. 367). There is a potential within Rasta teaching to view other races as inferior, in line with some of the teachings of Marcus Garvey, but this is, by and large, not the attitude taken by the majority of Rastafari. Having suffered injustice they are less likely to replicate it.

This idea of black liberation is inextricably linked to the messiahship of Haile Selassie I. For a messianic figure to be needed, there had to be something from which people needed liberation. In Rastafari terms the rescue was needed from Babylon. Babylon is a

Rastafari

biblical reference and image symbolic of the 'world' and the idea of the Jews, as the chosen people of God, who found themselves in bondage to Babylon. Hence the Psalm which remembered better days when Israel was free and pointed to the defeat of Babylon:

> By the rivers of Babylon, there we sat down, yea, we wept, when we remembered Zion.
> We hanged our harps upon the willows in the midst thereof.
> For there they that carried us away captive required of us a song; and they that wasted us required of us mirth, saying, Sing us one of the songs of Zion.
> How shall we sing the Lord's song in a strange land?
> If I forget thee, O Jerusalem, let my right hand forget her cunning.
> If I do not remember thee, let my tongue cleave to the roof of my mouth; if I prefer not Jerusalem above my chief joy.
> Remember, O Lord, the children of Edom in the day of Jerusalem; who said, Rase it, rase it, even to the foundation thereof.
> O daughter of Babylon, who art to be destroyed; happy shall he be, that rewardeth thee as thou hast served us.
> Happy shall he be, that taketh and dasheth thy little ones against the stones (Psalm 137).

This Psalm speaks of the bondage that Jews/Africans found and find themselves in, and also of a future time when Babylon will be destroyed. The applicability of such a text to the Rasta understanding of their identity as descendants/reincarnations of the exiled people of Israel, how history is being repeated and how they can find liberation is the setting of the words to a song 'By the Rivers of Babylon'. This Rastafari song was written and recorded by Brent Dowe and Trevor McNaughton (The Melodians) in 1970, and popularised in Europe by Boney M in 1978. In the original version of the song by the Melodians, the references to the Lord were changed to 'Far-I' and 'King Alpha', both references in Rasta theology to Haile Selassie I.

Babylon thus becomes, in Rastafari teaching, reference to any system that seeks to subjugate the rights of individuals. Murrell suggests that rather than sitting and accepting the lot and the promise of a better future, a Rasta reading of Psalm 137 calls a person to immediate action:

> Psalm 137 thus becomes a call not to capitulate in silence to Babylon or assimilate its cultural values; not to wallow in the mire of hopelessness and self-pity or wish for the former days of the nation's glory; not to offer imprecations to a God who is not there for Rastas, silent, hidden (deus absconditus), and indifferent to the people of African descent; but a militant song to rub Babylon's nose in the dust – to chant down Babylon in "ah ridim" – and effect social change (Murrell, 2000).

What this meant for Rastafari is multifaceted; Cashmore recognises this in the suggestion that:

> ... some regarded it as a mandate for attacks on any manifestation of Babylon, whether the police, store owners or property; some understood their role as more passive, comforting themselves in the belief that Jah would reconstruct society and elevate them from their lowly positions. In between these two there lay a plethora of variegated responses organised around Rastafarian principles (2013, p. 94).

The reality of liberation is made possible through the messianic figure of Haile Selassie I. He inaugurated a time in which 'Zion' could be found and Babylon destroyed. Ennis Edmonds has suggested that the Rastafari ideal of Zion stands in stark contrast to the idea of Babylon:

> In contrast to the Babylonian West, with its alienating and oppressive social institutions, Rastas invoke the term 'Zion' as the ideal to which they aspire ... it represents justice, harmony, and community ... The positing of Africa as Zion, the true home of Rastas and all black people, speaks to a desire to escape the domination and degradation experienced under the Babylonian system of the West (Edmonds, 2012, pp. 40–41).

For some Rastas, the reality of Zion is found within Ethiopia and repatriation there is seen to be an ideal. For others the repatriation is the restoration of African identity and pride, which is seen to be most important and more realistic in the living of a Rasta way of life today.

Rastafari

Nature of God

Jah is a contraction of the Hebrew name for God, Yahweh, often rendered in English as Jehovah. In Rastafari God is Jah. Jah is both transcendent, meaning that he is above and beyond the world; yet at the same time Jah is immanent and involved in the day to lives of people. Thus every circumstance is an opportunity to commune with, and experience, Jah. Jah is found throughout the natural world and can be experienced in nature:

> The word "nature" implies not only the cosmic creative force, "the light of this world, the first without last, the beginning without end" and the fruits of that creation, but also the inner power and vitality of all created things, including man and the spirit of man, and the force of sex (Kitzinger, 1966, p. 37).

In Rastafari belief, it can be seen that many believe that Haile Selassie I is God. Linked with this belief, and the idea that humanity is created in the image of God, then the assumption is that God is black. In some forms of Rasta there is the establishment of the Trinity with Haile Selessie I as God; in other forms he is the Holy Spirit. Writing when Haile Selassie I was still alive, Kitzinger (1966) outlined the difference between the Rasta God and the Christian God:

> Rastafarians speak scornfully of the white man's God in the sky and laugh about the Jesus of Sunday School books. "They say that Jesus is a white man with blue eyes and He lives in the sky," said one religious leader amidst hilarious laughter, "but you have to die before you can see that God ... Yet the Bible say ... 'I am a God of the living.' Not a God of the dead!" They do not see that a God in Ethiopia is just as ridiculous, but this may be partly because to them the physical person of the Emperor is but one manifestation of the Godhead (p. 36).

Jah had become for Rastafari intimately involved in their lives, and just as the Old Testament God he had a chosen people of Black Africans as the reincarnation of Israel. He would destroy Babylon, the enemies of the black people. He is the fulfilment of the prophecy of Revelation 19:

> And I saw heaven opened, and behold a white horse; and he that sat upon him was called Faithful and True, and in righteousness he doth

> judge and make war ... And out of his mouth goeth a sharp sword, that with it he should smite the nations: and he shall rule them with a rod of iron: and he treadeth the winepress of the fierceness and wrath of Almighty God. And he hath on his vesture and on his thigh a name written, King Of Kings, And Lord Of Lords ...
>
> And I saw the beast, and the kings of the earth, and their armies, gathered together to make war against him that sat on the horse, and against his army. And the beast was taken, and with him the false prophet that wrought miracles before him, with which he deceived them that had received the mark of the beast, and them that worshipped his image. These both were cast alive into a lake of fire burning with brimstone. (Revelation 19:11, 15-16, 19-20).

The arrest and death of Haile Selassie I caused issues for some Rastas, with some suggesting it might be a conspiracy of Babylon to hide the truth of his identity. As Rastas came to terms with it, the belief that Jah is within everything, and within the heart of people became most important; but this did not contradict the idea, for many, that Haile Selassie I is Jah.

The identity of Haile Selassie I as the reincarnation of Jesus Christ is an area where there is no necessary agreement. Within the Twelve Tribes, Bedasse (2010) has noted:

> There are basically two different viewpoints: on one hand, those who believe that Haile Selassie is the final Christ who represents the second advent of Jesus Christ and, on the other hand, those who see Haile Selassie as one who embodies the spirit of Jesus Christ and is the representative of Christ's throne on earth but not the second advent of Christ. For the former, Haile Selassie is seen as the living God, the final Christ of which the Bible speaks. The latter maintains that while Haile Selassie and Christ represent the same spirit, they are not of the same flesh (p. 964).

Another group associated with Rastafari, the Ethiopian Zion Coptic Church:

> ... recognize that Haile Selassie is of a Solomonic dynasty that links him to King David, and therefore to Christ, but for them he is not divine, he is not the second coming of Christ (Barnett, 2005, p. 74).

This seems to be a common theme among Rastas that may be seen to be removed from Jamaica and the roots of the religion. Middleton (2006) argues that for Rastas in Ghana while recognising "the ultimacy of Jah he cannot be contained and that Haile Selassie is God's emissary, 'like Kwame Nkrumah,' a noble man, sent to proclaim liberty, chiefly mental emancipation, but he is not Jah-in-the-flesh" (Middleton, 2006, p. 160). This does not negate his importance and stories of his greatness and power as the 'Lion of Judah' remain. But Bedasse does note that the change from the identification of Haile Selassie I as Jesus is the result of an evolution of belief:

> They attribute the change in their outlook to their own spiritual development or evolution, many of them using the term *progressive revelation* to describe the process by which they moved from one interpretation to the next (Bedasse, 2010, p. 968).

For members of the Twelve Tribes, while there may have been an evolution in the identifying of Haile Selassie I as a reincarnation of Jesus, there is no ambiguity in the statement that 'Haile Selassie is Jah'. There are various themes that can be outlined for certain within Rasta theology:

- Jah is black.
- Jah is helping to re-establish the identity of the black race and seeks to destroy Babylon.
- Jah can be experienced everywhere, as he is within everything.
- Haile Selassie embodied the characteristics of Jesus – the implications of this are different for different Rastafari.
- Haile Selassie is Jah (some expressions might reject this, for example the Ethiopian Zion Coptic Church', though Barrett (1997) suggests that recognition of them as 'Rastafari' has been not forthcoming from other Rasta houses, and he sees the identification of Selassie as Jah as a core belief of Rastafari.

Nature of humanity
Livity is a word that is often used to describe the lifestyle that might be followed by Rastafari. It has a much wider meaning, however, in the

sense that it is life force or energy that is sent by Jah in all living things. It is an expression of divinity that can be found within humanity, and all of the natural world. This finds expression in the Rasta belief of 'IandI' where the first I is Jah and the second is humans; through this the nature and reality of human existence is described. Cashmore has explained that:

> I and I is an expression to totalize the concept of oneness. 'I and I' as being the oneness of two persons. So God is within all of us and we're one people in fact. 'I and I means that God is in all men. The bond of Ras Tafari is the bond of God, of man. But man itself needs a head and the head of man is His Imperial Majesty Haile Selassie of Ethiopia' (2013, p. 67).

This unity with Jah raises the status of humans, and helps black people to reclaim their identity. This enables them to take control of their lives and have a knowledge of their destiny.

> For members of a group whose self-worth had been immolated in the altar of profit-making during the colonial enterprise, and whose marginalised existence in the underside of Jamaican society had been criminalised, the profession of InI consciousness repudiates all negative perceptions of their African past, their underclass status in Jamaican society, and their subjugation to the capitalist world order (Edmonds, 2012, pp. 37–38).

Within the exploration of Rastafari, the message of Jah is sent to help reclaim black identity. Cashmore has outlined, for this reason, that IandI, and its expression in livity, has "become arguably the most important theoretical tool apart from the Babylonian conspiracy in the Rastafarian repertoire" (2013, p. 66). It also provides an important link with the rest of the natural world, with which Rastafari seek to live in harmony (see below, Expression: Diet/Ital).

A Rastafari view of life after death is hard to articulate. For some the belief of a Day of Judgement is a day when Babylon will be destroyed and Rastas among a small number of other people would survive. The world would then be ruled by Black Africans as foretold in Daniel 2:37–38:

> Thou, O king, art a king of kings: for the God of heaven hath given thee a kingdom, power, and strength, and glory. And wheresoever the children of men dwell, the beasts of the field and the fowls of the heaven hath he given into thine hand, and hath made thee ruler over them all. Thou art this head of gold.

This time would be a time of peace and happiness in Africa, and specifically Ethiopia. The righteous will be able enter into this 'Paradise'. In this view, there is a possibility of reincarnation, where the soul and its attendant identity will be reborn and be able to participate in this paradisiacal existence. Thus, it can be seen that "while Rastafarians … believe in reincarnation they reject the notion of an afterlife" (Clarke, 1986, p. 74).

This belief is not universal, and Roskind relates a conversation with Rastas who articulate a more conventional form of reincarnation, that finds its fulfilment in the casting off of the body:

> "Well, de spirit of a man cayn nevah die but de physical body is 'ere ta fade away. It is like a butterfly … Woman and mon supposed ta change in de spirit."
>
> "We're not supposed to be limited to a body forever. We must transform into the spirit," Julia said.
>
> "So if we keep evolving spiritually, we drop the body?" I asked.
>
> "Yeah, mon. And change inta a new body," Scram said. "Dat means if it's up ta de power to exist and someone else ta born, ya live, mon."
>
> "Do you mean in another physical body, like reincarnation?" I asked.
>
> "Yeah, mon. Dat is my belief."
>
> As Bob Marley said, "I've been here before and will come again, but I'm not going this trip through" (2001, p. 213).

Recognising this diversity within the Rastafari community is important. One of its main features is the fluidity of belief, and the lack of dogma. It is a religion that seeks to empower, and as such personal responsibility is key in every aspect of life. There are various practices that tie adherents together, but in the main the search for the true black identity is personal.

Scripture
There are important books/writings within Rastafari that are linked with its identity as a modern-day reincarnation/expression of Israel as the chosen people of Jah. Specific examples which help articulate elements of Rastafari belief and theology include:

- The King James Version of the Bible.
- *The Holy Piby.*
- *The Royal Parchment Scroll of Black Supremacy.*
- *The Promised Key.*
- *Kebra Negast.*

King James Bible
The King James Version is the Bible used by Rastafarians. Rastas belief that all versions of the Bible are corrupt, but the King James version is the least so. While recognising the importance of the Bible as a source for Jah's action in the world they interpret many elements in light of Rastafari beliefs. The daily reading of the Bible is an important aspect of Rasta practice on a daily basis.

The Rasta interpretation of the Bible as originally given tells the story of the black race, identity and destiny. The message of the black race as the chosen people of Jah has been lost. The original version was written in Amharic (the language of Ethiopia). It has been subsequently corrupted and the message changed to suit the needs of Babylon.

The Book of Revelation is a particularly important as it foretells of Haile Selassie I; their view of Jesus is also that he was black and that the message he brought of emancipation of Jah's chosen people has been similarly corrupted.

A further reason that the Bible is used is because Haile Selassie I, as an Orthodox Ethiopian Christian, used it.

Rastafari

The Holy Piby
The Holy Piby was compiled by Robert Athlyi Rogers, claiming it to be a translation from Amharic, and it was published in 1924. It is also known as the 'Black Man's Bible' in that it speaks of the destruction of Babylon (which is white), and the return of the Israelites (who are black) to Africa/Zion. Its influence on Rastafari thought is evident, but it is not seen as a Rastafari text. It is, however, an important document in the establishment of Rasta ideas.

The Royal Parchment Scroll of Black Supremacy
The Royal Parchment Scroll of Black Supremacy was published in 1926 and was written by Reverend Fitz Balintine Pettersburgh. It is a book that, along with the *Holy Piby*, is seen as an important document in the formulation of Rasta beliefs.

The Promised Key
The Promised Key is a writing by Leonard Howell (though it was published under the name Gangunguru Maragh, teacher of famed wisdom). It draws heavily on the Holy Piby and The Royal Parchment Scroll of Black Supremacy. The book is seen to be an outlining of Rasta ideas especially with regard to black supremacy, the messiahship of Haile Selassie I, and the redemption from oppression.

Kebra Negast
The *Kebra Negast* (Glory of the Kings) was originally written in Amharic and tells the story of Ethiopia. It traces the lineage of Solomon through the Ethiopian line, and establishes the supremacy of Ethiopia over Israel. Rastafari use it to establish the blood line of Haile Selassie I and the native people of Ethiopia as the descendants and chosen people of Jah.

Religious expression

Dreadlocks
One of the most identifiable features of Rastafari identity is the growth

of dreadlocks. They serve as both an identifier of someone as a Rasta (though non-Rastafari may wear dreadlocks, and not all Rastafari will) and as a symbol of some of the most deeply held beliefs of Rastafari.

Firstly, they are seen as a rejection of the norms established by Babylon. The idea of beauty and grooming established in Babylon usually involves straight and well-groomed hair. The use of dreadlocks as a hairstyle celebrates and reclaims the features of African beauty. Those people of African descent that straighten their hair, or conform to the social norms are striving for an unattainable whiteness, and a rejection of their identity as Africans. As a part of the regality of African identity, dreadlocks are seen to be reflective of a lion and as such are seen to indicate the qualities of boldness, uprightness and confidence. They give the Rasta the strength to stand up in the face of injustice and oppression. In this way they could be seen to reflecting the identity of Haile Selassie I who is known as the 'Lion of Judah' and Samson whose strength came from his hair.

The wearing of dreadlocks also links Rastafari with their identity as descendants of the chosen people of Jah. Just as the Jews were instructed to grow their hair, so this injunction is in effect for Jah's chosen people today. The practice draws on the biblical record:

> All the days of the vow of his separation there shall no razor come upon his head: until the days be fulfilled, in the which he separateth himself unto the Lord, he shall be holy, and shall let the locks of the hair of his head grow (Numbers 6:5).

Within all of this symbolism is the connection that hair makes with God. The dreadlocks are "a mark of InI consciousness and a connection of the individual to Jah's power that pervades the universe like radio waves" (Edmonds, 2012, p. 45). Through their hairstyle, a Rasta is able to access the divine power and channel/transmit it as a creative or destructive power.

In exploring the use of dreadlocks as a hairstyle by Rastas, it is possible to overlook it as a cultural identifier rather than as an expression of Rasta beliefs. In this practice, and that of Dreadtalk (see

Rastafari

below) various elements of the Rasta worldview find their most vivid representation.

Dreadtalk

In a similar way to dreadlocks, Dreadtalk is reflective of the rejection of Babylon and its systems of oppression, and is also an assertion of a Rasta worldview. The language of Jamaica is English, and is seen to be the language of the oppressor. In the 1940s Rastas began to develop a language that is variously known as Dreadtalk or Iyaric to reflect their developing separate identity from Babylon. The use of received and 'proper' English is seen as a way to progress and reinforce repression; the use of Dreadtalk is the opposite – it is a physical expression of a rejection of all the structures of oppression. Thus Rastas have developed English into a language of their own, utilising various religious principles, (see below), the patois language, and different African languages such as Twi.

The language is reflective of the principle of 'Word, Sound and Power', a belief that words have power and that the phonetics of the words should be closely aligned with their meanings. Examples of Dreadtalk include:

- The replacement of certain features of words with 'I' to symbolise both the presence of the divine within the universe and also a person as closely linked with Jah. Examples of 'I' words are:
  - I instead of 'me'.
  - I and I (InI), which symbolises the unity of a person and Jah. Indeed, I is added to Haile Selassie to symbolise his unity with Jah.
  - I man, which refers to the inner self within each Rastafari believer.
  - Irie, which is used for positive emotions (perhaps linked to alright).
  - Irator instead of creator.
  - Iration instead of creation.
  - Itinually instead of continually – symbolising the eternity of I.

- The rejection of certain syllables that do not enable the word to function as it does:
    - Oppression is replaced by downpression, as 'op' sounds like up and could be used to suggest a positivity. Downpression is more descriptive of the pressure that people are feeling as it is imposed from above.
    - Hello is replaced by lo; because it contains the word 'hell'.
    - Overstand instead of understand – symbolic of the knowledge necessary for enlightenment or the raising of a person's consciousness.
- Other words that have a distinctly Rastafari understanding:
    - Babylon meaning oppressive structures. In Jamaica this has entered into the vernacular, as the police are sometimes referred to as Babylon.
    - Politricks to reflect the idea that politicians, especially British politicians, are tricksters who cannot be trusted.

It is interesting in the exploration of Dreadtalk to notice the fusion of existing cultural norms such as language with the expression of a religious identity. A large number of the developments of language in response to religion are perhaps evident in history, but this is an expression that has developed in the last century and observers will be able to see the importance of language in the establishment of a religious identity.

Music

Possibly the expression of Rastafari that has done more to establish Rasta identity in the public consciousness is its music, and most particularly reggae. This is not to suggest that reggae is the most important form of music for Rastafari, rather that it gave expression to elements of Rasta teaching and created a wider audience for it, it is important to note the links between Rasta and reggae, but not to overplay them.

Perhaps the most important form of music within Rastafari is Nyabinghi rhythm. This is drum music that is played at Rasta gatherings and celebrations by men in the community. There are three types of drum that are used: the bass (also known as the

'Vatican Basher' indicative of a rejection of Babylon and its systems of oppression), the funde, and the akete (also known as the 'repeater'). The first two drums keep the beat, while the akete is played solo and is fairly improvisational. This type of music built upon existing forms of drumming evident in Jamaica such as Burru. This link with traditional drumming is an expression of a reclamation and assertion of African identity which is a central focus of Rasta belief.

The Nyabinghi drumming is accompanied by chants that are usually taken from Psalms or from Christian hymns. These are given a Rasta interpretation and often focus on the themes of black liberation and repatriation. The chants have a specific rhythm and the communal nature of them in the gatherings help to reinforce Rasta identity and bring elements of the community together. Rasta gatherings still use this style of drumming and chanting today.

The use of drums is an important part of an individual's religious expression. Most Rasta homes will have a drum, often a funde which can be played at any time. It can be seen that the playing of a drum and the accompanying chants can be healing, both mentally and spiritually. One Rastafari has suggested:

> Suppose, for argument sake, I come home one evening and I really feel downpressed – like I don't make no scufflings [money] all day… I tek out a drum and start a little riddim, yuh know Before yuh know what jappen, the whole yard is wid I. Yuh no see it? Next thing yuh know I man mind come off the worries so much so, sometimes I get a little insight into how fi tackle me problems next day (in Reckford, 1998, p. 242).

Or another:

> The drum can work like that, yes. Yuh just feel youself lif outa downpression (in Reckford, 1998, p. 242).

In the mid twentieth century the figure associated most with the development of Nyabinghi drumming was Count Ossie. As Ossie's music reached the 'mainstream', elements of its style were developed into ska music by Ossie himself and others. In ska the bass drum of

Nyabinghi formed a background for a new style of popular music. In common with Nayabinghi, the lyrics of ska were often in the form of a protest against social and political inequalities.

These, and other musical forms evident in Jamaica, provided the backdrop for the development of reggae. Most importantly though for the development of Rastafari in the public consciousness was the inclusion of Rasta ideology and social commentary in the lyrics. Count Ossie had laid the groundwork in including Rastafari themes into the mainstream in songs such as 'Another Moses' and 'Babylon Gone, but the radical aspects of the social commentary and religious ideas found their widest expression in reggae music. Bob Marley and the Wailers were the most well-known of the reggae artists of the 1960s and 70s. The titles of some of his songs point towards the many Rasta themes that found their expression in his music:

- Oppressor Man.
- Rightful Ruler.
- Downpressor.
- African Herbsman.
- Lion.
- Satisfy My Soul Jah Jah.
- I Shot the Sheriff.
- So Jah Seh.
- Jah Live.
- Exodus.
- Rastaman Live Up.
- Blackman Redemption.
- Redemption Song.

The use of music to explore Rasta teachings and the importance of Rasta beliefs engages people in elements of the expression that are most recognisable, but it is important to realise the beliefs are what are key. The liberation and realisation of African identity is the most important element of Rasta music of all forms. The use of drums in Nyabinghi music reclaims African identity, but it is incomplete without the chanting. This style of music and protest is replicated in some forms of reggae music. Edmonds comments that in reggae:

> The Nyabinghi bass drum was imitated by the bass guitar and the bass drum of the trap set; the 'funde' syncopation was reproduced in the 'skeng-ay' rhythms on the keyboard and the rhythm guitar; and 'peta' improvisations found their way into the phrasings of the lead guitar. Rastafarian chants were often arranged and presented as reggae, often accompanied by the unadulterated Nyabinghi drumming style (2012, p. 117).

Diet/Ital

Ital is the Dreadtalk equivalent of 'vital' and is an approach to diet and living based on the concept of livity. The idea that Jah has imbued all of nature with his divine power means that there is a strength associated with natural living. Everything that a person eats becomes a part of who they are. For this reason most Rastafari will avoid all processed food, or products that have been subject to chemicals and artificial developments. There is an associated belief that human disease and harm to the environment is caused by relying on unnatural chemicals that have been added to food, products and the environment. The approach to diet is perhaps best described by Nicholas and Sparrow (1979):

> If you are going to teach into life everlasting, you must eat divinely of life everlasting. It's that simple (p. 62).

As an outworking of the beliefs outlined above the natural based diet would be variously interpreted but could include a strict vegetarianism, though this does differ between individual Rastafari. Those who adopt a strict vegetarianism will suggest that the eating of dead flesh is forbidden, as only life can give life. Some will extend this to a rejection of the use of dairy as this is also unnatural for human consumption.

All canned goods, refined sugars, food with additives, and in some cases rock salt will be avoided in a strict Rastafari diet. There will also be some Rastafari who will only use 'natural' materials within their cooking such as clay pots, wooden utensils rather than the manufactured metals and glass.

Also avoided by most Rastas is the use of alcohol. Though there will be some who drink alcohol in moderation, it can be seen to have negative effects on those who use it.

As inheritors of the chosen people of Jah, many Rastas will also follow the dietary laws outlined in Leviticus, where the eating of pork, fish without scales and shellfish is forbidden.

The use of herbs is central to natural living. Although a major focus of observers of Rastafari is the use of marijuana, the use of other herbs is an important part of an ital diet. The use of herbs of all kind builds on the command given to Adam:

> And God said, Behold, I have given you every herb bearing seed, which is upon the face of all the earth, and every tree, in the which is the fruit of a tree yielding seed; to you it shall be for meat (Genesis 1:29).

Herbs are a source of the natural energy with which Jah has imbued the natural world. Though some might suggest that the use of herbs might advocate drug use, Rastas would oppose the use of what they see to be manufactured drugs such as cocaine, heroin and, for some Rastas, tobacco because of the negative impacts on the body.

The use of ganja as the 'supreme herb' is potentially the most well known but potentially misunderstood practice of the Rasta community. The use of ganja by Rastafari builds upon Genesis 1:29 outlined above, and a distinctly Rasta interpretation of Revelation 22:2:

> In the midst of the street of it, and on either side of the river, was there the tree of life, which bare twelve manner of fruits, and yielded her fruit every month: and the leaves of the tree were for the healing of the nations.

It is a herb that, in the Rasta view, elicits feelings of peace and love. It also helps a person discover a higher state of consciousness and understanding of the reality of IandI. There will be Rastas who do not use ganja at all because they will feel that they can attain this higher consciousness without it. Although most often used in groundings,

Rastafari

ganja will also be used in teas, in cooking as a spice, and as a part of a medicine. One Rasta has explained:

> We use this herb as medicine and for spiritual experiences. It helps us to overcome illness, suffering and death ... We use our herb in our church – as incense for God, as the Roman Catholics use incense in their church. We burn our incense in order to venerate our God through spiritual experience ... It gives us spiritual comfort, we praise God in peace and love, without force ... When we are depressed, when we are hungry we smoke our little herb and we meditate on our God. The herb is a true comfort to us (in Kitzinger, 1971, p. 581).

When smoked in a grounding it may be smoked as a spliff, but on other occasions a chalice (water pipe) may be used. There are different types of chalice including kutchies, chillums, and steamers. The various rituals around its preparation and use are found below in the discussion of groundings.

Every aspect of an ital diet reflects Rastafari identity and belief. The goal of a realisation of an IandI consciousness remains the central feature of all of the practices. A reclamation of African identity as the chosen people of Jah is similarly expressed in aspects of the food laws.

Grounding

A grounding is a meeting of Rastafari which takes place in a commune or a yard presided over by an elder of the community. They 'ground the nation to the foundation'; this is a common Rasta saying that identifies Rastafari as the nation and the foundation as the principles of Rasta and Jah himself. For the most part groundings are male only. The elder's role is to oversee the grounding and ensure that all are able to participate and no one disrupts the gatherings. A grounding can involve a small or large number of Rastas. The larger groundings have become known as Nyabinghi Issemblies (through previously they were known as groundations). The larger Issemblies are usually associated with important dates such as Haile Selassie I's coronation (2 November), birthday (23 July) and visit to Jamaica (21 April).

At a grounding there are opening and closing prayers; Barrett has commented on the structures of the prayers being 'classical':

There is adoration to the supreme being *Ras Tafari;* then there is supplication for the hungry, the sick, the infant and for the destruction of the enemy, and finally it closes with adoration. The last paragraph of the prayer is repeated over and over again in meetings where the Bible is read. The Rastafarians are also in the habit of expressing evocatively 'Jah! Ras Tafari!' throughout a ceremony ... (Barrett, 1997, pp. 125–26).

After the opening prayer there may be various activities that take place during the grounding:

Reasoning – During this period there is a discussion about the intersection between Rasta principles and current events. These discussions are supposed to be friendly, though fallacies in arguments can be identified. The purpose is to push the boundaries "of understanding until the entire group achieves deeper or clearer insight into the topic under discussion" (Edmonds, 2012, p. 57). This is never the final word, as Rastas recognise that there can always be a deeper understanding at a future point.

Drumming – This is the Nyabinghi drumming explored above (see Religious expression: Music on p. 314).

Singing of hymns/reciting of poetry – These often utilise Psalms, or themes surrounding the emancipation of Israel re-enacted in the lives of Israel reincarnated in the people of Black Africa.

Smoking of ganja – It should always be recognised that the smoking of ganja is a way for a person to become introspective and reflect on the depths of their understanding. It is also an effective way for IandI to become realised, as the smoker can feel closer to Jah. There are particular rituals associated with the use of ganja in a grounding.

- Headwear is removed before smoking.
- A prayer is offered while the ganja is prepared.
- It can be smoked as a spliff or in a chalice (water pipe).
- The pipe is passed around the circle in an anti-clockwise direction.

The smoking of ganja usually accompanies the reasoning portion of the grounding.

Rastafari

A Rastafari grounding highlights the various elements of Rasta belief. It develops a sense of community that reinforces the ideals that are taught throughout Rastafari. Elements of black identity, the reality of Jah, and the distinctive practices of ital find an expression in a grounding and can be seen to 'ground' the Rasta in the community.

Ideas for the RE Classroom
There are many aspects of Rastafari belief and practice that could find a place within the RE classroom. There are some aspects that should be considered age-appropriate – for example the smoking of ganja is not something to be explored by younger children. It is very important to note, especially in the teaching of Rastafari, that we do not teach it to sensationalise lessons, or to try and engage the disaffected. There are legitimate reasons, and ways, to include Rastafari in the classroom and we do not need to sensationalise to be able to justify their inclusion. Possible ways include:

- Perhaps in Key Stage 4 or 5 an exploration of a Marxist interpretation of religion could lead to an interesting discussion of the theology of Rastafari. It arose to challenge the established systems of power within society and religion. It sought to throw off the shackles that seemed to bind black people down. In a Marxist critique, religion would be relegated, but in a Rastafari application, religion became/becomes emancipatory.
- The place of music in worship and as an expression of identity. Many religions have songs and hymns that reflect beliefs and Rastas are no less enthused by music and the identity that it expresses. Reggae is not the sole property of Rasta, but the influence of each on the other is undeniable. Exploring the beliefs that are expressed in the songs would engage pupils, and help them become interested in the study of distinctive Rasta beliefs. Exploring songs like 'Redemption Song' can help pupils understand the deeper message of Rasta.
- Symbols of identity. Care should be taken in an exploration of Rasta symbols, in the sense that the object or symbol can become an end in itself. What do Rastas believe? That 'they should wear dreadlocks and play reggae music' is not the end of the discussion. What are

dreadlocks a symbol of? How does it reclaim the identity of the black man and reject the norms of Babylon? The colours that Rastas use are deeply symbolic, along with the language that they use. It is crucial that the deeper beliefs are used to underpin any exploration of practices and symbols.
- The ital diet and livity way of life. Rasta is an Abrahamic religion that seeks to live in harmony with nature and the natural world. The way that they live goes beyond the ideas of stewardship usually developed within Judaism, Christianity and Islam. Learning how to recognise the livity in all creation enables a Rasta to articulate a way of life that is both counter-cultural and also an expression of beliefs. At all ages, aspects of diet and the reasons behind them can be explored.
- The way of worship within Rastafari and especially the grounding ceremonies are away to explore issues of 'reasoning' and boundaries of acceptability in worship. This will counter aspects of a narrative about Rasta in the media and the zeitgeist. The purpose of worship is both communal and individual.
- There are many aspects of ethical living that could be explored, from the environmentalism evident in livity to issues of race.
- The inclusion of Rasta portrayals of Jesus can also challenge the narrative that he was a white man. The use of such images can be used to raise discussion, and also explore the motivations of artists in the art they produce.

Useful websites

Websites about Rastafari do not tend to be very user friendly. Instead, the further reading for Rastafari includes some very good introductions that can be found in the following books.
- Barrett, Leonard E. (1997) [1988]. *The Rastafarians*. Boston, MA: Beacon Press.
- Edmonds, Ennis (2012). *Rastafari. A very short introduction*. Oxford, UK: Oxford University Press.
- Murrell, Nathaniel Samuel, Spencer, William David, & McFarlane, Adrian Anthony (Eds.). (1998). *Chanting down Babylon: Rastafarian reader*. Philadelphia, PA: Temple University Press.

References

Barnett, Michael (2005). The many faces of Rasta: Doctrinal diversity within the Rastafari movement, *Caribbean Quarterly, 51*(2), 67-78.

Barrett, Leonard E. (1997) [1988]. *The Rastafarians*. Boston, MA: Beacon Press.

Bedasse, M. (2010). Rasta evolution: The theology of the Twelve Tribes of Israel. *Journal of Black Studies, 40*(5), 960-973.

Cashmore, Ellis (2013) [1979]. *Rastaman: The Rastafarian movement in England*. Abingdon. UK: Routledge.

Clarke, Peter B. (1986). *Black paradise: The Rastafarian movement*. New Religious Movements Series. Wellingborough, UK: The Aquarian Press.

Garvey, Marcus (1920, 3 August). *New York Times*.

Edmonds, Ennis (2012). *Rastafari. A very short introduction*. Oxford, UK: Oxford University Press.

King, S. (1998). International reggae, Democratic socialism, and the secularization of the Rastafarian Movement, 1972-1980. *Popular Music and Society, 22*(3), 39-64.

Kitzinger, Sheila (1966). The Rastafarian Brethren of Jamaica. *Comparative Studies in Society and History*, 10, 9(1), 33-39.

Kitzinger, Sheila (1971). The Rastafarian Brethren of Jamaica. In Michael M. Horowitz (Ed.). *Peoples and cultures of the Caribbean* (pp. 580-588). Garden City, NY: Natural History Press.

Middleton, Darren (2006). As it is in Zion: Seeking the Rastafari in Ghana, West Africa, *Black Theology, 4*(2), 151-172.

Murrell, Nathaniel Samuel (2000). Tuning Hebrew Psalms to reggae rhythms: Rastas' revolutionary lamentations for social change. *CrossCurrents, 50*(4). Retrieved from http://www.crosscurrents.org/murrell.htm

Murrell, Nathaniel Samuel, Spencer, William David, & McFarlane, Adrian Anthony (Eds.). (1998) *Chanting down Babylon: Rastafarian reader*. Philadelphia, PA: Temple University Press.

Nicholas, Tracy, & Sparrow, Bill (1979). *Rastafari: A way of life*. Garden City, NY: Anchor Books.

Reckford, Verena (1998). From Burru Drums to Reggae Ridims: The evolution of rasta music. In Nathaniel Samuel Murrell, William David Spencer, & Adrian Anthony McFarlane, (Eds.), *Chanting down Babylon: Rastafarian reader* (pp. 231-251). Philadelphia, PA: Temple University Press.

Roskind, Robert (2001). *Rasta heart: A journey into one love*. Blowing Rock, NC: One Love Press.